Anthropology
and Religion

BOOKS BY ROBERT L. WINZELER

The Architecture of Life and Death in Borneo

Indigenous Architecture of Borneo, editor

Indigenous Peoples and the State: Politics, Land and Ethnicity in the Malay Peninsula and Borneo, editor

Latah in Southeast Asia: The History and Ethnography of a Culture-Bound Syndrome

The Seen and the Unseen: Shamanism, Mediumship and Spirit Possession in Borneo, editor

Ethnic Relations in Kelantan: Malays and Non-Malays in an East Coast Malay State

Anthropology and Religion

What We Know, Think, and Question

Robert L. Winzeler

ALTAMIRA
PRESS

A division of
ROWMAN & LITTLEFIELD PUBLISHERS, INC.
Lanham • New York • Toronto • Plymouth, UK

AltaMira Press
A division of Rowman & Littlefield Publishers, Inc
A wholly owned subsidiary of The Rowman & Littlefield Publishing Group, Inc.
4501 Forbes Boulevard, Suite 200, Lanham, MD 20706
www.altamirapress.com

Estover Road, Plymouth PL6 7PY, United Kingdom

British Library Cataloguing in Publication Information Available

Library of Congress Cataloging-in-Publication Data

Winzeler, Robert L.
  Anthropology and religion : what we know, think, and question /
Robert L. Winzeler.
      p. cm.
  Includes bibliographical references and index.
  ISBN-13: 978-0-7591-1045-8 (cloth : alk. paper)
  ISBN-10: 0-7591-1045-X (cloth : alk. paper)
  ISBN-13: 978-0-7591-1046-5 (pbk. : alk. paper)
  ISBN-10: 0-7591-1046-8 (pbk. : alk. paper)
  1. Ethnology—Religious aspects. 2. Religion. I. Title.

  BL256.W56 2008
  306.6—dc22
                                        2007024726

Printed in the United States of America

∞™ The paper used in this publication meets the minimum requirements of
American National Standard for Information Sciences—Permanence of Paper
for Printed Library Materials, ANSI/NISO Z39.48-1992.

For Judy

Contents

Preface and Acknowledgments

This book is intended to be an overview of what anthropologists know, think, and argue about religion. My original reason for writing it was to have something for students to read that was well suited to the sort of course in the anthropology of religion that I have been teaching for many years. It is also meant for anyone interested in religion in the most broadly comparative and inclusive terms, with the kinds of information that anthropologists and others working in the anthropological tradition have accumulated and how they have explained or interpreted this information. My goal has also been to go beyond cultural and social anthropology or ethnology and to incorporate relevant information and insights from other fields of anthropology including archaeology and physical anthropology, and I have done so at several points. I begin in chapter 1 with the basics of how religion is to be defined, the types of anthropological studies that have been done, and the main overall types of religion. In chapter 2 I offer some generalizations about what Westerners (especially Americans) seem to think that religion is all about and then discuss the extent to which such views hold up (not very well I argue) when applied more broadly.

The chapters that follow these consist of summaries, arguments, generalizations, and propositions about topics and issues that I consider to be central to the modern anthropology of religion. Some of the issues involved (for example, the primacy of ritual or belief or the relationship of religion and morality) have been around for a long time while others (such as religion and ecology or the effects of religion on the environment) are more recent. Most topics are introduced in historical terms and with reference to seminal theorists and key studies. Some of the matters covered would be included in any book attempting to provide an overview of the anthropology of religion, while others are more distinctive to this book. I know of no existing efforts to bring together and discuss, as I have done in chapter 3, the very different efforts that have been made to explain the origin, prehistory, and evolution of religion. This is also true of my evaluation of work on anthropology, ecology, and the environment in chapter 4 and consideration of natural symbols in religion in chapter 5.

My consideration of all topics and issues is illustrated wherever possible with examples, some well-known, others familiar mainly to specialists, and some from my own experiences. These examples are drawn from various sources. Some topics seem to require discussion of specific regions of the world, including Africa in relationship to traditional witchcraft and Native North America and Melanesia regarding religious movements. In addition to such considerations, many of my examples concern East Asia and Southeast Asia, the latter being one of the main crossroads of the major religions of the world and the realm of my particular research interests and experiences.

ACKNOWLEDGMENTS

I am indebted to the many students who have over the years listened to my discussion of the issues and information presented here, and especially to those who have responded in person to what I have said or to what they have read. The book was accepted on the recommendation of several anonymous readers whose positive responses to an early and partial draft are much appreciated. David Whitely, who read and approved a later, full version, was critical of my rather negative discussion of the issue of shamanism and prehistoric art, which led me to rethink, revise, and—I hope—improve what I had said. My friend and archaeological colleague Gary Haynes kindly read and commented on the chapters on the evolution of religion and on religion, ecology, and the environment as well as the later section on shamanism and rock art, which also contributed to my refinement of this material. I am above all indebted to my wife, Judy Winzeler, who is among other things an excellent editor; she read the entire manuscript at least twice in addition to discussing countless specific matters with me from the beginning to the end. As for the personally gained knowledge that has gone into this book, I offer thanks to the many friends, acquaintances, assistants, and colleagues I have had in Southeast Asia—for what I have learned from them with their help and for enriching my life. I have already acknowledged in other books my thanks and appreciation to the various foundations and agencies for the financial assistance that has helped me over the years and do so here again without naming them.

I wish to thank especially my friend Lim Yu Seng and the Sarawak Museum for the use of several of the photos that appear in the book. Finally, it has been a pleasure to work with the people at AltaMira Press, whose professionalism, cooperative spirit, and consideration of my preferences are much appreciated. I thank in particular Rosalie Robertson who accepted the book for AltaMira at an early point and Alan McClare, Executive Editor, and Jehanne Schweitzer, Senior Production Editor, at Rowman & Littlefield for their very capable handling of its publication.

1

_oᔕ௦_

Anthropology and Religion

What is religion? Everyone can give some kind of definition of this term or at least describe the things associated with it, such as believing in God or going to church. But what is religion in terms of the wide range of societies known to anthropology? Is religion as Westerners know it a human universal—something found in all known societies? I sometimes begin my course on the anthropology of religion by saying that this is a course in something that may not even exist.

WORDS AND THINGS

One way of responding to this assertion is to say that if we have a word for something it must exist in some sense, if only in the sense that people believe it exists. But assuming that something exists just because there is a word for it is an elementary fallacy (known as nominalism). The fact that we have words for ghost and Martian does not mean that ghosts or Martians exist, except as beliefs or fantasies. Human thought and human language enable us to imagine and name all sorts of things that may not otherwise exist. Putting the word "religion" in the same category as "ghost" or "Martian" may seem absurd when we can point to so many real things (e.g., churches or people praying) that are concrete, factual indications that religion exists in a way that ghosts or Martians do not. There clearly is something in society that we can call religion, although exactly what it is may not be that simple to specify.

1

What about religion in societies that have no such word in their vocabulary? Can you have something if you do not have a word for it? Certainly you can, at least as far as some things are concerned. People can have viruses without having words for them. We had the AIDS virus before we had a word for the syndrome; we created the word (an acronym) after we became aware that people were becoming ill and dying of something (the effect of that particular virus) no one had known about. But the question of whether a society can have a religion if it has no term for religion has important implications for understanding the nature of the anthropological study of religion. I shall return to this matter later, but suffice it to say at this point that the issue of societies without words for religion is not hypothetical. Nonmodern terms for religion hardly exist beyond the world religions and are not necessarily the same within all of them. Neither the Chinese nor the Japanese have a single traditional term that is the simple equivalent of the Western notion of religion. In Chinese the modern term is *tsung chiao*, which means in English "doctrine of faith," but according to C. K. Yang (1991: 2), different traditional terms were used for different systems of belief and practice. There was no overarching version of religion and therefore no single abstract concept that identified religion as a thing itself. The situation among the Japanese is much the same—different terms for different religious traditions but nothing for religion in general. Of course, some Chinese and Japanese and many other peoples in the world have been long aware of the modern Western notion of religion and have either taken on the term itself or have developed an equivalent word. Even in Western society the notion of religion as a noun or thing is fairly recent (in terms of the long history of Christianity), according to the distinguished historian of religion Wilfred Cantwell Smith (1963). The term itself comes from the Latin *religio*, which means pious or devoted to the gods. Smith thought we would be better off without the term, but, for better or worse, four decades later there is little sign that it is likely to go away.

Probably most anthropologists would take the position that we can have useful articles, books, and university courses involving topics for which there may be no words among the kinds of nonmodern, non-Western societies in which anthropologists have traditionally had a strong interest. If we did not do this, anthropology would be mainly out of business, at least in terms of books and courses, for many or most of the societies anthropologists have often focused on also have no general words for art, social organization, economy, ecology, or environment.

There are two points here. One is that course labels or book titles should not lead us to expect that there is anything out there in comparative terms that closely or explicitly corresponds to what we think it is simply because *we* have a word for it. The second point is that if we are to pursue the question of whether all societies have some kind of religion or understand what religion is in some particular society that lacks a word for religion comparable to our modern Western one, we need to understand what we mean by "religion" in the first place. And what we generally mean by religion in modern Western society may not be very useful in broad comparative terms, a matter that will be explored more fully in the next chapter.

IS RELIGION A HUMAN UNIVERSAL?

In the past claims were often made that religion was lacking in various societies. E. B. Tylor began his book on religion (first published in 1871 as the second volume of *Primitive Culture*) with the question of whether all known human societies had religion and noted many claims about the total absence of religion among various peoples. Such assertions had been made over several centuries or more and continued into the time that Tylor wrote. He cited examples of statements about the absence of religion in societies in North and South America, Polynesia, Australia and Africa, Southeast Asia, and elsewhere. Tylor attributed such claims partly to negative prejudice, partly to a lack of understanding or the inability to communicate with the group in question and partly to a tendency by observers "to do scant justice to the facts before their eyes." But he also concluded that part of the problem was the absence of a definition of religion other than the implicit notions based on the religious background of the observer—ethnocentrism.

Today neither anthropologists nor, probably, any other scholars would accept claims of the sort reviewed and rejected by Tylor about the absence of religion in various societies. Anthropologists are now confident that religion is present in all human societies, even though some or many traditionally lack a word for religion in their own language and therefore do not separate "religion" from other realms of culture. This does not mean, however, that all societies are equally religious. And those that are not include not only communist or other modern societies, but also indigenous traditional ones. Here are a few examples from the literature.

The French anthropologist Bernard Sellato, an authority on the Punan (nomadic hunter-gatherers of Indonesian Borneo), concludes that while these groups are by no means devoid of religious beliefs and practices, "nevertheless I would tend to view the Punan band as a 'secular' society, pragmatic and little given to religious belief or behavior" (1994: 208). The Punan are not a single ethno-linguistic group and appear to differ from one group to another. Further, the various Punan groups have been influenced by the surrounding farming, village-dwelling peoples, although the latter groups tend to have elaborate ceremonies and associated beliefs, and therefore the effect of this influence would seem to be toward the adoption of more rather than less religion. It is also possible that for researchers who (like Sellato) are familiar with the highly developed religious traditions of the horticultural, longhouse societies of Borneo, those of the Punan are meager in comparative rather than in absolute terms. For his part, however (and he is not alone), Sellato (1994: 204–8) concludes that the Punan are not very religious by any standard.

Sellato goes on to note other societies with minimal religion. These include the Basseri, Shiite Muslims who were studied and written about by anthropologist Fredrik Barth (1961), among whom "ritual life is remarkably sparse." They also include the Siriono of Bolivia, the Pinatubo of the Philippines, and the BaMbuti of Africa (and according to one authority African hunter-gatherers in general). All of these examples concern societies that are nomadic hunter-gatherers or (in the case of the Basseri) at least nomadic. Sellato therefore seems to be hinting that nomadic hunter-gatherers are often likely to be minimally religious. Any anthropologist would probably be able to rattle off a list of counterexamples—of nomadic hunter-gatherers that have rich and elaborate religion. But let us grant the point that not all, even traditional, people are very (or "deeply") religious.[1]

THE MEANING OF RELIGION

But exactly what is it that all societies are supposed to have, even if some may not have much of it? That is, what do anthropologists mean by religion in the first place? When I read or peruse books about religion in broad comparative terms, I begin with what the author thinks religion is, although some prominent scholars of religion refuse to provide an explicit or succinct definition or have avoided the issue.

When anthropologists use the term "religion" they usually do so in a broadly inclusive manner. Anthropology courses on religion, at least as taught in American colleges and universities, often have magic and witchcraft in the title as well as religion. The current title of the course I teach is Magic, Witchcraft, and Religion, although magic and witchcraft do not get separate and equal treatment along with religion. When anthropologists speak of religion they often mean it to include magic and witchcraft, even if the two latter topics may also be considered each on its own. Religion is not considered a subtopic of either magic or witchcraft but is the more fundamental, inclusive concept.

What religion, magic, and witchcraft have in common is that they involve things (beings, processes, events) that are held to be unseen—

outside of the realm of ordinary waking experience and normal physical cause and effect. In modern Western traditions of thought, we tend to draw sharp lines between religion, magic, and witchcraft and between all of these and science, or empirical knowledge. The former are things about which Westerners have beliefs or in which they have faith, as opposed to assumed, taken-for-granted, proven, or certain knowledge. We should not assume, however, that all peoples make sharp distinctions between forms of knowledge and ways of knowing and believing.

As already noted, the problem of defining religion in broad comparative terms has been present since the beginning of modern anthropology in the late nineteenth century. While there are various approaches, most belong to one of two traditions or schools of thought, one deriving from Tylor and focusing on the supernatural and the other from Emile Durkheim and focusing on the sacred.

Tylor's Definition

Tylor's 1871 definition of religion is the oldest in anthropology, at least the oldest that anyone now pays much attention to. It consists only of the proposition that religion is "the belief in spiritual beings." Part of the virtue of this definition is its simplicity. It makes no distinction between beliefs in spirits and in gods or between polytheism and monotheism. It does not specify any other criteria that need to be met for something to qualify as religion. For example, it does not assume that religion must have a social dimension or a moral one, and it does not distinguish between beliefs in important sorts of supernatural beings and trivial ones. All beliefs in supernatural beings constitute religion. Tylor proposed a definition that would solve the problem of whether there were societies that did not have religion by arguing that if a society had beliefs in spiritual beings it had religion, and that was all there was to it. Beyond this, however, Tylor also held that if belief in spiritual beings is the central feature of religion, then understanding how religion had first developed in human society was a matter of understanding how humans first came to have beliefs in such things.

To oversimplify a bit, anthropologists and other scholars and researchers of comparative religion are of two minds regarding Tylor's well-known definition: those who basically agree with it or find it useful or necessary as a starting point and those who would prefer another way of going at it. Those who follow Tylor tend to improve on his simple definition. For one thing, the very notion of belief may be misleading. The existence of spirits, though ordinarily unseen, may be less "believed in" than taken for granted as part of the real world, and so may other things that we call religion, magic, and witchcraft. However, it is not easy to do without the notion of belief as a way of referring to the assumptions that various peoples hold about the nature of reality. Aside from calling attention to the problem, no one has come up with a suitable alternative.

At five words, Tylor's definition seems too minimal. Many anthropologists would be inclined to add "behavior" or "ritual," as in the phrase "beliefs and behavior, especially ritual, involving supernatural beings." However, while an improvement, this is still perhaps too minimal. Should religious beliefs be said to be limited to beliefs in spiritual beings? The answer would seem to be no. By "spiritual beings" Tylor presumably meant a separate being or agent possessing both will and some degree of intelligence, along with spiritual or superhuman powers or qualities of some sort. If the belief in spiritual powers beyond the belief in specific spiritual beings or agents is a fundamental part of religion, then we need a broader term such as "spiritual." The term that anthropologists came to prefer is "supernatural," as in Anthony Wallace's (1966: 5) definition of religion as "behavior that can be classified as belief and ritual concerned with supernatural beings, powers and forces." Most anthropologists (including me) think that Tylor was on the right track and would probably accept "supernatural" as a more desirable alternative.

Do All Peoples Distinguish between "Natural" and "Supernatural"?

The Tylorian approach to religion seems to assume that societies which have religion distinguish between spiritual beings and nonspiritual or "ordinary" ones and, more broadly, the "natural" and the "supernatural." If religion as Tylor defined it is found in all human societies, then so (it would seem) is some sort of distinction between the natural and the supernatural. To what extent is such a distinction always present among human groups?

The question of whether various people distinguish between natural and supernatural remains controversial. Anthropologists may say that some group doesn't distinguish between natural and supernatural realms or that they regard spirits as a part of the "natural" world. How well do such statements hold up to close examination? E. E. Evans-Prichard addressed this question in his pioneering study of the Azande of central Africa. He began by noting that Europeans are fond of asking whether people like the Azande distinguish between the natural and the supernatural. The correct answer in his view depends on how the question is asked. If you are asking about whether the Azande make an *explicit* distinction between natural and supernatural, the answer is, they do not. But Evans-Prichard goes on to say that this does not mean the Azande make no distinction between natural and supernatural. If you pose the question in a different way, you get a different answer.

If [the Azande] do not give to the natural and supernatural the meanings which educated Europeans give to them they nevertheless distinguish between them. For our question may be formulated, and should be formulated, in a different manner. We ought to rather ask whether primitive peoples perceive any difference between the happenings that we, the observers of their culture, class as natural and the happenings which we class as mystical. Azande undoubtedly perceive a difference between what we consider the workings of nature on the one hand and the workings of magic and ghosts and witchcraft on the other hand, though in the absence of a formulated doctrine of natural law they do not, and cannot, express the difference as we express it. (Evans-Prichard 1937: 81)

Can what Evans-Prichard says of the Azande—that while they do not make an explicit or formal distinction between natural and supernatural they undoubtedly do make a fundamental implicit one—be said to apply generally? Or are there human societies that make neither an explicit nor an implicit distinction between natural and supernatural? Keep in mind what is at issue here. To put it in simple terms, "natural" and "supernatural" as categories are logically meaningful only in relation to each other. You cannot have an idea of the natural without also having the idea of the supernatural, and vice versa. To say that a human group makes no distinction between natural and supernatural is tantamount to saying they do not recognize supernatural beings, happenings, or processes. To put it slightly differently, to say that a people recognize no implicit distinction between what we explicitly call natural and supernatural would be to say they do not recognize any difference between a normal living person and a ghost, between a human being or an animal and a spirit or a god, between normal material cause and effect and mystical influence or causation, magic, or witchcraft. To my knowledge, no anthropologist or other reliable observer has ever described such a people—the once common claims about one or another society having no religion notwithstanding. All existing peoples appear to make such distinctions. They probably appeared at an early point in time in the evolution of modern humans in association with the development of language and would seem to have been necessary for the emergence of what we call religion.

For many peoples—including the Azande, who do not make a formal, explicit, categorical distinction between natural and supernatural—the boundaries between the two realms may be fuzzy or interpenetrating or difficult to determine. If you are inclined to believe in spirits and you see something move in the forest, you may think you have seen an animal or a spirit in the form of an animal. People may—indeed often do—believe that humans and other living creatures (and perhaps all things) have both a natural and a supernatural dimension.

Beyond having a soul, some people may also be assumed to be super-natural beings. For example, during first contact episodes involving West-erners and indigenous societies in the New Guinea highlands the native highlanders believed that the white outsiders who suddenly appeared among them were "sky people" or spirits of some sort rather than ordi-nary humans who differed from them. The highlanders also assumed that the lowland natives who accompanied the whites were ancestors return-ing from the land of the dead. The same claim (though disputed) has been made regarding Hawaiian beliefs about Captain Cook, the first Western voyager to reach them. In this instance it has been argued that Cook was believed to be the returning god Lono (Sahlins 1995; Obeyesekere 1992). This sort of claim has also figured prominently in explanations (again dis-puted) of the Spanish conquest of the Aztec, Maya, and Inca empires (Re-stall 2003: 108–20).

Westerners are fascinated by the idea of going off to remote places and being taken for gods by credulous natives. For example, in Rudyard Kipling's story *The Man Who Would Be King* (later made into a Hollywood film starring Sean Connery and Michael Caine), two ne'er-do-well ex-British soldiers in colonial India set out to become kings of Kaffiristan (in present-day northern Pakistan) They succeed for a while because one of them (Daniel Dravitt, played by Sean Connery) is initially identified by the natives as a god (because he is wearing a Masonic ring and is there-fore believed to be the returning Alexander the Great who had first been there more than two thousand years before).

In most such stories it does not take long for the natives to learn that the Western newcomers are all too human. In the Kipling tale this occurs when the divine European king decides to take a beautiful native woman as a wife. But the woman is terrified (presumably of marrying a god) and during the wedding ritual scratches his face, thus revealing to the assembled crowd that his blood is red rather than white and there-fore that he is really mortal rather than divine. In the documentary ac-count of first contact in highland New Guinea, the natives in the Mount Hagen area learn the white men are ordinary humans in a more prosaic manner involving a different body substance. As one highlander wryly recounted long after the event, everyone was curious to see if the white men relieved themselves, and if so how, since their bodies were covered with clothing. One man sneaked up and watched as one of the Euro-peans defecated, and then inspected the results and learned, as he put it, that "their skin might be different but their shit smells like ours" (Con-nolly and Anderson 1987: 44). Some natives did not entirely give up the notion that Europeans were not simply ordinary people. But the point is that while mortal humans may be taken for spirits or divinities in some instances (or to have supernatural powers—the original meaning of

Max Weber's famous term *charisma*), the assumption could only have been made if a distinction between normal mortals and supernatural beings existed among those involved.

Anthropologists are often unhappy with drawing a simple dichotomy between natural and supernatural and the beliefs of non-Western or nonmodern peoples, and therefore with defining religion in ways that seem to assume such an explicit distinction. Many appear to favor distinctions between "seen" and "unseen" dimensions of reality, or statements to the effect that there is "more to the world than meets the eye" as a way of trying to get closer to what modern Westerners mean when they speak in explicit terms of natural and supernatural. However, people do not necessarily see their own beliefs and practices in terms of a plain distinction between natural and supernatural. Most people are probably aware of the categories of natural and supernatural and might be willing to apply them to some of their religious beliefs and practices, while perhaps preferring other terms for the latter, such as "faith" or "spiritual." Ordinary people, in contrast to anthropologists, scientists, or philosophers, likely don't think of reading and believing in horoscopes or engaging in various other popular forms of what anthropologists would call magic as delving into the supernatural, let alone into superstition. And people who go to church would certainly not think of themselves as worshipping a supernatural being.

The Durkheimian Approach

Anthropologists who do not favor some version of Tylor's approach to religion take various positions. As we shall see in the next chapter, some have argued that religion is more a matter of ritual, or formally patterned behavior, than of belief. However, most scholars who consider religion in broad comparative terms and do not favor a Tylorian approach prefer to emphasize meaning and emotion rather than specific types of supernatural belief. This position can be traced to Emile Durkheim, an early French sociologist who made extensive use of comparative or ethnological material and heavily influenced the anthropology of religion. Durkheim formulated his own definition early in the twentieth century in the opening section to his *Elementary Forms of Religious Life* (a translation from the French), a landmark study that focused on the religious life of the indigenous peoples of Australia. He developed his own approach in part in opposition to that of Tylor and other scholars of the time who approached religion in terms of the presence of supernatural beliefs. Durkheim rejected references to the supernatural as useful criteria on several grounds. For one thing, he argued that that the distinction between natural and supernatural that Tylor and others took for granted was a modern notion.

(As we have seen, this was probably so in terms of explicit distinctions but not implicit ones.) Further, he held that religion does not require a belief in supernatural beings and went on to claim several examples of Eastern religions that did not have such beliefs, at least as central doctrinal principles. The best known of the "atheistic" religions that Durkheim cited was Buddhism (another was Jainism). He acknowledged that both of these religions as believed and practiced in some regions (northern Asia, including Tibet, China, Japan, and Korea, in contrast to Southeast Asia) or by some peoples (ordinary villagers in contrast to learned monks and scholars) had ceased to be atheistic. For some devotees the Buddha had been changed from a normal flesh-and-blood mortal, who had achieved enlightenment and taught others how they could do the same, into a god, but this was not the original or pure form.

Durkheim's final point was that while most religions involve a belief in supernatural beings, some of what was practiced included few references to the supernatural. He summarized his objections by saying that "religion is more than the idea of gods or spirits, and consequently cannot be defined exclusively in relation to these latter" (Durkheim 1965: 50). As discussed above, most anthropologists would agree with the assertion that Tylor's formulation needs to be expanded.

For Durkheim the necessary characteristic of religion was the "sacred," which is special, awesome, or revered, while the profane is ordinary and mundane. In all human societies, he argued, there is a sharp and pervasive dichotomy between the sacred and the profane.

> The division of the world into two domains, the one containing all that is sacred, the other all that is profane, is the distinctive trait of religious thought; the beliefs, myths, dogmas . . . express the nature of sacred things . . . But by sacred things one must not understand simply those personal beings which are called gods or spirits; a rock, a tree, a spring, a piece of wood, in a word, anything can be sacred. (1965: 52)

While Durkheim perceived some overlap between the sacred and the profane, on the one hand, and the supernatural and the natural, on the other, the two sets of distinctions did not map the same realm—not all that was supernatural was sacred and not all that was sacred was supernatural. Some spirits may be regarded as sacred but others not. Alternatively, people may hold some things sacred that they do not regard as belonging to the realm of the supernatural. Westerners, for example, regard their national flags as sacred but not supernatural objects.

Perhaps Durkheim's central proposition about the sacred is that it is associated with society. Religious beliefs are *collective* representations, and the most essential rites are performed together. A group of people who hold beliefs in common and participate together in rituals form what he called a church. Although Durkheim seemed to be projecting a specific Western institutional form onto all religions, he was simply claiming that religion is social and organized. Religion in Durkheim's view therefore does not include magic. A lot of people practice magic but when they do they are not engaged in religion, since magic is individual while religion is social. *"There is no Church of magic,"* he wrote in italics in order to stress the point.

Defining religion in terms of the sacred became a prominent alternative to Tylorian approaches in the 1960s. In anthropology, Clifford Geertz's definition of religion as consisting of sacred symbols is perhaps the most important example of such thinking. This goes as follows:

> Religion is: (1) a system of symbols which acts to (2) establish powerful, pervasive, and long-lasting moods and motivations in men by (3) formulating conceptions of a general order of existence and (4) clothing these in conceptions in such an order of factuality that (5) the moods and motivations seem uniquely realistic. (Geertz 1973: 4)

Geertz's approach to religion stresses meaning and derives especially from the ideas of Max Weber (a founder of modern sociology who wrote extensively about religion but did not influence the anthropology of religion as to the extent that Durkheim did). For Geertz, "meaning" involves both cognition and emotion; that is, in terms of knowing, believing, or supposing on the one hand, and feeling or experiencing on the other. However, he emphasizes emotion over cognition, which puts him in the Durkheimian camp.

Geertz's definition leaves out any reference to supernatural beings or the supernatural (however defined); this also aligns him with Durkheim and in opposition to Tylor. Leaving beliefs in supernatural beings and processes out of the equation, however, loses a way of distinguishing religion from other things that we might not want to consider religion. In explicating his definition, Geertz acknowledges that some people might think that, according to his definition, baseball is a religion, and therefore feels the need to assure his readers that it is not. Perhaps the more serious problem lies in distinguishing religion defined in terms of the sacred from the great secular ideologies (and their symbolism and ceremonies) of the nineteenth and twentieth centuries—socialism, communism, fascism, and perhaps capitalism. Perhaps nothing so exemplifies Geertz's formulation of religion as one of those than the great Nazi rallies of the 1930s preserved in newsreels—the vast crowds, the huge banners, the goose-stepping SS parades, the martial music, and the mesmerizing speeches. Perhaps you want to think that such ideological ceremonies are just as much religion as the installation of a new pope, a Balinese royal cremation, or an Aztec rite of human sacrifice. Or perhaps you want to argue that the ideologues and demagogues of recent history—Marx, Stalin, Hitler, Mao, and others— came to be regarded as supernatural figures by their followers. In Cambodia, for example, some villagers came to regard Pol Pot as superhuman— in which case we have gotten back to Tylor.

The idea of approaching religion in terms of the sacred (or in terms of meaning) rather than as beliefs and practices involving the supernatural also underlies the notion of civil religion as developed by the sociologist Robert Bellah (1967), whose work has also influenced anthropology. American civil religion includes both spiritual symbols that transcend particular religions as in various sacred phrases ("one nation under God," "in God we trust," "endowed by our Creator with certain unalienable rights") as well as sacred but nonsupernatural ones like the flag. It also includes national holidays, some of which (like Christmas and Easter) are optionally religious in a conventional sense, others of which (like Thanksgiving and the Fourth of July) are definitely not. The idea of a civil religion (that of some things held sacred in the Durkheimian sense, and felt and practiced by all Americans no matter what their particular conventional religious beliefs and practices, or lack thereof) has lost much of its appeal given the current political divisiveness of religion in American political and cultural life. Americans now appear to be more divided than united by religious symbols.

Durkheimian approaches, including Geertz's notion of religion as meaningful sacred symbols and Bellah's concept of civil religion, continue to be influential. However, most anthropologists who produce religious ethnographies or who attempt to advance theoretical interpretations of religion in recent years seem to favor Tylorian approaches. What appears to interest modern anthropological scholars of religion at the present time involves religion and cognition, the matter of how or why humans can hold supernatural beliefs at the same time they depend on "real" knowledge about the natural world. This has been a major issue in the anthropology of religion for a long time. It has returned to the forefront as anthropologists and others ask how supernatural beliefs could have evolved.

THE ANTHROPOLOGY OF RELIGION

Many people study and write about religion. Journalists and popular writers aside, these include sociologists and historians of religion and specialists in Judaism, Buddhism, Hinduism, or Islam or one of the other world religions, not to mention theologians and philosophers and the occasional political scientist or area specialist. What distinguishes anthropological approaches from these others?

To begin with, if religion needs to be defined in broad terms, so also does anthropology. Much of what will be said about anthropology and religion involves cultural anthropology—also referred to as ethnology. However, religion has also been dealt with in other branches of anthropology, including physical anthropology, on the one hand, and archaeology and prehistory, on the other. This information is important to questions about the origins and evolution of religious beliefs and practices and will be considered in chapter 3.

Anthropology can be called a theoretically oriented discipline, which means taking some care with how terms are defined and concepts are applied. It also means that, as researchers and scholars, anthropologists operate with general strategies of interpretation or explanation, either in the form of specific arguments or in terms of a general tendency to stress certain kinds of factors. (Studies that offer little explicit interpretation or explanation are said to be "descriptive.") But being a theoretically oriented discipline does not distinguish anthropology from other academic fields. Nor are the particular theories that anthropologists utilize to interpret or explain religion or most other matters very different from those of other fields.

The differences between anthropological and other approaches to religion mainly involve methods of study and the kinds of peoples or religions that are studied. Anthropology as we know it took shape in the late nineteenth century, with a further crucial development around the beginning of the twentieth century that involved formal training and fieldwork as an essential part of the process in both the United States and Great Britain, and somewhat later in other places. Many or most of the notions, concepts, and theories that have been important in the anthropology of religion were formulated in the earliest period of anthropology, before fieldwork became an established part of the process. Early scholars such as Edward B. Tylor and James Frazer relied on descriptive accounts that they then sifted, synthesized, and interpreted. Some of this information came from the writings of precolonial travelers and explorers, but much of it had a colonial context. It is not an accident that anthropology as a research discipline developed at a comparatively early point in England and the United States. Great Britain at the turn of the twentieth century presided over the most far-flung empire (and the most disparate range of peoples) in history, while the states and territories of the United States contained many diverse native groups in various states of subjugation and acculturation and, in some instances, annihilation.

Great Britain and the United States were of course not the only countries in such a position in the nineteenth and twentieth centuries. Several other Western European countries, most notably France and the Nether-lands, also had colonial territories filled with a variety of peoples who stimulated anthropological or ethnological inquiry in regard to religious beliefs and practices and other matters. The vast Russian empire extended from Europe to the Pacific and encompassed a great number and variety of Siberian and Central Asian peoples. Many of these peoples practiced versions of shamanism, a religious complex or tradition that eventually became important in anthropological and other studies of comparative re-ligion and a topic that attracted the interest of Russian observers (includ-ing the later detailed attention of Russian ethnologists and psychologists) over many centuries.

In colonial settings individuals, including military officers, government officials, missionaries, and explorers, were apt to gather and publish in-formation on the native peoples they encountered. The religious beliefs and practices of the indigenous peoples were only one of various topics that drew attention, but they held a special interest for practical and in-tellectual or mystical reasons. Where religion was thought to be associ-ated with native resistance, rebellion, or unrest, as was not uncommonly the case in colonial and other situations of contact, acculturation, and sub-jugation, it became a matter of general concern. In the United States, the Ghost Dance religious movement of the western Great Plains attracted the attention of James Mooney of the Smithsonian Institution. Mooney de-voted several years to studying the Ghost Dance of the late 1800s, includ-ing lengthy field trips to many of the places and groups involved (in-cluding central Nevada, where he interviewed the founding prophet Wovoka) in order to gather firsthand information. Beginning with some of the earliest known Native American religious movements in the colo-nial period of eastern North America, he wrote a highly detailed, sympa-thetic account of the Ghost Dance, blaming whites for the Sioux outbreak of 1890 and ensuing massacre of Big Foot's band of men, women, and children at Wounded Knee. *The Ghost Dance Religion and the Sioux Outbreak of 1890* was originally published in 1896 (Mooney 1973).

In the early decades of the twentieth century, anthropology became in-creasingly professionalized. This involved university courses of study, graduate degrees, academic positions in museums and universities, and especially fieldwork. In order to complete graduate degrees and establish professional qualifications, aspiring anthropologists did lengthy field studies that involved living with a group of people and getting to know them as individuals and learning and ideally using their language. In the case of British anthropology, this almost always involved some group and place in a colony or protectorate of the empire (on which "the sun never set"), while American anthropology usually involved one or another Na-tive American group. In either case, fieldwork was supposed to be a scientific enterprise. If what was being studied was undertaken at the initiative of, or with financial support by, a colonial regime or government agency wanting information for a practical purpose, it was still supposed to be done according to established professional standards. Fieldwork was based on some problem or hypothesis and the use of established methods, the most important of which in American anthropology was systematic work with informants; for the British, it was a more general activity called participant observation. The observer lived with and participated, to the extent that he or she could, in the activities being studied. Whatever was studied in particular was supposed to be studied in the context of a more general understanding of the society and culture of the group in question.

Partly at least because of the kinds of groups involved (or at least the kinds of groups that attracted the attention of early observers and then early anthropologists), anthropology became overwhelmingly associated with the study of peoples referred to as "primitive." This term was eventually abandoned or repudiated, but in the nineteenth century and the first seventy-five years of the twentieth century anthropologists, other scholars, and the general public used it to refer to peoples now called tribal, preliterate, prestate, small-scale, or indigenous.

Consequently, for a long period of time the anthropological study of religion was largely, if not entirely, the study of primitive religion. Until several decades ago courses in the anthropology of religion commonly had the term "primitive" in their titles, as did courses in the anthropology of art and other topics for which there was a perceived need to distinguish an anthropological approach or topic from that of other academic disciplines. However unfortunate or embarrassing such terms for small-scale societies now seem to anthropologists and others, and however unfortunate the circumstances of study may have sometimes been, the enduring contributions that anthropology has made to the understanding of religious beliefs and practices among small-scale societies is considerable.

TYPES OF ANTHROPOLOGICAL STUDIES OF RELIGION

Anthropological studies of religion form several types. The most important, ethnographies, are contextually developed accounts of the religious beliefs and practices (or anything else) of particular groups that are usually based on firsthand research and knowledge—fieldwork among the people in question. They are usually focused not only on a particular people but also on a particular place, often a specific village or other circumscribed location. In this regard, Mooney's study of the Ghost Dance was based on fieldwork but not exactly ethnographic fieldwork. Ethnographic accounts are distinguished by their detail and degree of thoroughness. These accounts, in turn, provide the basis for more theoretical or comparative ones.

Beyond ethnography there are various sorts of comparative study. Any study that draws on either published or unpublished information on a variety of different societies in order to make comparisons, note contrasts, explore a theme, or provide examples that illustrate a point is comparative rather than ethnographic in nature. The late-nineteenth- and early-twentieth-century armchair studies of religion done by Tylor, Frazer, and others of magic and religion are early examples, but there are more recent ones as well.

Some of the most important comparative studies have been carried out by scholars of comparative religion. Probably the best-known study in comparative religion is Mircea Eliade's seminal *Shamanism: Archaic Techniques of Ecstasy*. This work was originally published in French (1951) and later in English (1964). It is a vast study based on accounts in many languages in which Eliade sought to establish the basic features of shamanism in Siberia and Central Asia and then sought comparisons across the world. It is controversial among anthropologists, partly for the same reasons as were the earlier great armchair studies. But this work is to a substantial extent responsible for the enormous scholarly interest in shamanism that has developed over the past several decades and seems likely to continue.

There is another type of comparative study that is formally constituted and aspires to something closer to science than humanistic scholarship, though whether it does so successfully is controversial: cross-cultural study. The term "cross-cultural" refers to a research effort or account that is comparative in nature but also refers to something more particular. A cross-cultural study goes more or less as follows: A sample of societies is created, usually by drawing from the human relations area files (a huge database of ethnographic accounts of societies throughout the world). Some effort is usually made to make the sample broadly based; that is, to include societies from throughout the various parts of the world in equal proportion (so many from North America, South America, Africa, Asia, the Pacific Islands), though actually doing this in a satisfactory manner is difficult. An effort is also made to exclude any or many societies that are from the same local geographic area. Once the sample of societies (usually fifty or more) has been created, research questions or hypotheses are posed and information is sought from the database or from this and other ethnographic sources that will, it is hoped, answer them. The answers to the questions are sought by counting the bits of information from each society in the sample that supports one or another possible interpretation or conclusion. The results are seldom (if ever) absolute but instead find greater or lesser support for an interpretation; therefore they usually have to be established statistically, in terms of probability. Such studies have been done by researchers outside of anthropology as well. Many anthropologists are skeptical of the results or general value of such studies either because of the various difficulties involved or because of a more pervasive disinclination to think that research in cultural anthropology can or should be "scientific" in nature.[2]

TYPES OF RELIGION

For the purposes of this book the religions of humanity can be put into several broad categories. There are many ways that religions can be divided up for purposes of identification and comparison. The one that is used here is not based on a single criterion such as the nature of the central beliefs (animism, pantheism, polytheism, monotheism). It is simply an overall way of identifying kinds of religion in terms of how anthropologists and other scholars deal with the topic.

Prehistoric Religion

The religious beliefs and practices of prehistory are known only in fragmentary terms as a result of archaeological discovery and inference, although they tend to be of considerable hypothetical importance in relation to the question of when religion first appeared in the human past. The matter of when religion may have first come into existence, of how this can be known or inferred, of how it may have occurred, and what early religion may have been like, is looked at in chapter 3. Some scholars believe that the various religious practices around the world have deep prehistoric origins. Shamanism is an example that will be discussed in detail later on.

Ancient Religions

Ancient religions belonged to past civilizations. They include the religions of the pre-Christian Greeks and Romans and the Egyptians in the times of the pharaohs and the religions of the pre-Columbian Aztecs, Maya, and Incas. In much of the world the religions of these past civilizations have been replaced by or absorbed into succeeding religions (see below). This did not occur everywhere. In India and China the religions of antiquity continued to exist—though not in an unchanging form—to be supplemented rather than replaced by later religions. However, even when supplanted, many of the beliefs and practices of the older religion survived, especially among villagers. Some examples of this will be discussed in later chapters, but at this point let us assume that the ancient religions are gone. While anthropologists may be interested in these ancient religions and sometimes write about them they do not—except for anthropological archaeologists—study them extensively because they lack the research skills or knowledge of languages and scripts needed to do so. Of the studies of ancient religion that have been done, William Robertson Smith's *Lectures on the Religion of the Semites* (1901), has been of greatest importance by far, for Smith established a line of interpretation that continues to be of fundamental importance to the present.

Indigenous Religions of Small-Scale Societies

As already noted, the religions of the smaller societies of the world, along with their other dimensions, were formerly referred to as "primitive." This term was generally accepted in anthropology into the 1960s. Some scholars preferred "savage" to "primitive" but meant the same things by it. Both terms came to be regarded as pejorative and ethnocentric and went out of use after the 1960s. However, their passing created the problem of how to refer to the kinds of religions, cultures, and societies that had formerly been referred to as primitive or savage. "Small-scale" is probably the preferred term, but it may be misleading if it is applied directly to religion (as in "small-scale religion") rather than to the religion of such a society (as in the "religion of a small-scale society"). "Tribal" is another term used for such societies, but it has several problems, including its widespread popular use to refer to clans, ethnic groups (e.g., in present-day news stories about Iraq), or other social divisions of large and complex societies.

It is also misleading to refer to "tribal religion" as a general type, since societies that are tribal in a political sense (e.g., autonomous or semiautonomous) may be adherents of a major or world religion. This is especially true of the Islamic world. While many small-scale societies follow distinctive religions traditions, many others adhere generally to one or another of the world religions. It is also true that religion in large-scale societies (e.g., China and Japan) may include distinctive indigenous traditions or dimensions as well as those associated with one or another of the world religions.

Such labeling problems notwithstanding, much of the contribution that anthropology has made to the understanding of the nature of religious belief and practice and their role in human life, much of the theorizing about religion, and many important ethnographic accounts of religion have involved such indigenous religions of small-scale societies. Anthropologists are not the only scholars with an interest in these kinds of religions but they are usually recognized as special authorities on them. Until the middle of the twentieth century, anthropological interest in religion was directed largely at these types, since anthropology in general was mainly concerned with small-scale indigenous societies. Such religions are referred to throughout the book.

The World Religions

The last type of religion includes the various named religions to which a large portion of the world's population now belongs (or at least with which it identifies). These are the so-called world religions (the preferred term), the "great religions" or the "world's major religions," the "universal religions" or sometimes "religions of the book." These religions have spread far beyond their places of origin and over many geographical zones and across innumerable ethnic and linguistic boundaries. They are based in part on written texts, have lengthy known histories, and tend to be proselytizing and competitive. The main world religions are Christianity, Islam, Judaism, Buddhism, and Hinduism, all of which include countless regional and local divisions and varieties that constantly grow and change. The world religions have been spreading over a long period of time. But colonial rule and postcolonial globalizing trends have helped them become established throughout many areas of the world in which the inhabitants had formerly adhered to local religious beliefs and practices.

Anthropologists began to do research that involved the world religions mainly after World War II, first in places like Latin America, India, China, and Southeast Asia, then in eastern and southern Europe and finally in Western society itself. If nothing else, the extensive conversion of the native or indigenous inhabitants of Southeast Asia, the Pacific Islands, Africa, and North and South America has meant that any study of the religions of these peoples has to take account of the world religions, even if they do not amount to the totality of their religion. Such anthropological studies involving the world religions will be mentioned at various places throughout the book and then discussed more fully in the final chapter. Anthropological interest in the world religions has concerned especially the ways they are believed and practiced locally rather than globally. The result is that the "same" religion may be interpreted and practiced very differently in different places.

RELIGIONS VERSUS RELIGION

The importance of the differences among the various religions is not something everyone would agree on. Some anthropologists take the position that religion is not that different from one people or place to another. For them, what is most interesting about religion is what all religions have in common (such as the assumption that there is more to reality than is experienced through the senses, or that supernatural beings tend to be thought of in similar ways in many societies) than in the differences that make it useful to put the many varieties of religion in different categories. Obviously it is worth making distinctions among different forms of religion, but there is little value in making distinctions for their own sake. Those who stress that what is important or interesting about religion is a matter of commonalities rather than differences have important points to make (e.g., in trying to understand how religion may have developed in the first place).

There are also reasons for looking at differences. For example, in trying to understand religion in very broad comparative terms it is useful to begin (as will be done in the next chapter) by examining the distinctive features of Western views of religion. But in doing this, it is generally necessary to go beyond a simple us-versus-the-rest approach. While some Western ideas or orientations to religion (e.g., the general tendency not to see it in what I call "practical" terms) can be usefully contrasted with those of most other peoples, such a distinction is usually too crude. Often I find myself saying that some notion or generalization (e.g., about religion and morality) tends to work well for the world religions in general but not for others. I also note contrasts among the world religions and among the various levels or forms of practice that exist within them, but this does not negate the general value of generalizing about the world religions.

NOTES

1. The prominent anthropological scholar of religion Mary Douglas goes much further than this. She writes that "the idea that primitive man is by nature deeply religious is nonsense. The truth is that all varieties of skepticism, materialism and spiritual fervour are to be found in the range of tribal societies" (Douglas 1973: 36–37).

2. One well-known cross-cultural study of religion was done by the sociologist Guy Swanson and published as *The Birth of the Gods* (1960).

REFERENCES AND FURTHER READING

Banton, Michael, ed. 1966. *Anthropological Approaches to the Study of Religion*. London: Tavistock.

Barth, Fredrik. 1961. *Nomads of South Persia: The Basseri Tribe of the Khamseh Confederacy*. Boston: Little, Brown.

Bellah, Robert. 1965. "Religious Evolution." In *Reader in Comparative Religion*, edited by William A. Lessa and Evon Z. Vogt, pp. 73–87. New York: Harper & Row.
———. 1967. "Civil Religion in America." *Daedalus* 96 (Winter): 1–21.
Carstairs, G. Morris. [1957] 1967. *The Twice Born: A Study of a Community of High-Caste Hindus*. Bloomington: Indiana University Press.
Connolly, Bob, and Robin Anderson. 1987 *First Contact: New Guinea's Encounter with the Outside World*. Harmondsworth, U.K.: Penguin.
Douglas, Mary. 1973. *Natural Symbols: Exploration in Cosmology*. New York: Vintage.
Durkheim, Emile. [1915] 1965. *The Elementary Forms of Religious Life*. New York: Free Press.
Eliade, Mircea. [1951] 1964. *Shamanism: Archaic Techniques of Ecstasy*. New York: Pantheon.
Endicott, Kirk. 1979. *Batek Negrito Religion: The World-View and Rituals of a Hunting and Gathering People of Peninsular Malaysia*. Oxford: Clarendon.
Evans-Prichard, E. E. 1937. *Witchcraft, Oracles, and Magic among the Azande*. Oxford: Oxford University Press.
Firth, Raymond. 1968. *Tikopia Ritual and Belief*. Boston: Beacon.
Geertz, Clifford. 1973. *The Interpretation of Cultures*. New York: Basic Books.
Glazier, Stephen D., ed. 1997. *Anthropology of Religion: A Handbook*. Westport, Conn.: Greenwood.
Guthrie, Stewart. 1993. *Faces in the Clouds: A New Theory of Religion*. New York: Oxford University Press.
Holmberg, Alan R. 1950. *Nomads of the Long Bow: The Siriono of Eastern Bolivia*. Washington, D.C.: U.S. Government Printing Office.
Hultkrantz, Åke. [1967] 1979. *The Religions of the American Indians*. Berkeley: University of California Press.
———. [1987] 1998. *Native Religions of North America*. Prospect Heights, Ill.: Waveland.
Keesing, Roger M. 1982. *Kwaio Religion: The Living and the Dead in a Solomon Island Society*. New York: Columbia University Press
Lienhardt, Godfrey. 1961. *Divinity and Experience: The Religion of the Dinka*. Oxford: Oxford University Press.
Metcalf, Peter. 1989. *Where Are You/Spirits: Style and Theme in Berawan Prayer*. Washington, D.C.: Smithsonian Institution Press.
Mooney, James. [1896] 1973. *The Ghost-Dance Religion and the Sioux Outbreak of 1890*. Fourteenth Annual Report of the Bureau of American Ethnology. Glorieta, N.M.: Rio Grande.
Obeyesekere, Gananth. 1992. *The Apotheosis of Captain Cook: European Mythmaking in the Pacific*. Princeton: Princeton University Press.
Reichel-Dolmatoff, Gerardo. 1971. *Amazon Cosmos. The Sexual and Religious Symbolism of the Tukano Indians*. Chicago: University of Chicago Press.
Restall, Matthew. 2003. *Seven Myths of the Spanish Conquest*. New York: Oxford.
Sahlins, Marshall. 1995. *How Natives Think: About Captain Cook, for Example*. Chicago: University of Chicago Press.
Sellato, Bernard. 1994. *When Nomads Settle: The Economics, Politics, and Ideology of Settling Down*. Honolulu: University of Hawaii Press.
Smith, Wilfred Cantwell. 1963. *The Meaning and End of Religion: A New Approach to the Religions of Mankind*. New York: Macmillan.

Smith, William Robertson. [1889] 1901. *Lectures on the Religion of the Semites*. London: Adam and Charles Black.

Swanson, Guy E. 1960. *The Birth of the Gods: The Origin of Primitive Beliefs*. Ann Arbor: University of Michigan Press.

Tylor, Edward B. [1871] 1889. *Primitive Culture: Researches into the Development of Mythology, Philosophy, Religion, Language, Art, and Custom*. 2 vols. 3rd American ed. New York: Holt.

Wallace, Anthony F. C. 1966. *Religion: An Anthropological View*. New York: Random House.

Yang, C. K. [1961] 1991. *Religion in Chinese Society*. Prospect Heights, Ill.: Waveland.

or husband) only one at a time. To use the most common denominations, an American identifies himself or herself as a Christian, a Jew, a Muslim, a Buddhist, or a Hindu, and so on, and labels others in such terms as well. More particular identities may be even more important. To leave out the fast-growing new religions, a Christian can be a Roman Catholic (or less commonly Eastern Orthodox) or a Protestant, and a Protestant can be a Methodist, Lutheran, Baptist, Presbyterian, and so on, while a Muslim may be Sunni or Shiite. Whether one wishes to use broad or more specific designations, the principle of mutual exclusiveness applies. Although there is (at least in the United States) no law that says a person cannot be a Jew and a Catholic at the same time and alternatively attend Jewish and Catholic services, such a person would be seen as someone who had not yet made up her or his mind or else as being confused. People of different religions who marry may (and often do) devise wedding ceremonies that combine elements from each tradition and otherwise work out which religious holidays are to be celebrated in which ways and with whose relatives. But such practices do not negate the general cultural principle of exclusive religious identity. People who change their religious affiliation are said to "convert" and thereby cease to be what they had been. Persons who claim to hold no religious beliefs and follow no religious practices are so labeled as atheists, agnostics, or (more positively) as nonbelievers or freethinkers.

Religious identities are separate from and therefore not mutually exclusive with other sorts of identity, including gender, sexual orientation, class, occupation, political affiliation, and ethnicity. Although there are some associations between religion and these other sorts of identities, none can be assumed. Finally, religion tends to be very important in terms of a person's overall notion of what sort of person he or she is, and of how she or he is viewed by others. In the United States religious identities are highly politicized, as we are constantly being reminded.

Westerners are hardly exclusive in having specific and exclusive religious identities. Such identities appear to be characteristic of Christians, Muslims, and Jews everywhere and probably of many of the present-day adherents of all of the world religions. Such explicit, mutually exclusive religious identities are not usually found among people who are adherents of indigenous religious beliefs and practices. Once a world religion such as Christianity or Islam has spread into an area, all people are identified accordingly. However, while it is easy to identify and label people who have become Christians or Muslims, there is often a problem of how to refer to those who have not. In many places in the world where Christianity has been introduced or widely accepted by indigenous peoples, those who have not converted are referred to as "pagans," a term introduced by missionaries or colonial officials. In my experience in Southeast Asia, this term is often used by local persons without negative prejudice, for families as well as villages may contain some members who are Christian and some who are not. However, Westerners are likely to be uncomfortable with this term, regard it as pejorative (as it was generally intended to be by those who introduced it) and not wish to use it unless they do so negatively. Indigenous tribal peoples normally lack a term for persons who are *not* converts to an introduced religion or for those who continue to follow traditional beliefs and practices. In Southeast Asia, except for the term "pagan" or similar introduced notions, there are generally no single words by which to label non-Christian, non-Muslim, non-Buddhist peoples. Anthropologists, who are uncomfortable with terms like "pagan," generally have recourse to awkward phrases such as "followers of custom," "customary religion," or "ways of the ancestors" if these have become locally accepted.

Even if there is no single word for a religious identity, however, such identities are now present and highly important throughout most of the world. Such labels as Christian, Muslim, and Buddhist or pagan do not necessarily mean much in terms of the content of religion—what people actually know, believe, and practice—but they have become increasingly pervasive as identities, often with major (and bloody) political consequences as well.

Nonetheless, in some places where the world religions may be well established, people do not regard religious identities in exclusive terms. Asian religions in general do not fit easily with the notion that people adhere to one or another specific religion to the exclusion of others. In much of East Asia, Buddhism has been well established a long time, but people in China, Japan, and Vietnam generally do not regard themselves simply as Buddhists to the exclusion of other traditions. In the case of all of the various world religions, what people actually believe and practice is considerably more diverse and complex than the labels by which they identify themselves, but in East Asia people tend not to even accept the term Buddhist as an adequate label for the whole range of their religion. Because of this and because of the variety of historically established and widely practiced non-Buddhist traditions, scholars tend to speak of "Chinese religion" or "Japanese religion" rather than simply identify these countries or civilizations as part of the Buddhist world.

RELIGION IS A SEPARATE REALM OF LIFE

The third characteristic Western view about religion is that it is largely separate from other realms of life. In intellectual terms "religion" as belief and knowledge is distinguished from "science," and in occupational terms religious specialists are differentiated from doctors, lawyers, professors, plumbers, politicians, social workers, and so on. Religion is also seen as something that is done on a special separate day of the week—mainly Sunday in the case of most Christians—but most people know that different religions have different special days of the week.

To say that Westerners view religion as largely separate from other realms in these and other ways is not to say that religion is much different than anything else. If you want to say that institutions, occupations, behavioral patterns, forms of social organization, and whatever else are also marked by separation from one another, you would be correct, although the separation is particularly significant where religion is concerned. Also, in this instance the prevailing cultural view is largely correct. In comparative terms, religion in Western society really *is* largely separate from other realms, its high level of (and increasing) politicization notwithstanding. This is partly a matter of language, a matter of having a word for religion in contrast to words for entertainment, art, government, education, government, economy, literature, medicine, science, and so on. Words create reality (or help to at least) even if they also create fallacies. The way we think about religion, even to the point of having it as a major category of culture, is in part a matter of having the word bequeathed to Western society by several centuries or more of written history.

Many people would hold that the separation of religion from other aspects of life is not all a good thing, reject it entirely, and do what they can to diminish or eliminate it—the separateness—from their lives. Further, many people in the United States who see themselves as very religious might claim that religion is not that separate from other things in their (or their families' lives); rather, it pervades all they do. But even persons who would claim it is not so in their own lives would probably not dispute the proposition that religion tends to be separate from other things in American life as far as most people are concerned.

Again, assuming that religion is separate from other things is not a very useful approach to understanding it in broad comparative terms. Of course, religion is separate in other modern Western societies and probably to some extent among followers of the various world religions (and Christianity and Islam are spreading rapidly into the various corners of the world). But the assumption that religion can be separated from other realms of culture is misleading when we come to the kinds of traditionally preliterate, small-scale, or indigenous societies, the study of which have been until recently the special province of anthropology.

RELIGION IS ASSOCIATED WITH A SPECIAL BUILDING

One of the main ways that religion is differentiated from other things in Western society is that much of it takes place in special buildings, for example, synagogues, mosques, temples, and so forth. Of course, not all religious activity takes place in a dedicated building. Religiously oriented weddings among Christians traditionally are held in churches but may be held elsewhere, for example, out of doors in a beautiful setting. This is also true of funerals, since the graveside service cannot be held in or even near a church or other religious building because cemeteries are no longer located on church grounds as they once were, except perhaps in some rural areas. Nor, if people say daily prayers or invoke blessings before meals would they be doing so in a church, temple, mosque, or synagogue except on special occasions. Muslims are required to pray five times a day or thirty-five times a week, of which only the special prayer at noon on Friday is supposed to be done by men in a mosque or prayer house, although any of the daily prayers may be done in these places and doing so is common for people (especially men) who live nearby and have the time.

The special buildings for religion are not used much for other purposes. They are regarded as sacred and their primary purpose is for ritual, especially, as Westerners say, for worship. They are not used only for ritual of course. There is an ancient association in most of the world religions of using religious buildings as places of teaching, a practice that survives among American Christians in the form of Sunday school, adult Bible study classes, and so on. And many other activities take place in present-day religious buildings, but they are all related to religion in one way or another.

Religious buildings pervade our view of what religion is all about. People use the term "church" to refer not only to the building but also (as is true also of houses, banks, and may other things) to the organization or institution that it embodies, as in the phrase "my church does this or that"). Churches, mosques, synagogues, and temples are therefore highly important symbols. If we are on a road trip and drive through a town and see an unusually large number of churches, we will take it as an indication that it is a particularly religious sort of town. Conversely, one of the favorite observations made about the old gold rush mining town of Virginia City, Nevada (and probably similar towns in the West), concerned the low ratio of churches to saloons and other architectural embodiments of sin and degradation.

The association of special buildings with religion is hardly rare in comparative terms. It is true of all of the various world religions and probably of all of the ancient religions of both the Old and the New Worlds. Much of the monumental architecture of antiquity was religious.

The presence of a special building for religion seems so obvious and well-known that it may not appear worth noting. Except, again, it is not always the case. Within the religious practices of small-scale or tribal peoples, we find a mixed pattern of religious architecture. The Polynesian societies of the Pacific had a well-developed tradition of elaborate temples (Oliver 1989), but many (perhaps most) other small-scale societies do not. This comes as no surprise in the case of those hunting and gathering groups and other nomadic peoples whose architecture is limited to what they can take with them or what can be created anew each time a move is made to a new place. But the absence of dedicated religious buildings is by no means limited to such groups. It is also common among many peoples who make substantial or even massive buildings to live in. Among Native Americans the Pueblo dwellers of the Southwest did build separate ritual structures generally referred to as *kivas*, but the groups of the Northwest Coast who built massive wooden houses of cedar logs and planks did not create separate, permanent ritual structures (Nabakov and Easton 1989).

Nor do the Dayak groups in the interior of Borneo, who build some of the largest wooden dwellings of all small-scale societies (Winzeler 2004). These take the form of massive longhouses up to several hundred meters in length containing up to fifty or so family apartments. While some Dayak ritual activities take place outside the longhouse either in the open air or in special temporary shelters, most take place in the longhouse. Nor are there any rooms or places in a longhouse that are dedicated to ritual activities for either the whole group or for individuals, or any places that are more or less sacred, except perhaps for certain hearths above which the skulls taken in head-hunting were hung, or conversely the unclean areas where women give birth or the area beneath the longhouse where human garbage and waste is deposited and where pigs, chickens, and dogs forage. Most ceremonies take place in the covered front veranda of the longhouse, but some occur also inside the private apartments of families or outside on open platforms. All of these places are used for everyday work, socializing, and life in general. It could be argued that the longhouse in the interior of Borneo (and the same point could be made regarding the massive houses of northern Pacific Coast) is really a ritual structure in which people also happen to live and work. Longhouses are ritual structures in some ways, but the point is that unlike the churches, temples, mosques, and synagogues we are familiar with, they are not separate or dedicated religious structures.

RELIGION CONCERNS TRANSCENDENTAL
RATHER THAN PRACTICAL MATTERS

Another way of saying that Westerners tend to see religion as separate from other realms of life is to note that for many it does not have much to do with practical matters as opposed to "spiritual" ones. This is to invoke a distinction that anthropologists and other scholars sometimes make between the transcendental, metaphysical, or otherworldly dimensions of religion and the more "practical" or "worldly" ones (Mandelbaum 1964). Such a separation can never be complete, and statements about the extent to which Westerners (or anyone else) have a well-developed practical orientation to religion can only be made in relative terms and need to be qualified in ways that will be discussed below.

It is relatively easy to understand what is meant by the transcendental or otherworldly dimensions of Christianity, for example. This includes what people variously believe or do not believe about God, Jesus Christ, Mary, the Saints, the devil, the ultimate nature of the universe as having meaning and human life has having divine purpose, the human soul as something separate from the body that will continue after life and will be rewarded or punished according to how life has been lived and to the will of the Almighty. The ritual or behavioral side of such beliefs includes all the prescribed or patterned things that people do as individuals and in groups to act on such beliefs, to communicate with God and other superhuman beings such as saints, to invoke divine blessings, and to ask forgiveness for transgressions. Such ritual activities include prayer, grace before meals, and attending religious services, routinely and on special occasions, including the great holidays and important life events, especially weddings and funerals. They also include pilgrimages (though religious as opposed to secular pilgrimages are far less important in America than in some countries, including many Western ones) to sacred places, the performance of penance, and acts of charity.

All of this constitutes what Westerners are generally inclined to regard as "religion," and not only Westerners, of course. It would not be difficult to give a similar summary of the transcendental dimensions of the religious beliefs and activities of other religions, especially the other world religions, though many things would be different. For example, religion as most Westerners practice it does not include blood sacrifices or the ritual killing of animals as offerings to spiritual beings, but animal sacrifice is very important in some non-Western religions, as was human sacrifice in some ancient religions. In Islam animals are sacrificed as a part of several important ceremonies, including the annual pilgrimage.

Westerners generally do not think of religion in terms of its practical side. Indeed, the phrase "transcendental religion" would generally be regarded as redundant. Why bother with the "transcendental" part? Of course, if religion is said to include both a transcendental and a practical side, many Americans would claim that their religious beliefs and participation in ritual activities are enormously practical in that these are vital to their happiness and sense of well-being, that their faith and prayers get them through difficult times, help them cope with the death of friends and loved ones and with the inevitability of their own demise. Nonetheless, much of the practical side of religion has largely disappeared from what many Westerners commonly think religion is all about.

Although there are various important exceptions (noted below), practical religion has declined as Westerners have largely come to rely on other forms of knowledge and practice—especially science, technology, and social services—in living their everyday lives and in coping with illness and other misfortune or problems. Put more abstractly, the space for practical religion in modern Western life has greatly narrowed.

Modern-day religious specialists, including ministers, priests, and rabbis, do certain practical things including visiting the sick, counseling the troubled, and helping the homeless and impoverished. Charity or giving is generally considered mandatory for church members, and charity is a matter of practical or material assistance. Faith healers, astrologers, spiritual advisers, and other practitioners also offer various sorts of practical assistance. Overall, however, much of what is done in many places in the world realm of practical religion by religious specialists or by relatives and neighbors using religious ritual is now done in the West by secular specialists, including medical doctors, psychiatrists, marriage counselors, psychologists, social workers, and other therapists. Funerals have both practical and transcendental dimensions, and are handled largely by nonreligious mortuary specialists.

In comparative terms, practical religion includes various concerns. In Malaysia these include protection for a journey, finding a winning lottery number, passing school exams, attracting or getting back husbands and wives, becoming pregnant and bearing children. Two concerns that are particularly important in many places in the world are curing and food production. Religion in Western society continues to have some association (perhaps a growing one in the case of rapidly spreading Pentecostalism and the introduction of healing activities in some mainline religions) with the former, but little with the latter. Most Westerners who seek assistance when sick or injured go to a doctor or the hospital (at least in the United States if they have insurance). Religion for some people is left entirely out of the process. The church services I am familiar with include prayers for the sick and dying or the otherwise seriously troubled, and ministers and other religious specialists visit the very ill or injured and provide counseling to those who wish it. Faith healing is important for religious groups as documented in a recently published collection of articles (Barnes and Sered 2005). But generally, physical and psychological healing and counseling are the province of medical doctors, psychologists, counselors, social workers, and other secular specialists.

Religious institutions are involved in the distribution of food and meals as charity to the poor. However, in contrast to the distribution of food, religious belief and ritual in Western society has little to do with the production of food. Food production has become a highly specialized activity carried out by a small number of farmers and ranchers.

The contrast with what occurs in other places can be striking. In many other places in the world, growing crops or hunting animals is a religious activity. In Southeast Asia the cultivation of rice is sometimes referred to as a major cult. What is meant by this assertion is that the growing of rice is an important dimension of the religious practices of many groups, sometimes as much a ritual activity as a technological one. This has changed with the spread of Western influence and the world religions and with the adoption of new seed varieties and scientifically developed forms of cultivation, but it can still be found. The last time I was in Sarawak (one of the two Malaysian states in Borneo) I was photographing a swidden (slash and burn) field in a Bidayuh village that had been recently burned and was being tidied up in preparation for planting. I noticed that a small cross made of two sticks tied together with a piece of vine had been placed in the middle of the field after it had been burned. It reminded me of small wooden crosses placed along highways in the United States to mark the sites of fatal traffic accidents. I asked farmers who were working there what it was for. They replied it was to protect the field. They told me they were now Christian, and therefore it was appropriate to put the cross up. In the past, they had followed the traditional ceremonies involved with the production of rice but after converting no longer did so. They supposed that having prayers in the field and putting up the cross would protect the rice and help it grow. The growing of rice had been a major dimension of traditional Dayak religion. The simple ritual actions were meager in comparison to the elaborate traditional cycle of religious ceremonies (*gawai*) involved with rice growing that begin with the clearing of the fields and culminate in the harvest festival. The cross in the field was a modest reflection of traditional belief and practice.

Practical Religion among Latin American Immigrants in Los Angeles

Although practical religion has greatly diminished in the West, it is alive and well among some groups and in some areas. In the United States, immigrants from Latin America, the Caribbean, Southeast Asia, and elsewhere have brought their religions traditions with them (including vernacular versions of Christianity), and these traditions tend to have well-developed practical dimensions. For example, a recent account of Latin American immigrants from Mexico and Central America in Los Angeles vividly describes the various folk or popular practical beliefs, ritual practices, and groups that comprise a large part of the religious life of the several million Hispanics in the city. The authors of this account report that Hispanic immigrant religion focuses on two popular religious divinities. One is El Santo San Niño de Atocha, who is thought to be an incarnation of the Christ Child and who is shown in posters sold everywhere as an angelic adolescent in pilgrim's clothing. The other is Hermano San Simón (also known as Maximón), a folk saint of uncertain Guatemalan origin who is unrecognized by the official Catholic Church but "is fast becoming one the most familiar of the multitude of immigrant gods, spirits, and saints whose icons are used to mark sacred space in Los Angeles" (Polk, Jones, Hernández, and Ronelli 2005: 111). The popularity of both of deities is linked to a belief in their effectiveness in dispensing practical assistance to those in need:

> Although the Vatican does not recognize him, San Simón is nonetheless greatly revered. Offerings consist of cigarettes, liquor, money, tamales, and fruit accompanied by prayers and candles intended to safeguard or enrich the petitioner. A red candle stands for love, green symbolizes prosperity, white guards children, yellow protects adults, pink secures health, blue brings work and luck, and sky blue assures money and happiness . . . Brother Simón can also cause harm to enemies; one sometimes sees black candles in front of alters, often with a name scratched on the surface . . . One may petition him for things one would not ask of other saints, for example, sexual success, revenge on enemies, overlooking of debts and so on. (Polk, Jones, Hernández, and Ronelli 2005: 112)

In modern urban Los Angeles practical religion among Latin American immigrants seems to be as fully and richly developed as anywhere in the world. The general range of concerns and needs it embodies are much the same as those to be found anywhere else, although some things vary according to cultural traditions and local circumstances. On the one hand, rituals or petitions to make the crops grow are not common in urban areas where people are not farmers but farm laborers. On the other hand, people who live and work as urban, suburban, or rural laborers and are often undocumented immigrants whose lives include dangerous travel over great distances and through a heavily fortified and guarded border face practical difficulties of their own. Asked why she was devoted to San Simón, one Guatemalan immigrant woman replied:

> The first thing he did for me was to help me pass the citizenship test, when I didn't know how to speak a bit of English. There was also another time when I crossed the border through Tijuana with two kids [her niece and nephew]. They didn't do anything to me. They just arrested me and took one of the kids with them and I had prayed so much to him that nothing really happened. I could have lost my green card. (Polk, Jones, Hernández, and Ronelli 2005: 116)

Older ethnic minorities in the United States have continued to adhere to practically oriented religion's traditions. Here (as perhaps to some extent also among the dominant Euro-American sectors) the orientation to supernaturally focused curing and other forms of practical religiosity tend to be linked to socioeconomic status; the better-off and more formally educated sectors have tended to turn away from practical religion while the poorer sectors, who have much less control over their lives, have continued to adhere to it.

RELIGION IS THE BASIS OF MORALITY

Westerners assume that morality (or ethics) is one of the most important dimensions of religion. Americans commonly believe that Western morality is based largely or entirely on biblical (i.e., Judeo-Christian) religious principles, as reflected especially in the Ten Commandments. Of course, what this should mean in political terms in the present-day United States is controversial, the focus of "culture wars" over gay rights, school prayer, and so on. Even people who favor the total separation of church and state or are indifferent to religion are inclined to grant the religious origins of much of Western morality.

When anthropologists address the question of religion and morality, they are asking whether or not relations among humans (what they do to or with one another, how they regard and treat one another, with kindness or cruelty, help or exploitation) are of concern to the gods and spirits that they believe in; or, if not, whether there are other sorts of connections between religious beliefs and practices and the do's and don'ts of social life. One possibility is for people to believe that God is concerned with human conduct with other humans and dispenses rewards and punishment accordingly. The opposite possibility is that the gods and spirits don't really care what humans do among or to themselves as long as they respect and deal with the supernatural beings in a proper manner (e.g., referring to and addressing them correctly, making offerings and sacrifices, invoking their blessings). Morality in such circumstances is said to be mainly secular.

The Judeo-Christian religious view is the first. The basic idea is that moral transgressions are sins, offenses to God, and will be punished accordingly, especially in terms of what happens to the soul after death. God cares about how people treat one another and acts accordingly by rewarding people for not doing evil deeds and for doing good ones. Salvation is a complicated matter involving grace and forgiveness, but the religious importance of moral behavior is usually emphasized.

In other world religions, the link between religion and morality is also clear. In Islam it is, if anything, even more emphatic than in Christianity.

In the Eastern world religions, the relationship of morality to religion is somewhat different but also very strong. In Buddhist doctrine the principle is not that God is angered by human misconduct toward other humans and pleased by kindness, selflessness, charity, and other positive forms of behavior but rather that good and bad conduct are a matter of karma (to use the term in its general sense), the impersonal moral law of the universe that is the sum total or balance of a person's good and bad acts, both in this life and in all pervious ones, and that determines fate in this life and future lives.

It is what happens beyond the realm of the doctrines of the world religions that raises a problem about religion and morality. The issue is an old one in anthropology. E. B. Tylor raised it at the very beginning:

> So far as savage religion can stand as representing natural religion, the popular idea that the moral government of the universe is an essential tenet of natural religion simply falls to the ground. Savage animism is almost devoid of that ethical element which to the educated modern mind is the very mainspring of practical religion. (Tylor 1958: 446)

Tylor went on to say that it was not that savage society lacked moral standards or codes. These codes were highly developed, as they would have to be, even in the simplest society. It was rather that morality stood on its own and was handled by tradition, mediation, public opinion, and retribution rather than by religion.

To the extent that Tylor is correct we should not expect to find that religion and morality are closely associated beyond Christianity and the other world religions. But Tylor's claim has long been controversial. Some anthropologists familiar with indigenous religions have expressed agreement with him, either in general terms or specific ethnographic accounts, while others have taken the opposite view. Malinowski (1935), a founder of modern British social anthropology who wrote famous accounts of magic, science, and religion, held that Tylor was wrong and that morality was always closely connected with religion, although he discussed the matter in generally abstract terms rather than of specific examples that make his argument less than clear.

Many ethnographic studies discuss the issue, although they do not always resolve it in either/or terms. To take another example from the Azande, Evans-Prichard says that their moral notions of good and bad conduct are not very different from our own. But such notions do not have the kind of religious basis they do in the world religions:

> The ghosts of the dead cannot be appealed to as arbiters of morals and sanctions of conduct, because the ghosts are members of kinship groups and only exercise authority within these groups among the same people

over whom they exercised authority when they were alive. The Supreme Being is a very vague influence and is not cited by the Azande as the guardian of moral law which must be obeyed simply because he is its author. (Evans-Prichard 1937: 110)

Evans-Prichard goes on to assert a connection between morality and religion that lies in the "idiom of witchcraft." Bad actions and evil thoughts are condemned mainly because they lead to witchcraft—and witchcraft can kill or bring other misfortune including accidents, illnesses, and crop failures. Witchcraft-related beliefs, fears, accusations, and gossip thus tend to encourage the Azande to behave in moral terms. Other accounts of non–world religions also tend toward the general conclusion that there *is* a connection between spiritual beliefs and practices and morality but the connection is likely to take a very different form than in Christianity or the other world religions (Swanson 1960: 153–74).

Among indigenous peoples of Southeast Asia, there are links between proper and improper behavior and spiritual beliefs, although not of a familiar sort. In Borneo such links often involve the notion of what is sometimes referred to as taboo and "pollution." The idea is that bad acts or improper behavior has harmful spiritual consequences for the community that are quite separate from the "natural" or social consequences of what has been done, such as killing someone or engaging in incest. It requires a ritual response of sacrifice or cleansing in addition to whatever is involved in the way of "secular" punishment or compensation.

In the interior of Borneo, notions about the spiritual state of a community—traditionally often a longhouse—are sometimes expressed in humoral terms or as a matter of balance. In humoral terms the desirable state of a longhouse or other community is to be "cool." This means that things are in spiritual balance and life is good: the rice grows well, there are wild pigs around to hunt, people are healthy and get along, women succeed in becoming pregnant and bearing live children, and so on. If the village becomes "hot," bad things (crop failures, disease, quarreling, miscarriages) happen. Among the Iban of northwestern Borneo, according to Derek Freeman,

> When the Iban speak of the ritual condition of a long-house they liken it to the temper of a human organism. When in sound and normal health, a man's body is said to be *chelap*, or cool and when it is afflicted by disease or disorder, *angat*, or feverish. These same terms are applied to the long-house. Ritually, it may be in a "cool" and benign state (*rumah chelap*), or, what is greatly feared, it may become ritually "heated" (*rumah angat*), charged with a kind of evil and contagious essence that threatens all of its inhabitants. The danger is not physical but spiritual—though to an Iban mind physical and spiritual events are but different aspects of the same continuum—and its agency is

mystical. This dreaded state of affairs—*rumah angat*—is liable to be brought
about by any serious transgression of a ritual prohibition (*pemali*); but the
danger can be averted by the paying cf an expiatory fine to the *tuai burong*.
Such a fine . . . always includes a fowl (or a pig) which is sacrificed, to excul-
pate the transgressor, and free the community from any threat to its well-being. (Freeman 1970: 122–23)

In the case of the Bidayuh of the same general region, spiritual pollution or danger is also expressed in terms of balance. According to a recent Sarawak (Malaysian) government manual on Bidayuh customary
law (*adat*):

The primary function of the *adat* in the Bidayuh society is to maintain a har-
monious relationship among the members of the community and to preserve
the physical and spiritual well-being of the *kupuo* (village, longhouse or community). Proper conduct . . . is believed to maintain the community in a state
of balance or ritual wellbeing with the gods and spirits. Any breach of conduct may threaten individual relationship[s] and the spiritual wellbeing of
the community, such as the health and material prosperity of the people.
Therefore, remedial action must be taken immediately by offering [a] ritual
propitiation." (*Adat Bidayuh* 1994: i)

To take one further example from the same area, in his account of the
Kayan, Jérôme Rousseau writes that "religion has relatively little to do
with morals. Adultery, theft and murder are essentially secular matters
with only incidental religious aspects (thus a murder within a longhouse
pollutes it). However, habitual thieves may suffer supernatural punishment" (Rousseau 1998: 75). Perhaps the starkest contrast between Kayan
religious beliefs and morals (i.e., traditional or indigenous beliefs; most
Dayaks are now Christians) and those of Christians, Muslims, or adherents of world religions involves the afterlife. People live in longhouses
along rivers, procreate, grow rice, go hunting, and even have religious rituals and quarrel. The land of the dead does have different regions and
some places are better than others. However, where one ends up has nothing much to do with how one has behaved in life but rather mainly with
how one has died (Rousseau 1998: 97–98).

Kayan morality, like that of some other Southeast Asian societies, pro-
scribes the mockery of animals (Rousseau 1998: 105–6). With the exception of the monkey and the frog (which had angered an important god) it
is absolutely forbidden to show disrespect for wild or domestic animals,
including pigs and dogs. Mocking animals, among the Kayan, falls into
the same category as incest and brings forth the same spiritual response.
It is punished by Thunder, a spirit that transforms itself into thunder and
sends heavy rain and lightening. At the worst, an offender can be turned

into stone (and the Kayan can point to various rock formations to show that this has happened to both individuals and entire longhouses). The proscription (which also occurs among the indigenous peoples of the interior of the Malay Peninsula) has long puzzled Westerners because it has no obvious rational basis. The taboo, which is explained by a myth, does not include hunting wild animals or killing domestic ones.

Clearly the matter of religion and morality is more complicated than Tylor claimed. But it also seems clear that the sort of moral codes Westerners associate with religion do not extend beyond the world religions to all others.[2]

NOTES

1. Although he states it less strongly than Raglan, the American anthropologist Anthony Wallace (1966: 102–4) also takes the position that ritual is more important than belief. Wallace's reasoning is based partly on what he thinks has occurred in evolutionary terms, which is to say that ritual was present long before belief.

2. Guy Swanson (1960) in his statistical cross-cultural study discusses religion, morality, and evidence in more detail.

REFERENCES AND FURTHER READING

Adat Bidayuh 1994. 1994. Kuching: Majalis Adat Istiadat Sarawak.

Barnes, Linda, and Susan S. Sered, eds. 2005. *Religion and Healing in America.* New York: Oxford University Press.

Evans-Prichard, E. E. 1937. *Witchcraft, Oracles, and Magic among the Azande.* Oxford: Oxford University Press.

Freeman, Derek. [1955] 1970. *Report on the Iban.* London: Athlone.

Malinowski, Bronislaw. 1935. *The Foundation of Faith and Morals: An Anthropological Analysis of Primitive Beliefs and Conduct with Special Reference to the Fundamental Problems of Religion and Ethics.* London: Oxford University Press.

Mandelbaum, David. 1964. "Introduction: Process and Structure in South Asian Religion." In *Religion in South Asia*, edited by E. B. Harpur, pp. 5–20. Seattle: University of Washington Press.

Nabakov, Peter, and Robert Easton. 1989. *Native American Architecture.* New York: Oxford University Press.

Needham, Rodney. 1964. "Blood, Thunder, and the Mockery of Animals." *Sociologus* 14(2): 136–49.

Oliver, Douglas L. 1989. *Oceania: The Native Cultures of Australia and the Pacific Islands.* 2 vols. Honolulu: University of Hawaii Press.

Polk, Patrick A., Michael Owen Jones, Claudia J. Hernández, and Reyna C. Ronelli. 2005. "Miraculous Migrants to the City of Angels: Perceptions of El Santo Niño de Atocha and San Simón as Sources of Help and Healing." In *Reli-*

gion and Healing in America, edited by Linda Barnes and Susan S. Sered, pp. 104–20. New York: Oxford University Press.

Raglan, Lord Fitzroy R. S. 1949. *The Origins of Religion*. London: Watts.

Rousseau, Jérôme. 1998. *Kayan Religion: Ritual Life and Religious Reform in Central Borneo*. Leiden: KITLV Press.

Ruel, M. 1982. "Christians as Believers." In *Religious Organization and Religious Experience*, edited by J. Davis, pp. 9–31. London: Academic.

Swanson, Guy E. 1960. *The Birth of the Gods: The Origin of Primitive Beliefs*. Ann Arbor: University of Michigan Press.

Tylor, Edward B. [1871] 1958. *Religion in Primitive Culture: Part 2 of "Primitive Culture."* New York: Harper & Row.

Wallace, Anthony F. C. 1966. *Religion: An Anthropological View*. New York: Random House.

Winzeler, Robert L. 2004. *The Architecture of Life and Death in Borneo*. Honolulu: University of Hawaii Press.

3

⚭

Religion, Evolution, and Prehistory

How and when did religion begin and how has it changed over time? In this chapter we shall consider a series of questions about the origin and development of religion. First, is there some biological-evolutionary basis for religious beliefs and behavior, given their presence in all known societies? And if there is a bio-evolutionary basis for religion (i.e., one that is more specific than the evolutionary development of such general capacities as those for language and symbolic or abstract thought), is it a direct or an indirect result of biological evolution? While some anthropologists would probably dismiss such questions out of hand as either having the obvious answer of no or as being unanswerable, they have recently been examined at length from the perspective of bio-evolutionary theory.

Second, when did religion begin? At what point in human prehistory does evidence of supernatural or spiritual beliefs and practices first appear? While this question is more the province of physical anthropologists, archaeologists, and prehistorians than cultural anthropologists, it has also been dealt with by the latter as well, often in introductory anthropology textbooks and sometimes in more advanced or specialized works. Interestingly enough, over the past several decades, conclusions by specialists about the antiquity of evidence for religion have changed in favor of a later point in time and a later stage of evolutionary development than accepted previously.

Third, how did religious beliefs and practices originate? This is a question that early armchair anthropologists were fond of asking and answering but later critics regarded as foolish because they considered it unanswerable. However, the question has continued to be asked and answered

41

in various ways. Such answers refer to possible precursors to religious behavior among nonhuman animals, to the evolution of human cognition,
to abnormal mental conditions involving delusions, or to altered states of
consciousness induced through hallucinatory substances.

Further, what was early religion like? The evidence here is of two sorts.
The first concerns the archaeological record, including ancient human and
prehuman burials and grave goods, the images found on the walls of
caves in southwestern Europe and on boulders, rock faces, and shelters
throughout the inhabited world. This evidence also includes various artifacts taken to have been made or embellished wholly or in part for religious purposes. The identification and interpretation of such materials
has been controversial, especially that concerning the religious beliefs and
practices of existing (or recently existing) peoples, specifically the inferences that can be made from such evidence concerning early religion.

Finally, once religion emerged and became a part of human culture, did
it develop in regular ways over time that can be said to be evolutionary—
or has it, instead, remained the same basic thing from first to last? Interest in this question has waxed and waned over time and efforts to ask and
answer it have again elicited controversy. Answers are partly a matter of
how religion is defined in the first place or of what is supposed to be most
important about it.

THE BIO-EVOLUTION OF RELIGION

The possibility that religion may have a biological-evolutionary or genetic
basis is currently a popular topic. Efforts to relate religion to a specific
area of the brain controlled by one or a few genes promise much but deliver little. For example, biologist Dean Hamer in his popularly oriented
book with the provocative title *The God Gene: How Faith Is Hardwired into
Our Genes* purports to show one thing but what actually emerges in the
text is a very different matter. In order to make a connection between a
specific, genetically based area of the brain and faith it is necessary for the
author to define faith in vague psychological terms as a feeling of con-
tentment about the universe as revealed by asking subjects questions
about their emotional states. The relationship between such emotional
states and a belief in God or spirits is not shown. Using this approach it
would also be possible to show a genetic basis for belief in Satan by defining such a belief as a feeling of anger or fear and then showing that such
an emotion can be located on a map of the brain.

There have been more serious scientific or scholarly efforts to study and
explain the relation of some dimensions of religious experience to cognitive and emotional makeup of humans, including specific areas of the

brain.[1] Trance or altered states of consciousness, not to mention dreams, have been studied from this perspective, but they do not amount to religion in any society but only an aspect of religion. Is it possible to show that religion, defined as beliefs and practices involving unseen or supernatural beings, forces, or dimensions of the world, can be explained in bio-evolutionary terms? This complex matter has been explored at length by Scott Atran, an evolutionary anthropologist. Atran seeks to explain what he refers to as the "evolutionary landscape of religion." He begins with the proposition that human religious practices constitute an evolutionary dilemma, something that according to the straightforward logic of evolutionary cost-benefit principles of adaptation and selection should not exist. He defines religion as "a community's costly and hard-to-fake commitment to a counterfactual and counterintuitive world of supernatural agents" (by agents he means intelligent, motivated, effective beings). One may quibble about this definition, but his main point is that religion is costly in various ways and therefore should not exist as an evolutionary development. He writes that "the reasons religion should not exist are patent: religion is materially expensive and unrelentingly counterfactual and even counterintuitive. Religious practice is costly in terms of material sacrifice (at least one's prayer time), emotional expenditure (inciting fears and hopes) and cognitive efforts (maintaining both factual and counterfactual networks of beliefs)" (Atran 2002: 4). Sacrifice also includes material expenditures, bodily mutilation, the killing of animals and humans, and celibacy. The willingness to hold to counterfactual and counterintuitive beliefs and to make sacrifices on the basis of such beliefs is a measure of faith and piety—the more extreme the commitment and the greater the willingness to sacrifice, the greater the faith and piety.

None of this makes evolutionary sense, he argues: "Imagine another animal that took injury for health, or big for small, or fast for slow, or dead for alive. It is unlikely that such a species could survive competition with many other species, or that individuals that acted this way could proliferate among conspecifics that did not act this way" (Atran 2002: 5).

There are two possible solutions to the problem Atran poses. One is the conventional utilitarian or functionalist explanation that the selective costs of religion are offset by benefits of enhanced survival, either for the individual or the society, or both. For the individual, religion provides meaning and compensation for loss. For the society, religion has often been claimed to do many useful things:

It benefits elites. It benefits the downtrodden. It intensifies surplus production. It wastes surplus production. It fosters cooperation. It drives competition. It binds society. It cements the self. It is the opiate of the masses. It is the motor of the masses. It is the warhorse of war. It's a player for peace. It's the mouthpiece of monarchy. It's the oracle of oligarchy. It's a friend of fascism. It's a foe of communism. It's the spirit of capitalism. It's whatever money can't buy. (Atran 2002: 7)

As should be clear from the way he has put all of this—following of one sort of claim with its opposite—that Atran does not buy social utilitarian arguments about religion, though in his conclusion to the book he seems to be accepting individually oriented ones when he asserts the greater appeal of religion over science not only for most ordinary people but for many scientists as well. He also concedes that almost any such proposition about the useful things religion does for a society may have been true at one time or another. But aside from the general principle that any proposition which explains almost anything, including opposite kinds of things, really explains nothing, he asserts that all such propositions could be made about nonreligious cultural phenomena as well as religious ones. Further, such utilitarian propositions about the individual or group consequences of religious beliefs and practices do not predict "the cognitive peculiarities of religion," such as the emphasis on supernatural agents in all religions.

It is therefore, according to Atran, incorrect to suppose that religion is something that has evolved in the sense of being a genetically based and selected-for pattern of belief and behavior that helps individuals and societies adapt and compete because its benefits surpass its costs. It is also incorrect to conclude that religion as such has evolved in that "religion" is not a single thing to begin with, but rather a variety of different things. Such different things do have certain characteristics in common and if they did not, the concept of religion would be meaningless in scientific or scholarly terms. The main characteristic that religious patterns have in common is belief in the supernatural and especially in supernatural agents—Atran is a follower of Tylor.

This brings us to the second possible solution to Atran's evolutionary problem: religious beliefs and behavior are things of a sort that have been *indirectly* selected for. That is, they are by-products of other evolutionary developments, ones involving human emotion and cognition, the mind or intelligence, all of which *have been* selected for. These developments include some general capacities, such as language-based communication, which are uniquely human. More specifically, religion reflects several sets of panhuman emotional faculties and cognitive abilities. Some human emotions, such as surprise, fear, and anger, date at least to the emergence of the reptiles, while grief and guilt, for example, may be unique to humans. The early cognitive developments include the ability to detect predators and protectors. Of these, the first is more obvious than the second, which, however, would include the calls or movements of animals or birds that warned of predators or indicated the presence of food. Although in general this ability goes far back in evolutionary time, it has some distinctly human aspects.

Atran attempts to explain the development of the human religious intellect in terms of several cognitive models. These include folk mechanics (presumably, some awareness of how things work in physical terms, that is, of physical cause and effect), folk biology (some awareness of the differences among animals and their characteristics), and folk psychology (or a theory of mind, the attribution of intentions, beliefs, desires, etc., to the minds of other creatures). Of these three cognitive modules, folk mechanics is the oldest, perhaps stretching back to amphibian brains (but since he does not discuss or even really define it, it is difficult to know why he thinks this). Folk biology appears to emerge with primates (distinct calls of alarm for many different species of predators) but is much more highly developed among humans—among whom it is cross-culturally similar—as is of course also true of folk mechanics. Folk psychology is distinctly human, with at most some elementary foreshadowing among the nonhuman higher primates. "Only humans. . . seem able to formulate the abstract notion of controlling force that applies to agents and without which religion is inconceivable. Only humans can conceive of multiple models of other minds and worlds, including those of the supernatural" (Atran 2002: 265).

Folk psychology, the ability (and compulsion) to attribute intentions, beliefs, and desires to other minds, is the crucial evolutionary development unique to humans that underlies religion. The crucial feature of all religion is the belief in supernatural agents, including spirits and souls. The inclination to detect or imagine supernatural agents is a natural and inevitable consequence of the human ability and inclination to detect natural agents, including other humans and animals. Souls and spirits are nearly universal candidates for elaboration in part because they resemble the disassociated thoughts of dreams and the disembodied movements of shadows. Souls, spirits, dreams, and shadows have important thematic associations, including immateriality, unworldliness, and death.

In linking the origins of religion in the development of beliefs in supernatural agents (i.e., souls and spirits) and in deriving such beliefs in part from dreams, night, and shadows, Atran is offering a neointellectualist view of religion, one that seems to be an update of what Tylor and others proposed more than 130 years ago. However, he also relates the development of such beliefs to other evolutionary attributes of the human mind. This is our naturally selected for "agency detection system," which is fine-tuned or trip-wired to respond to fragmentary information. This system inclines us to see things lurking in the shadows that may or may not be there and to develop feelings of dread and awe about them. Insofar as humans evolved in circumstances that included both predatory (or other dangerous) animals and human enemies, an inclination to react quickly and emotionally to threats both real and imagined would have been adaptive. Mistaking a nonagent for an agent or a nondangerous one for a dangerous one would do little harm. Failing to detect in time the presence of a dangerous agent, either human or animal, could prove fatal; so better safe than sorry. "The evolutionary imperative to rapidly detect and react to rapacious agents encourages the emergence of malevolent deities in every culture, just as the countervailing imperative attached to care givers favors the apparition of benevolent deities" (Atran 2002: 267).

Such assertions about the evolutionary role of fear and alertness regarding predators and other dangerous agents in the formation of religious beliefs and practices fits with the commonness of serpents in religions throughout the world (discussed in chapter 5). Emotional and behavioral reactions to dangerous agents would appear to be well developed throughout much of the animal kingdom and thus very old in evolutionary terms—far older than any indication of religion. Therefore there must have been other crucial developments as well, including the evolution of other emotions and mental abilities, not to mention language, without which the culture of religion is inconceivable. In other words, the development of religion was a part of the broader development of the humanness, including mental abilities, dispositions, emotions, symbolic reasoning, communication, and so on. Put in such general terms, this is not exactly news, although Atran's efforts to show how the human mind developed in terms of its various specific cognitive abilities and their role in the development of religion is detailed and specific.

WHEN DID RELIGION DEVELOP?

This brings us to the question of when in the human past religion first appeared. Atran says little about the actual evolutionary history of religion. All that can be said on the basis of his discussion is that religion is present in all human societies and absent in all other animal groups, including, as far as we know, the higher nonhuman primates. In terms of evolutionary time, this leaves a wide gap of many millions of years. Some of the kinds of developments Atran sees as crucial to the emergence of religion are ones which occurred over the 5 to 10 million years that separate modern humans from the other existing higher primates.

The question of when, in terms of time and the sequence of human development, religion first appeared raises the matter of how this can be known. It certainly happened in prehistory, which means that the evidence is indirect, a matter of making inferences from the archaeological record, of interpreting limited and often ambiguous material remains as signs of religious practices and indicators of beliefs. On the basis of such evidence we can infer that the origins of religion lie in the Paleolithic (which dates from 2.6 million to about 15,000 years ago), before the advent of agriculture or settled life in villages. But the question of whether religion can be traced to Middle Paleolithic (from about 200,000 to about 40,000 years ago), or if instead it can be traced only as far back as the subsequent Upper Paleolithic (from about 40,000 to about 15,000 years ago in the Old World) is disputed.

At one time there was some inclination to think that the earliest signs of religion could be found in the Lower (or earliest part of the) Paleolithic, but this now seems to have been ruled out. This possibility involved Peking Man (*Sinanthropus pekinensis*, now *Homo erectus*). In a book on religion in prehistory published in Dutch in 1952, in German in 1956, and in English in 1960 (*The Gods of Prehistory*) Johannes Maringer (1960) seeks to show that Peking Man engaged in ritual practices involving veneration of the bones of the dead including cannibalism. This inference is based on several assumptions. One is that the bones, among which skulls are said to be particularly common, show signs of being opened to obtain brains, which is taken to be evidence of cannibalism. A further assumption is that since other food sources were thought to be abundant, the likely motivation for the assumed cannibalism was not the need or desire for food but rather the spiritual energy contained in the brain and marrow of the dead. The author assumes, finally, that an analogy can be drawn with the mortuary practices of some contemporary societies involving skulls. Insofar as knowledgeable physical anthropologists and archaeologists ever took such assertions seriously, they now seem to have discarded them.

Neanderthal Burials, Ritual Cannibalism, and Cave Bear Cults

Until more recently it seems to have been widely accepted in anthropology that religion has existed since the Middle Paleolithic. Specifically, for many years Neanderthal archaeological sites throughout Europe and the Middle East were held to provide the earliest indications of religious behavior and belief. In addition to burials, the practices that were included in the realm of religious behavior involved ritual cannibalism (and perhaps human sacrifice)—the same idea that had, for a time, involved *Homo erectus*. Cannibalism was again inferred by the presence of Neanderthal skulls in which the foramen magnum (the hole at the base of the skull through which the spinal cord passes) had been enlarged, presumably in order to extract the brains for consumption, and by bones broken open to extract the marrow, presumably again for consumption. The notion of ritual cannibalism involves the assumption that brains and marrow were

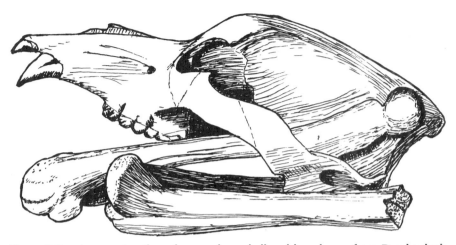

Figure 3.1. A reconstruction of a cave bear skull and long bones from Drachenloch cave in Germany. Formerly offered as evidence of a cave bear cult among European Neanderthal inhabitants, the deliberate arrangement of the bones is now doubted.

eaten in order to gain the spiritual power of the person or for some other magical or religious reason.

Other possible Neanderthal religious practices included cults of animal worship, especially of the cave bear. Such cults were inferred from the apparent arrangement of the skulls and other bones of the giant bears in altar-like settings found in the excavation of caves. The first descriptions of cave bear ritual practices came into existence with the excavation of the Drachenloch ("Dragon's Cave") site in Switzerland between 1917 and 1921 (Tattersall 1995: 94–95). Although lacking burials or other Neanderthal remains, the cave contained, in addition to Middle Paleolithic Mousterian tools, the remains of many cave bears. Finding some of the cave bear skeletal material apparently piled up with stone blocks, the amateur archaeologist Emil Bächler, who excavated the site, inferred a cult involving the worship and perhaps the sacrifice of the giant bears. After this other excavators began to find similar evidence of cave bear cults at other sites.

By far the most important and widespread evidence of possible Neanderthal religion was the apparent burial of the dead in the caves and rock shelters, presumably the same ones in which those who did the burying were also living. The burials were held to have been carried out in such a way that they were assumed to be deliberate and to have contained offerings or objects apparently intended to aid the journey of the deceased to the land of the dead. In one famous instance, interment had even included flowers, these indicated by the extensive presence of pollen from brightly colored flowers in soil surrounding the remains.

Claims or assumptions about the similarities of Neanderthal religious practices to those of ethnographically known peoples are common in general anthropology textbooks published in earlier decades. The most extravagant account of Neanderthal ritual burial and other religious practices is perhaps to be found in George Constable's *The Neanderthals* published in 1973 by Time Life Books in the popularly oriented Emergence of Man series. This extensively illustrated volume had an introduction by the archaeologist and Neanderthal expert Ralph Solecki of Columbia University, who ends with a personal testimony of the impact that the apparent evidence of flowers had on him: "And then when a Neanderthal burial in the same cave turned out to have been accompanied by the flowers of mourners, the last barrier of understanding between me and Neanderthal man broke down." This is very touching. The scenes illustrating Neanderthal life that accompany the text show a Neanderthal man, woman, and child grieving over the burial of a child. There are also illustrations of other imagined religious ritual activities, including one that shows a group of men dancing around a dismembered deer carcass, and another in which earnest-looking worshipers are setting up a cave bear head on a stone altar by torchlight.

The different claims of apparent Neanderthal religious practices seem to have been mutually reinforcing. The acceptance of ritual burial enhanced the likelihood of religious cannibalism and these practices, in turn, enhanced the plausibility of the reported practice of worshiping and perhaps sacrificing cave bears, and so on. All of these apparent practices were taken as evidence that Neanderthals had at least a rudimentary symbolic ability and therefore culture, and if culture was present it would presumably vary because it is learned, which would in turn explain why some practices were found in some places but not others.

By the late 1980s, however, such inferences about Neanderthal religious practices were challenged as the archaeological specialty of taphonomy was developed and applied to existing sites and claims. Taphonomy is the study of how things found in sites (e.g., sediment deposition) are formed and affected (by later disturbances, for example) and how the evidence has been—often wrongly—interpreted. The challenges have involved questions of two sorts. The most basic issue is whether the practices (cannibalism, deliberate burial, the construction of cave bear altars) formerly inferred could even be discerned from the evidence in the first place. The second issue is whether, if a reported practice had occurred, it did so for the religious motives suggested or for some other reason. In the case of cannibalism the problem seems to be of the second sort—the question of whether marrow and brains were being extracted and eaten for religious motives or simply as "food."

In the case of the cave bear cults, the problem seems to have been of the more elementary first sort, according to modern critics, that is, whether the apparent arrangement of the bones was a consequence of human activity at all. The Neanderthal cave bear cults have now been dismissed as examples of bad archaeological method and unwarranted inference. In his recent account of the rise and fall of the cave bear cult, Ian Tattersall (1995: 96) reports that archaeologists are now unanimous in concluding that the Drachenloch and other supposed cave bear cult sites can be explained in terms of natural processes, that is, that the bears had simply died in the caves and their bones were arranged through normal processes of sedimentation rather than human handling, and that the bear-skull altars were therefore only imagined by overeager excavators.

The matter of Neanderthal burials as evidence of religion is somewhat more complicated, in part because of their widespread occurrence and diversity. In this case both sorts of issues have been raised; there is the question of whether the burials were deliberate and, if so, of whether they were carried out as a result of religious or of other motives. One claim is that burial could have been accidental (the result of death and interment as a result of falling rock from the roof of a cave or rock shelter), in which case the inference of deliberate burial was based on faulty excavation techniques, analysis, or interpretation. In the case of the pollen found in excavation of the burials at Shanidar cave that had been taken as evidence that flowers had been placed in the grave, the suggestion has been made that it was simply blown into the cave by wind or brought in later on the feet of workers at the site. Of the burials that do appear to be deliberate, some modern critics have concluded that religious motives cannot be taken for granted. Corpses decay and, aside from the likely unpleasant aspects of this, the attraction of dangerous scavengers might have been a nonreligious reason for early human burials. The creation of a burial chamber presumably involved some effort but so would the likely alternatives, which were the removal and disposal of corpses some distance from the living area or the abandonment of the place where the death occurred. Burial close to or within the living area might have also been the result of an attachment to the dead person that did not involve any beliefs about the soul or an afterlife. It can hardly be proved that early deliberate burials lacked religious motives, for sooner or later religious symbolism and ceremony came to be universally associated with death; but neither can it be assumed that these were present.

The issue of Neanderthal burial (and other previously accepted evidence of religion) has been controversial. Some researchers have argued that evidence for deliberate interment is widespread and undeniable but doubt religious intent. The Cambridge archaeologist and Neanderthal expert Paul Mellars says that it is not a simple matter. He concludes regarding the European sites that the evidence for deliberate burial remains strong, but that there is little evidence that burial involved what he calls symbolic (i.e., ritualistic or religious) behavior (Mellars 1996: 375). The assumption here is that the main evidence for burial as symbolic or religious behavior is based on the presence of deliberately placed grave goods, and such evidence is not really present. Artifactual (deliberately made) objects are commonly found in association with Neanderthal skeletal remains in burials but their presence is likely to be accidental—debris mixed with the backfill. Mellars also suggests that the often cited circle of ibex horns associated with the Neanderthal burial at Teshik Tash in Central Asia that had also been taken to be evidence of ritual activity has been called into question. The issue here is again the first—whether the horns were deliberately placed or not. The site was full of such horns and inferring a circle may be unwarranted.

Though now more cautiously phrased, the possibility or likelihood of Neanderthal religious burial continues to be raised. Some recent writers (including ones who write for nonspecialist readers for whom religious practices are part of the popular attraction of Neanderthals) still point to possible symbolic or ritual associations of burials. Paul Jordan, for example, notes that five of the burials at La Ferrassie in France are aligned on an east-west axis, as are those at some other Neanderthal sites as well. Such an alignment, he suggests, hints at an association of birth, death, and resurrection with the rising and setting of the sun. But he then goes on to acknowledge that whether Neanderthals were capable of such metaphorical thought is debatable (Jordan 2001: 104). Mellars (1996: 380) makes a similar point in noting that the only burials which strongly indicate symbolic offerings are those from two sites in Israel. Both are only ambiguously Neanderthal in terms of tool traditions and time (the late Middle Paleolithic) but not in terms of the skeletal remains; these are modern human rather than Neanderthal.

Religion in the Upper Paleolithic in Southwestern Europe

The shift away from the earlier conclusion that the Neanderthals of the Middle Paleolithic engaged in ritual practices and symbolic behavior that can be called religious moves attention forward to the Upper Paleolithic and the appearance of modern humans in Europe as the more certain period for the beginning of religion in Eurasia. The cultural transition from the Middle to the Upper Paleolithic (at least in Europe) is now viewed by some prehistorians as being abrupt and spectacular. The Upper Paleolithic "revolution" involved many things, including more sophisticated tools made of bone and ivory as well as stone, greater regional variation in tool-making traditions indicating localized cultural patterns, and the first real beginnings of art for personal adornment and other purposes, all of which suggest the presence of language. If true religion appeared at this time, it was in the context of these other developments and emergent abilities.

The evidence for religious belief and ritual in the Upper Paleolithic remains indirect and involves some of the same practices once accepted as present among the Neanderthals, as well as some that are unique to the later period. The earliest to emerge and probably most important of the Upper Paleolithic indications of religion are intentional human burial accompanied by deliberately placed grave goods, which are taken to indicate belief in an existence beyond death.

Another indication of religion is the appearance of symbolic art. This means material forms that cannot be explained at all (or at least not entirely) on the basis of physically utilitarian purposes but were created to represent something else. Some early Upper Paleolithic art may have been a matter of personal adornment carried out for aesthetic purposes or prestige. People have probably been decorating themselves for reasons of beauty and prestige for as long as they have had religion, and such efforts cannot be assumed to have necessarily had religious motives. At the same time, material objects that people in modern societies associate with nonreligious adornment may have had strong religious associations as well. Beads form a good example. In Borneo, for example, beads worn on bracelets, necklaces, and belts have simple aesthetic and prestige value but also strong magical meanings and uses. Here beaded bracelets worn by shamans and priestesses are "charm" bracelets in the older, literal meaning of this term. However, some objects such as the pregnant-looking "Venus" figurines would almost certainly appear to have had ritual purposes relating to fertility.

The most famous and spectacular manifestations of Upper Paleolithic art are the cave paintings of southwestern Europe. Designs made on stone faces of cliffs, rock shelters, and boulders are widely distributed in time and space, and they are often popularly assumed to be examples of ritual symbolism. The problem is, without ethnographic links, rock art images cannot necessarily or easily be regarded as instances of religious icons rather than something else, for example, as secular signals or markers of tribal or ethnic territories, calling cards or even plain old "Kilroy was here," or sexual graffiti. The polychrome paintings created deep in underground caves and visible only from within and by torchlight suggest ritual uses and religious purposes, though exactly or even approximately what these were is a different matter. Fertility, hunting magic, and shamanism have all been offered as interpretations, but lacking other evidence little is certain.[2]

THE ORIGIN OF RELIGION: HOW IT BEGAN

If as now seems likely, religion as we know it in ethnographic and historical terms first appeared in the Upper Paleolithic, several questions remain.
One of these is what the first religious beliefs and practices were like. An
even more basic question is, If religion involves beliefs and practices about
spirits, normally unseen worlds, and existence of life beyond death, then
how did humans first come to believe in and act on such notions? One sort
of answer is that such knowledge was revealed to humans by the spirits or
deities themselves, or that humans were created in possession of religion.
This of course is the answer provided by religious mythology itself, often
as a part of accounts of the creation of the world. Such answers may be intended as general explanations about how all humans, animals, plants,
and supernatural beings came into existence. But such answers are also
culturally specific and more or less particular to local groups or areas.
While anyone may choose to believe in such explanations as a part of his
or her general religious beliefs, they are beyond the realm of anthropological consideration, since accepting one particular explanation requires the
denial of others, without any basis other than faith for doing so.

Over the years anthropologists have offered various explanations of
how religious beliefs and practices could have come about. All such explanations are a matter of inference, since the beginnings of belief and
practice certainly lie deep in prehistory and are indicated only indirectly.
Some scholars have therefore argued that attempts to explain the origin
of religion are a foolish pursuit of questions that cannot be answered. But
the effort has continued. New and reliable archaeological evidence on
early human religious belief or practice would almost certainly be accepted for publication in the most prestigious journals of science, and hypotheses about how and why religion emerged and persisted have continued to be offered.

Anthropological explanations involve (1) various psychological and
sociological approaches; (2) alternative states of consciousness approaches that focus on hallucinatory experiences involving voices and
visions deriving either from "abnormal" mental states or episodes or
from the ingestion of mind-altering substances; and (3) ritual theories,
which hold that religion began with ritual activities or behavioral practices rather than belief.

Psychological and Sociological Theories

The various psychological and sociological explanations have already
been discussed and need be mentioned again only briefly. Of these, the intellectualist or cognitive approaches appear to have been most important

and enduring. Such explanations offer answers to the question of how human beings first acquired religious beliefs by suggesting they began as ways of explaining the otherwise seemingly inexplicable. In the earliest phase of the anthropology of religion, Tylor argued that the formulation of the notion of souls, ghosts, and spirits were the consequence of pondering dreams, illness, and death. Subsequently other scholars disputed this particular assertion or offered alternatives to it. These included Frazer's attempt to formulate the evolution of human efforts to understand and control the world as evolving from magic (the notion and practice of supernatural manipulation) to religion (the supplication of supernatural beings) to science (the realistic pursuit of the understanding and control of the natural world).

Though sometimes ridiculed (e.g., by Evans-Prichard as examples of if-I-were-a-horse [or a caveman] logic), intellectualist or cognitive explanations of the origins of religion have not disappeared and in fact have been favored in recent years. In addition to Scott Atran, the contemporary anthropological theorist of religion Stewart Guthrie (1993) takes an intellectualist approach. He argues that the origin of religion is based on human perception and imagination involving anthropomorphism, that is, the attribution of human characteristics (form, behavior, intelligence, emotion) to nonhuman animals or things (e.g., trees, volcanoes, rivers), along with various superhuman ones, thus creating spirits, divinities, or other supernatural creatures. Such beings, he claims, could have no existence in human belief or thought except insofar as they have at least some human attributes, such as self-awareness or motives (intentionality) that humans can only know of in relation to themselves. This is true even in the case of the supernatural beings that take the form of birds or other nonhuman creatures. Such an argument therefore negates Evans-Prichard's if-I-were-a-horse fallacy by asserting that all humans think alike (i.e., we are all horses or cavemen, as it were), at least in some respects, including a basic tendency to anthropomorphize. Early humans saw faces in the clouds and heard voices in the wind and concluded that they were spirits—human in some respects but superhuman in others.

Altered States of Consciousness Explanations

While cognitive theories of religion seek to explain the origin of supernatural beliefs as the result of conscious, rational human processes of perception and imagination, another line of argument asserts that such explanations are inadequate. Altered states of consciousness (or ASC) arguments hold that a key to understanding the origin of supernatural beliefs is that they are apt to be the result of *departures* from normal, awake, and conscious processes of human awareness and thought.

ASC states cover a range that begins with the normal ones that all humans (and evidentially other mammals) experience regularly, including dreams, semiconscious states at the edge of sleep and daydreams, and extend to hallucinations experienced as conscious, vivid, and extreme distortions of sensory experience. Both the mild and normal and the more extreme and abnormal ASC states have been held to be common and crucial sources of religious inspiration and perhaps of the origins of religion. As Tylor noted, dreams are widely held by adherents of indigenous religions to be points of contact with the supernatural or direct experiences of the supernatural and as previews of future experiences and events.

Visual and auditory hallucinations (or trances, ecstasy, or visions as they are commonly referred to in popular religious terms) include ones associated with abnormal mental states or cerebral pathology. They also include visions produced by the deliberate or accidental ingestion of psychotropic or mind-altering substances, as well as those resulting from physical illness, fever, and perhaps shock or extreme fear. Hallucinations can also derive from various assaults on the body, including extreme hunger and thirst, prolonged sleeplessness, exhaustion, or physical torture, all either experienced accidentally, inflicted by others for various reasons or deliberately self-imposed as penitence or as a means of achieving visions, or both. Rhythmic music, especially involving drumming and dancing, are common in ceremonies involving the achievement of trance states.

In many societies the occurrence of visual or auditory hallucinations that modern Western medicine would attribute to certain forms of epilepsy or to schizophrenia may be interpreted in religious terms, by the person experiencing them and sometimes by others, in which case these can become part of the religious structure of the community. Accounts of the visions of leading religious figures in history have been interpreted in this way. In Christianity the conversion of the Apostle Paul, as a result of his collapse and experience of visions on the road to Damascus, is the most famous example. In Islam the visions of the Prophet, through which Muslims believe that God conveyed the Qur'an to humans, are another example. In societies in which shamanism is practiced, visions or other signs of mental aberration are liable to be regarded as an affinity with the spirit world, evidence of shamanistic talent, or a call to become initiated as a shaman; however, this is not the only route to shamanism and all shamans are not necessarily afflicted individuals.

In addition to those associated with some forms of epilepsy or schizophrenia, vivid and powerful hallucinatory experiences can also be the result of the ingestion of chemical substances. Before they were synthesized by modern chemistry, hallucination-producing materials were obtained from various plants, especially certain funguses, cactuses, and members of the potato family. Since knowledge and the deliberate use of such plant substances is widespread in the world it is presumed to be also ancient and therefore possibly linked with the origins of religion. Hallucinogens are a subcategory of psychotropic (having an effect on mental states) substances.

Among cultural anthropologists, Weston La Barre has sought to link the origin of religion with shamanism and hallucinogenic experiences. He thinks both can be traced with relative certainty to the Mesolithic and probably to the earlier Upper Paleolithic. While La Barre concedes that the vast majority of ASC experiences can probably be regarded as naturally induced, he suggests that "the whole shamanic visionary complex of the Paleolithic Ur-religion" was probably based on psychotropic substances. "With some other anthropologists, I believe that the use of powerful botanical hallucinogens has been a real and important vehicle of shamanic ecstasy, not only in modern ethnographic time but also in pre-historic antiquity" (La Barre 1972: 270).[3]

But here La Barre points out an interesting anomaly involving the uses of hallucinogenic plants (including various others than mushrooms) in the New and the Old Worlds. Both the use of such plants and the number of plants involved are much more common in the New World than in the Old World. While indigenous New World peoples knew several hundred such plants, less than a dozen are (now) known in the entire Old World. There is reason to expect the reverse would be true in that the Old World of Europe, Asia, and Africa is much larger than the New World of North, Central, and South America, has more climatic zones and a much longer human presence. In addition, the number of ordinary domesticated food plants is more equally divided in terms of Old and New World origins. And further, Old World plants are at least as well-known to science as New World ones.

Two other differences may partially explain the disparity between the knowledge and ritual use of hallucinogenic plants in the Old and New Worlds. One of these is the much greater development and use of alcohol in the Old World, including its extensive use among tribal peoples in Southeast Asia, though alcohol does not have the same sort of psychotropic effects as do the powerful hallucinogenic plants. The other difference is the development and spread of the world religions. These religious traditions, though hardly associated with the total absence of alcohol or narcotic plant substances, are generally more hostile to altered states of consciousness induced by substances than are either the religious traditions of Native Americans or of tribal peoples elsewhere outside the embrace of the world religions. Perhaps as a substitute for the use of psychotropic substances, Islam, Christianity, and Buddhism have developed techniques of chanting, dancing, meditating, fasting and other deprivation, and sometimes mutilation that can produce varying altered states of consciousness.

If it is accepted that hallucinations experienced in association with abnormal psychological states are commonly interpreted across many religious traditions as evidence of supernatural contact and inspiration, it is not a great leap to suppose that such hallucinations could have given rise, or at least contributed, to the origin of notions of spiritual beings and experiences. Of course, the evidence for such a proposition is again strictly circumstantial: the widespread and presumably ancient occurrence of hallucination due to mental abnormality and the initially accidental ingestion of hallucinogenic plant substances combined with the widespread religious importance of visions. In any case, the role of either "natural" or induced visions is not a complete explanation of religion. Such experiences need to be accepted and interpreted both by the persons having them and others in order to become beliefs and acted on in other ways to become religion. No religious traditions known to anthropologists or other scholars consist simply of having or inducing visions. Much else is always involved.

Ritual as the Origin of Religion

Some anthropologists who have considered the origin of religion as a matter worthy of discussion have treated the question as one of explaining how humans first came to believe in the supernatural—souls, spirits, divinities, magic, and so on. Such an interpretation assumes, explicitly or implicitly, that belief takes precedence over ritual, that there could be no practices or ceremonies without beliefs, or at the least that ritual and belief would have emerged together.

Other scholars, including anthropologists, have taken the opposite view, however. The American anthropologist Anthony Wallace (1966: 224) suggests that religion more likely began as ritual because in evolutionary terms ritual as a general mode of behavior is older than symbolism and beliefs about the supernatural, which presumably require consciousness and language and are therefore a part of true culture. Wallace argues that animal rituals have been well studied under natural conditions. Mammals and birds commonly engage in stereotyped and repetitive behavior that does not itself constitute any of the biologically necessary activities of obtaining or eating food, nest building, fighting, mating, responding to danger, or caring for young. Ritual behavior does occur frequently in relation to these activities, especially to fighting or aggression and to mating, and therefore forms a part of the total behavioral pattern involving these activities. Such behavior is generally explained as something that may reduce anxiety or prepare the animal for some activity, or that constitutes communication between two or more animals, including courtship between male and female or aggressive encounters between two males.

Of particular interest are certain odd ritual reactions that cannot be simply interpreted as mating, fighting, or other biologically based patterns of behavior but that involve the performance of such behavior.

> The over-excitement induced in animals by a plane roaring above release mating actions as Lack saw from a low-flying plane in Kenya National Park: when this monster in the sky appeared, one male ostrich after another sank to the ground and spread his wings as if worshiping it. In such cases cats suddenly begin washing their fur; birds abruptly start singing or pecking on the ground without picking anything up; a turkey may go to a spring and make drinking movements without swallowing any water. (Portman 1961, as quoted by Wallace 1966: 221)

Such ritual behavior has also been reported for the higher primates, the most famous instance of which is probably the chimpanzee "rain dances" described by Jane Goodall that involved the repeated actions of a group of adult males in response to the onset of a violent storm (Lawick-Goodall 1971: 52–53).

Wallace asserts that in discussing either the normal or the apparently odd animal rituals he is not suggesting that "human religion is *nothing but* [italics original] an archaic primate, mammalian, or vertebrate behavioral characteristic that survives in humans by virtue of some sort of evolutionary lag." His claim is rather that ritual is a common form of behavior in animals to which both secular and religious ritual in humans is similar is some ways. What has happened in the case of religion is that at some point in the course of human cultural development some ritual *became* religious by being rationalized and explained in terms of beliefs about supernatural beings or magic.

THE NATURE OF EARLY RELIGION

What, then, can be said about early religion, that is, religion at the earliest points in time at which it can be safely inferred to exist, which would seem to be the Upper Paleolithic? Judging from burial practices, cave art, and other material remains, early religion involved beliefs and practices relating to death, probably including a belief in an afterlife or reincarnation and therefore in the existence of human spirit in some way separate from the physical body. The fertility of both humans and animals, as shown by the artistic depictions of pregnancy and the reproductive organs in cave paintings, was probably also a major concern of early humans. Judging from cave art of southwestern Europe, it does not seem farfetched to conclude that the successful killing of animals for food and for various other useful materials was another matter of importance. The depiction of animals pierced by spears is common—although as we shall see such literal interpretations have been challenged.

Beyond seemingly obvious or literal interpretations of prehistoric material evidence, what else can be inferred? Did efforts to cure the sick involve the same use of both material substances and supernaturally oriented practices that are so well-known in historical and ethnographic terms? In addition to mortuary practices, were rituals of initiation practiced? Were people worshiping the sun and moon? Were they more likely to have believed in a single creator god or in many different gods and spirits? Did they believe that alternative states of conscious were manifestations or modes of contact with supernatural beings, and if so did they

Figure 3.2.   An Upper Paleolithic shaman? The famous "sorcerer" figure of Les Trois Frères cave in the French Pyrenees first traced by Henri Breuil. Dating to about 16,000 years ago, it has sometimes been taken to be a shaman who wears a mask with antlers and a tail (Bahn 1998: 237). The image could also be that of a hybrid mythical creature combining human and animal features. Published in the *Cambridge Illustrated History of Prehistoric Art*, by Paul G. Bahn.

seek such experiences through the use of hallucinogenic plant substances? Anyone can look at the evidence (such as it is), pose such questions, and try to answer them.

A great deal of recent attention has been devoted to shamanism as a likely focus of early religion. While shamanism (discussed at length in chapter 9) has been defined or described in various ways, the most basic idea seems to be that the shaman is a human who has been selected by the spirits to be an intermediary and that once initiated he or she is able to cross cosmic boundaries, to visit the worlds of supernatural beings and the land of the dead, to deal with the spirits of animals, to retrieve the souls of the sick, and to help the spirits of the deceased with the difficult journey to the afterlife.

HAS RELIGION EVOLVED?

Has religion changed over the several tens of thousands of years that it now seems to have been around, and if so how much? No one can give a definitive answer to such questions because no one can know with any certainty what religion was like throughout much of this period. It has sometimes been argued that over the long term religion tends to have been very conservative (Knight 1991: 507). The French archaeologist and Upper Paleolithic cave art expert Leroi-Gourhan offers the interesting generalization that "models of weapons change very often, models of tools less often, and social institutions seldom, while religious institutions continue unchanged for millennia." Shamanism is (or was until the recent past) present and common throughout large areas of the world, and claims that it is the oldest or original type of religious belief and practice are in keeping with such an assertion.

But if religion has tended to change more slowly than other realms of culture—and the pace of change seems to have speeded up somewhat over the past several thousand years—this hardly means that it has not changed much at all. The present-day world religions differ in several obvious ways from those of antiquity. For example, theriomorphic deities—ones that take the form of animals—or hybrid ones that combine human and animal physical characteristics—seem to be less common than they were in the ancient religions. For another, blood sacrifice is now a rare practice, having been eliminated entirely for one reason or another from most of the universalistic religions (Christianity, Judaism, Buddhism, and Brahmanic Hinduism), to which a large part of the population of the world now adhere. And more generally, there is the sort of contrast that Roberson Smith pointed out as setting apart the ancient religions (dis-

cussed in chapter 6). These religions were made up mainly of ritual practices and varying myths but lacked much in the way of doctrine, creed, or
dogma (Smith 1901: 16–17).

The Evolution of Belief

Over the years there have been many efforts to show that religion has
evolved or progressed, that supernaturally oriented beliefs and practices
(and in some instances organization) have undergone systematic changes
from their first emergence to the present time. Many of these efforts involve dividing religions into types and arranging these into a hierarchy
from "lower" to "higher" forms.

The early phase of the anthropological study of religion was dominated
by such evolutionary arguments—that religion had begun as one thing
out of which then developed another. Tylor's scheme focused on religious
beliefs (religion is the belief in spiritual beings). It consisted essentially of
the simple proposition that beliefs in supernatural beings had developed
from lower to higher according to a principle of reduction and enlarge-
ment. The first beliefs took the form of animism, which had begun with
the notion of the soul, which then gave rise to the belief in independent
spirits of various other types. Eventually animism became polytheism as
a smaller number of divinities with great importance and specific powers
emerged. The next and final step was the emergence of monotheism (Tylor 1958: 417) among peoples with higher or civilized cultures or among
other peoples who had come under their influence.

Some scholars attempted to turn such evolutionary formulations
around. Wilhelm Schmidt (1931), an Austrian scholar, held that the earliest religions had been monotheistic and that animism and polytheism
were later developments. He claimed that the simplest—and therefore the
oldest—peoples all worshiped high gods. Such a high god is always believed by its adherents to be eternal, the creator of all things, omniscient,
beneficent, omnipotent, active in all matters of humans, and the basis of
morality—the sort of god believed in by Christians, Jews, and Muslims.

Such arguments do not seem to have held up well.[4] While it is possible
to find examples of technologically and organizationally simple peoples
who have beliefs in high gods, it is also possible to find more that do not.
Complex societies are more likely to have high gods than the simple ones.
In addition there is the problem of what monotheism is in the first place,
as distinct from a "high god." While high-god beliefs can sometimes be
found in the religions of small-scale, technologically simple peoples, these
are not the not the same as the more thoroughgoing monotheism of Judaism, Christianity, and Islam. High gods include any divinities that are

believed to have created the world, even if they have not continued to play an active role in it, or that simply occupy the supreme position in a hierarchy of divinities.

Religion and Society

Evolutionary claims about religion have often involved its relation to society or political organization. The general argument is that the kind of religious beliefs that people hold reflects the kind of society they live in; that beliefs about spirits, multiple divinities, high gods, or monotheism reflect forms of social and political rule, and that as social and political forms evolve religious belief does so as well. Such propositions invert the biblical assertion that God created man in his own image with the claim that man creates the gods in his image. This sort of idea is old in the history of human thought. Evans-Prichard (1965: 49) traces it back as far as Aristotle, who wrote in *Politics* that "all people say that the gods had a king because they themselves had kings; for men create gods after their own image, not only with regard to form; but also with regard to their manner of life." Tylor (1958: 334) also included such a claim in his evolutionary approach to religion:

> Among nation after nation it is still clear how, man being the type of deity, human society and government became the model on which divine society and government were shaped. As chiefs and kings are among men, so are the great gods among lesser spirits . . .
>
> With little exception, wherever a savage or barbaric system of religion is thoroughly described, great gods make their appearance in the spirit world as distinctly as chiefs in the human tribe.

In addition to such general propositions about the evolution of religious beliefs in relation to the evolution of society, there have been more specific efforts to locate the historical origins of monotheistic beliefs. The archaeologist James Breasted suggested that monotheistic beliefs are likely to have emerged under the influence of powerful human rulers who govern great and complex kingdoms or empires. He made this assertion in his study of the rise of the Egyptian high god Aton under the rule of the Pharaoh Ikhnaton (Breasted 1934: 272–302). Some have argued that societies which have developed social classes are more likely to have religiously based moral codes than are egalitarian societies. The idea here is that "one way to achieve conformity in stratified societies is to convince commoners that the gods demand obedience to the state" (Harris 1975: 551).

The general hypothesis that religious beliefs in spirits and divinities can be divided into types ranging from animism to monotheism and that such types correlate with political centralization and class stratification is controversial. Evans-Prichard (1965: 5C) found this line of interpretation naive and cited evidence of the sort noted by Lang and Schmidt—of peoples of the simplest and presumably oldest type believing in high gods. Swanson (1960: 65), on the other hand, was able to show in terms of cross-cultural evidence that belief in a high god is more strongly associated with greater social complexity than is the absence of such a belief; the societies (in his sample of 50, one from each of 50 areas of the world) with the least social complexity also had the fewest beliefs in a high god, that those of intermediate social complexity had an intermediate number of such beliefs, and that those in the highest category of complexity had the highest percentage of high-god beliefs. Social complexity, Swanson cautions, is not the same thing as strong centralized political leadership or despotic power. The latter may well give rise to high-god beliefs but does appear to be a required condition for them.

NOTES

1. For example, Michael Winkelman does this in his book *Shamanism: The Neural Ecology of Consciousness and Healing.*

2. The literature on the Paleolithic art of southwestern Europe is vast and beyond systematic discussion here. Paul Bahn's (1998) *The Cambridge Illustrated History of Prehistoric Art* provides a comprehensive, balanced overview of Paleolithic and other prehistoric art and of the history of religious (including the "hunting magic" hypothesis) and other interpretations that have been offered since the nineteenth century. Some of Bahn's other writings (e.g., about the literature on shamanism, as discussed in chapter 9) seem more polemical. R. Dale Guthrie's recent magnum opus *The Nature of Paleolithic Art* has as one of its main aims the demonstration that religious (or magico-religious) purposes and themes have been overemphasized in previous studies (2005: 8–10). Guthrie does not claim that Paleolithic cave art is devoid of religious content, but he seeks to diminish this in order to provide what he regards as a more balanced and complete understanding. He makes the interesting assertion that the tendency to view Paleolithic cave art in religious terms is partly a result of its geographical occurrence mainly in the context of the zone of conservative southern European Catholic culture. This, he suggests, led discoverers and interpreters to regard the art as a spiritual prelude to what came later. On the other hand, Guthrie (a zoologist by training and background) seems to have a limited knowledge of the anthropology of religion and a somewhat Western-centered and personally based view of religion as mainly spiritual rather than practical.

3. La Barre bases his own inferences on the work of several prominent ethnobotanists, especially R. Gordon Wasson and others (1986) and Richard Schultes (1990). Wasson's data, he thinks, demonstrates a Mesolithic age for the use of fly agaric (*Amanita muscaria*), a hallucinogenic mushroom, at remote enough dates to

make proto-Indo-European, Uralic, Paleo-Siberian, and American Indian use of narcotic mushrooms all related, that is, linked by migration or diffusion.

4. According to a later cross-cultural study by Guy Swanson (1960: 65), Schmidt's theory of religious devolution from monotheism to polytheism is not supported.

REFERENCES AND FURTHER READING

Atran, Scott. 2002. *In Gods We Trust: The Evolutionary Landscape of Religion*. New York: Oxford University Press.

Bahn, Paul. 1998. *The Cambridge Illustrated History of Prehistoric Art*. Cambridge: Cambridge University Press.

Boyer, Pascal. 2001. *Religion Explained: The Evolutionary Origins of Religious Thought*. New York: Basic Books.

Breasted, James Henry. 1934. *The Dawn of Conscience*. New York: Scribner's.

Constable, George. 1973. *The Neanderthals: The Emergence of Man*. New York: Time-Life Books.

De Rios, Marlene Dobkin. 1984. *Hallucinogens: Cross-Cultural Perspectives*. Albuquerque: University of New Mexico Press.

Evans-Prichard, E. E. 1965. *Theories of Primitive Religion*. Oxford: Oxford University Press.

Furst, Peter T., ed. [1972] 1990. *Flesh of the Gods: The Ritual Uses of Hallucinogens*. Prospect Heights, Ill.: Waveland.

Guthrie, R. Dale. 2005. *The Nature of Paleolithic Art*. Chicago: University of Chicago Press.

Guthrie, Stewart. 1993. *Faces in the Clouds: A New Theory of Religion*. New York: Oxford University Press.

Hamer, Dean. 2004. *The God Gene: How Faith Is Hardwired into Our Genes*. New York: Doubleday.

Harris, Marvin. 1975. *Culture, People, Nature: An Introduction to General Anthropology*. New York: Crowell.

Jordan, Paul. 2001. *Neanderthal: Neanderthal Man and the Story of Human Origins*. Phoenix Mill, U.K.: Sutton.

Knight, Chris. 1991. *Blood Relations: Menstruation and the Origins of Culture*. New Haven: Yale University Press.

La Barre, Weston. 1972. *The Ghost Dance: The Origins of Religion*. New York: Dell.

———. [1972] 1990. "Hallucinogens and the Shamanic Origins of Religion." In *Flesh of the Gods: The Ritual Uses of Hallucinogens*, edited by Peter T Furst, pp. 269–78. Prospect Heights, Ill.: Waveland.

Lang, Andrew. [1898] 2000. *The Making of Religion*. London: Longmans, Green.

Lawick-Goodall, Jane van. 1971. *In the Shadow of Man*. Boston: Houghton Mifflin.

Leroi-Gourhan, André. 1968. *The Art of Prehistoric Man in Western Europe*. London: Thames & Hudson.

Marett, R. R. 1914. *The Threshold of Religion*. New York: Macmillan.

Maringer, Johannes. 1960. *The Gods of Prehistoric Man*. New York: Knopf.

Mellars, Paul. 1996. *The Neanderthal Legacy: An Archaeological Legacy From Western Europe*. Princeton: Princeton University Press.

Mithen, Steven. 1996. *The Prehistory of the Mind: The Cognitive Origins of Art, Religion, and Science*. London: Thames & Hudson.

Raglan, Lord Fitzroy. 1949. *The Origins of Religion*. London: Watts.

Schmidt, Wilhelm. 1931. *The Origin and Growth of Religion*. New York: Dial.

Schultes, Richard Evans. [1972] 1990. "An Overview of Hallucinogens in the Western Hemisphere." In *Flesh of the Gods: The Ritual Uses of Hallucinogens*, edited by Peter T Furst, pp. 3–54. Prospect Heights, Ill.: Waveland.

Smith, William Robertson. [1889] 1901. *Lectures on the Religion of the Semites*. London: Adam and Charles Black.

Swanson, Guy E. 1960. *The Birth of the Gods: The Origin of Primitive Beliefs*. Ann Arbor: University of Michigan Press.

Tattersall, Ian. 1995. *The Last Neanderthal: The Rise, Success, and Mysterious Extinction of Our Closest Human Relatives*. Boulder: Westview.

Tylor, Edward B. [1871] 1958. *Religion in Primitive Culture: Part 2 of "Primitive Culture."* New York: Harper & Row.

Wallace, Anthony F. C. 1966. *Religion: An Anthropological View*. New York: Random House.

Wasson, R. Gordon, Stella Kramrisch, Jonathan Ott, and Carl A. P. Ruck. 1986. *Persephone's Quest: Entheogens and the Origins of Religion*. New Haven: Yale University Press.

Winkelman, Michael. 1997. "Altered States of Consciousness and Religious Behavior." In *Anthropology of Religion: A Handbook*, edited by Stephen Glazier, pp. 393–428. Westport, Conn.: Greenwood.

———. 2000. *Shamanism: The Neural Ecology of Consciousness and Healing*. Westport, Conn.: Bergin & Garvey.

4

⚜

Religion, Adaptation, and the Environment

For many years anthropology paid relatively little attention to the relationship of religion to human ecology or to the possible effects of religion on the environment. It was well-known that religion was often concerned with the fertility of plants and animals on which people depended, as well as of peoples themselves. Rain dances are probably the best known of all ritual practices carried out in "primitive religion." And scholars of comparative religion were well aware that shamans secure the cooperation of game animals and that rice growing in Southeast Asia is a ritual activity as well as a technological one. But religion was not recognized as having any real effect on patterns of adaptation. Religion could not really be doing what its practitioners appeared to be trying to do. Researchers sometimes even implied that the people who performed the rituals did not necessarily believe in them. Rain dances, iconoclasts pointed out, are only held during the rainy season or when it is probably going to rain anyway.

Such observations raised questions about the purpose of holding a ceremony in the first place. The answer was that *real* purposes of consequences of engaging in magical or religious rituals were of a psychological or social nature. Malinowski had notably argued long ago that magic relieved anxiety and fostered confidence and therefore helped people cope with danger and difficult situations, and religious activities promoted social solidarity. The general term for such a line of interpretation is functionalism. The basic idea is that actions or patterns of behavior can have important but unintended and unrecognized consequences (often referred to as latent functions). As a formal theory or mode of interpretation, functionalism was discredited for several reasons (for being overly optimistic, for underestimating conflict and the role of power, for incorrectly assuming the natural state of things is stability). But the general idea that patterns of behavior can have important unintended consequences (good or bad, useful or harmful) continues to be a fundamental part of the way that anthropologists and other social scientists—and to some extent everyone—understands how the world works (or doesn't work).

Several decades ago anthropologists began offering ecological interpretations of religious beliefs, practices, and taboos. Such interpretations seek to explain how various beliefs and practices can affect human adaptation in one way or another. Although they do not focus on the reduction of anxiety or the promotion of social solidarity, these interpretations are generally functionalist in nature. More recently (especially since the 1990s) ecological approaches have been supplemented by environmentalist or conservationist interpretations. These consider religious beliefs and practices from the perspective of their effect on other life forms in the environment, including game animals, fish or forests, or even the physical environment. Such interpretations are again functionalist in that they focus on unintended consequences—ones that can be either positive or negative. Further, the claims made by scholars and researchers may be echoed by more popular or political ones.

Neither of these approaches seeks to interpret religion in general or in particular instances in an overall way; both focus instead on how religion (or parts of it) concerns human ecology and environmental issues, especially degradation and sustainability. Some ecological and environmental claims about religion have been in conflict with others. Some observers have tried to make the case that various religious beliefs and practices promote useful adaptations or good environmental practices while others have asserted that this is not necessarily the case, or that religion has sometimes had a negative or even a disastrous effect on human adaptation. After discussing several studies purporting to show how various religious beliefs have played a positive role, we will consider some counterclaims.

ECOLOGICAL FUNCTIONALISM: NASKAPI HUNTING DIVINATION

Ecological interpretations of religious practices can be traced to an article published in 1957 in the *American Anthropologist* on divination and hunting practices among the Naskapi Indians, by Omar Khayam Moore. Moore was a psychologist working on human problem solving and became interested in magic as a "notoriously ineffective method," though one that could be explained in terms of its latent functions of inspiring confidence and so forth (Moore 1965: 378). He wondered if magic might also be explained by reference to other useful (if also unintended) consequences, including adaptive ones. He had read a published account of Naskapi divination and hunting practices by the American anthropologist Frank Speck. The Naskapi are a far northeastern Canadian Native American people who traditionally depended mainly on the hunting and trapping of animals, especially the hunting of caribou. Speck had written that, because of the importance and the uncertainty of hunting, Naskapi religion was dominated by divination, which was aimed above all at learning the whereabouts of caribou and other animals. When food became scarce, the Naskapi hunters would take sweat baths to induce dreams of animals, as well as drumming and shaking rattles. When someone had a dream of finding animals the next step was to divine where they were to be found, which could potentially be in any direction. Here the technique was to heat the cleaned shoulder blade of a caribou (if caribou were being hunted) over a bed of hot coals until cracks and other marks appeared. These cracks were then interpreted as a guide to where the animals were to be found, and the hunt was planned and carried out accordingly.

The patterning of the marks that appeared on the heated shoulder blade was probably not random. However, the general effect was like rolling dice as a means of deciding where to hunt. But other than giving confidence about the outcome of achieving a consensus about how to proceed (and perhaps absolving someone of making a bad decision in the event of failure), what good did it do to base a decision on a process that would supposedly yield only random results? Moore suggested that random choices may in fact be good choices in adaptive terms, in that they are better than choices made on the only likely other basis. That is, in the absence of confidence in divination as the best guide to decisions about where to hunt, hunters would likely return to places where they had most recently been successful. Success using such a strategy would sooner or later tend to failure as game animals in that area were depleted or became more wary. Divination thus prevented the depletion of animals and propelled hunters in potentially productive new directions. Further, the Naskapi really relied on divination in situations in which they realized they lacked good "realistic" information on the likely whereabouts of game. So magical divination was not really a matter of going against reasonably accurate rational knowledge based on experience. Moore suggested that the Naskapi approach was consistent with the theory of games as developed by Von Neumann and Morgenstern, though he did not pursue such a line of explanation. He also noted that hunting success is not exactly a matter about which the Naskapi could afford to be wrong very often, for their existence in such a harsh environment was precarious. If divination is useful in terms of its consequences, it can therefore be assumed that it has, in effect, been selected for in a process of cultural evolution, although it operates in a way that runs counter to the Naskapis' own beliefs about cause and effect in making choices (Moore 1965).

RELIGION AS A REGULATOR OF ECOLOGICAL PROCESSES

Moore's article was intended to be preliminary and hypothetical, but it seems to have set off lights in anthropological minds about unintended or latent adaptive consequences of religious belief, ritual, or organization. The results have included several widely noted studies of religiously based decision-making behavior and resource management.

Ritual as a Thermostat

The first of these studies was Roy Rappaport's (1967) analysis of the role of ritual in regulating the ecology of pigs and warfare among the Maring people of New Guinea. The Maring are a tribal people who live by a combination of slash-and-burn cultivation and pig rearing. Rappaport's account focuses on the interrelationship of pig rearing, pig slaughter and pig feasting, gardening, and warfare. These activities form a system of trophic (energy) exchanges that require regulation that goes beyond (or exists outside of) the cultural knowledge or understanding of the Maring natives themselves. It is ritual that provides the regulation. Ritual, Rappaport argues, functions as a kind of thermostat, turning on and off various activities in response to different kinds of pressure. The Maring raise pigs and keep as many as they can. Pig numbers increase but eventually become too large and create strains for those who care for them. Pigs also put pressure on the agricultural resources required to support them. Pigs are slaughtered and eaten only at ritual feasts, which are held in relation to warfare. Therefore when pig populations increase, Maring villages go to war with other villages. They also end their wars with pig feasts. The pig populations are thus depleted and have to be built up again, so the cycle starts anew and goes on repeating itself, enabling the Maring to live in harmony with their environment, if not with other people.

Balinese Temples as Regulators of Irrigation Systems

Stephen Lansing's (1991) account of water temples and wet rice irrigation in Bali is a later study of religion as a mechanism of resource management. The Balinese live in one of the most densely populated places in the world.

Much of the small, mountainous island of Bali (located just east of Java in Indonesia) is covered with terraces that have been developed over many centuries to grow several crops of rice a year. The provision and regulation of water in the terraces through an elaborate network of canals, weirs, and tunnels is crucial to growing enough rice to sustain the population. The main basis of the organization of the water system is the cooperative association (*subak*) of cultivators who own or work the lands that are involved. The Balinese were traditionally organized into a series of small competing states that had some limited role in managing the irrigation, as did colonial rule by the Dutch and then the postcolonial Indonesian state. All of this has been described and analyzed by various investigators.

Lansing has focused on the role of religion in the organization and management of irrigation. The Balinese are the last major population to remain Hindu in Southeast Asia, where most of the surrounding peoples converted to Islam several centuries ago. Balinese religion is unique and not very similar to the myriad forms of Hinduism practiced in India. In Bali, as elsewhere in Southeast Asia, the cultivation of rice is a matter of religious ritual as well as of practical or mechanical procedures.

Lansing's particular concern has been with the role of the water temple (one of several kinds of temples found throughout the island) in the operation of the irrigation system. Temples in general are staffed by priests and hold periodic festivals in accord with the complex set of Balinese calendars. He argues that religion and the temple system support the coordination and management of irrigation in several ways. For one thing, religious sentiments and ritual practice counter the potentially competitive or antagonistic tendencies among different water users. In addition, the calendar systems, which regulate the cycle of festivals, also facilitate the coordination of the opening and closing of the various gates and canals through which water is distributed. And finally the priests, who are supported by the authority of religion and who know how each water system works, serve as managers. Efforts to modernize and improve the traditional religiously organized system through modern engineering that have bypassed the priests and temples have therefore often failed.

CULTURAL MATERIALIST EXPLANATIONS OF SEEMINGLY MALADAPTIVE RITUAL PRACTICES (OR, SOLVING THE RIDDLES OF CULTURE)

By far the best known of the neofunctionalist interpretations of religious practices are those of Marvin Harris. In addition to being an influential faculty member in two important American anthropology departments, he uniquely combined two usually different sorts of career orientations—those of a relentlessly and often caustically polemical theorist, on the one hand, and of a very successful purveyor of popular versions of anthropological knowledge and argument, on the other. In the latter role (which appears to have engaged much of his energy in the latter part of his career) he wrote with great verve on various topics of a sort that had wide general appeal. His mission was to solve various "riddles of culture," especially concerning culinary practices and food taboos that had a religious basis or dimension. Why do some peoples do (and especially eat) some things that many others (often Westerners) do not—giving away or throwing away property, venerating cows, keeping or not keeping pigs, eating or not eating other human beings? His answer was largely or entirely the same in all cases (as it was also with other topics such as male chauvinism and tribal warfare that did not have a religious dimension). He looked for and propounded straightforward, if not obvious, economic (materialistic or utilitarian) explanations and referred to his general strategy as cultural materialism. Whatever people did or did not do was adaptive in the circumstances in which they lived, even if (as was usually the case) they did not understand the real reasons for their own behavior. Many of his topics came from the published research or arguments of others that Harris adapted or reinterpreted. He saw himself as a practitioner of hardheaded anthropological science and was disdainful of soft humanistic approaches and cultural relativism. Many of his best-known essays were collected and published in 1978 in *Cows, Pigs, Wars, and Witches*, which was followed by collections with similarly catchy titles, including *Good to Eat* in 1985.

Ceremonies Can Help Populations Adjust to Available Resources: The Potlatch

One of Harris's early essays concerned the potlatch held by the Kwakiutl and other groups of the Northwest Coast of North America. The potlatch is a competitive giveaway feast that had become well-known to ethnologists and others by the end of the nineteenth century. Potlatches were held on a variety of ritual occasions and included extensive feasting and the presentation of gifts to friends and rivals. The objective was to achieve high status and renown by outdoing rivals in the quantities of food consumed and property given away, and in some cases destroyed. Rivals who could not match a potlatch with one that equaled or exceeded what had been provided as food and gifts or destroyed were shamed. Potlatches became famous examples of conspicuous consumption and conspicuous waste—of irrational economic practices driven by the pursuit of prestige. The potlatch system was made possible by an abundant environment and resources, especially salmon and other fish that enabled the population to meet its needs and have time left for other pursuits. Ruth Benedict (1960) included a case study of the Northwest Coast peoples in her book *Patterns of Culture* in which she interpreted the potlatch in psychological terms as megalomania, a manifestation of an excessive drive for status.

Later, ecologically oriented anthropologists began to have doubts about such interpretations. It was pointed out that by the time Europeans had become familiar with the potlatch, conditions on the Northwest Coast had changed. Populations had been reduced by the arrival of infectious diseases, changing the ratio of people to resources—more food for fewer people. Moreover, the fur trade and other impacts had affected the local cultures as had European technology. It was therefore suggested that more traditional conditions in the past had been different. Food resources had probably varied from one location to another but had been less abundant overall. There had likely been occasional localized hardship or even starvation. Under such conditions, potlatch ceremonies could have played a more positive role than they had been reported in the later period of European contact. For one thing, by encouraging people to work hard and to produce more than they needed, they helped ensure that they produced enough. For another, they served to distribute food and other resources from those who had more than they needed to those who had less—that is they served as mechanisms of redistribution. And finally, the potlatch system encouraged people to move from areas of scarcity to areas of abundance by switching their loyalty from poor chiefs to rich ones. These revisionist ideas were in line with the ideas of economic anthropology in the 1960s and 1970s. They were developed and published by several scholars, including Andrew Vayda, before Harris turned them into a readable, provocative chapter.

Pig Hate and Pig Love

Harris's best-known ecological arguments about animals and religious beliefs and practices concern the pig and the cow. The pig is the most controversial of domestic animals. Unlike animals that provide several products (milk, hair or wool, labor, meat) it is of little intrinsic material value except as a source of meat. Jews and Muslims revile the pig and forbid it as food. At the opposite extreme, pigs are highly valued as a source of wealth, as well as food, by some other peoples. Many peoples fall somewhere between the two extremes and view the pig as just another animal that is raised or not according to (explicit) pragmatic considerations.

Unlike Rappaport's close analysis of one particular local instance of pig keeping in New Guinea, Harris's approach is large scale and comparative. He contrasts those areas of the world in which pigs are extensively or exclusively kept and pork is a highly important source of meat with those in which the opposite is the case. The geographical heart of pig love is Melanesia and Southeast Asia. The zone of pig hate is the Middle East, Central Asia, and North Africa, where pigs (though once abundant and important) are generally absent and pork is an abomination.

The taboo on pork has been a popular academic topic for centuries. Most people, including some anthropologists who have considered the taboo on pork, have focused on the religious proscriptions of Judaism and Islam. According to Mary Douglas (1984: 29–32), the taboo has long been explained from the perspective of *medical materialism*—the functionalist proposition that food taboos and other cultural practices can be explained by real if often unrecognized benefits to health or well-being. In the case of the pig, there are both older and newer medical materialist explanations. The older one, which goes back at least to the twelfth-century writer Maimonides, held that pork is unhealthy because pigs are dirty in terms of their food and their habits and surroundings. The newer version of the medical materialist explanation is that pork is an unhealthy food because the trichiniasis worm can infect it and then be passed to humans who have eaten insufficiently cooked pork. Douglas and Harris are united in their rejection of all such medical materialist explanations. They also both advocate a strategy of explanation that rejects only the consideration of the taboo of pigs and pork. Douglas argues that pigs have to be considered as one of many animals that are either permitted or forbidden to the Jews. When all of these forbidden animals are considered, in contrast to those that are permitted as food, a clear set of structural principles can be discerned (discussed further in chapter 5).

Harris's version of the comparative strategy is to consider areas of the world where the peoples who mainly have the taboo live with those where pigs are valued to the greatest extent. He claims that this reveals a clear ecological picture. He is uninterested in Douglas's approach apparently because the other animals forbidden to the Jews are all relatively or entirely insignificant as food resources. They are often not eaten by anyone anywhere, in contrast to the pig, which is one of the major domesticated animals of the world. Similarly, Douglas is apparently not interested in Harris's approach—to the extent that she was aware of such a line of explanation, which is not evident in *Purity and Danger*, which was published (in 1966) before *Cows, Pigs, Wars, and Witches*—because she is interested in symbolism and cultural systems of classification rather than ecology. The two strategies of comparison are not really incompatible in that the explanatory value of one does not necessarily mean the falsification of the other, and both reveal interesting results.

The ecological argument is that although pigs were evidently domesticated first at an early point in the Middle East, they were (or became as the climate changed) unsuited to its dry environment, in that they required the same vegetable foods (grains) that humans ate, in contrast to other domestic animals (sheep, goats, cattle, camels) that lived on grass and other foods that humans did not eat. Since pigs in such an environment were a luxury, it made ecological sense to ban them. The ban on pigs and eating pork was environmentalism in the guise of a religious taboo created by Judaism and perpetuated by Islam. For whatever reason, Christianity did not keep the taboo, which facilitated its development and spread as a world religion in regions where pig keeping is ecologically adaptive, for example, Europe.

Pig keeping therefore also has an ecological basis, Harris argues. Pig keeping works well in humid environments in which edible natural and cultivated vegetable foods are available. It is especially adaptive in circumstances where there are few other domestic or wild animals available as sources of meat. In the interior of New Guinea and some other islands of Melanesia that epitomize such conditions, pig raising is highly developed and the ceremonial sacrifice and consumption of pigs is a kind of cult.

The Pig and the Spread of Islam into Southeast Asia

How well does the argument really hold up in comparative terms? It is possible to look at other regions of the world in order to make relevant comparisons, at least regarding Islam. Muslims also took on the taboo of pigs and pork, and Islam is not limited to the arid regions of the world that, according to Harris, are the natural ecological home of pig avoidance. Southeast Asia is a very apt example. While it is a part of Harris's natural zone of pig keeping, part of its population has been Muslim since Islam spread into the region more than five centuries ago.

Southeast Asia would seem to be a challenge to Harris's argument. However, the historical and ecological basis of the development of Islam in this region is complicated in several ways. To begin with, historians of the region agree that the spread into Southeast Islam was peaceful, so that it cannot be said that the religion and its taboos were forced on people. Further, it did not involve large-scale migration of Muslims from other places where the pig taboo might have made the sort of ecological sense that Harris stresses.

The spread of Islam throughout Southeast Asia was far from uniform, however, and its distribution is of some relevance. To begin with, historians, geographers, and anthropologists divide Southeast Asia into two parts—an insular one and a mainland one. Insular Southeast Asia consists mainly of the island nations of Indonesia and the Philippines plus Malaysia. The mainland part consists of various countries that lay generally to the north of the insular ones and that are all part of the Asian continent. Malaysia is divided between insular and mainland Southeast Asia but is always considered part of the insular region in terms of language, culture, and history. The spread of Islam was limited almost entirely to insular Southeast Asia, including Malaysia. There are exceptions but they do not amount to much: relatively small, often urban, Muslim communities of some antiquity as well as others of more recent origin, in most of the mainland countries. The most substantial of the mainland Muslim communities is that of far southern Thailand, but this one is simply Malay and therefore also insular in terms of language, culture, and ethnic identity, as well as its modern religion. Without going into it here, the absence of Islam throughout most of mainland Southeast Asia and its presence in the insular region is not really a matter of differences in ecology in the sense of animals and crops or of geography in the sense of land forms, climate, and the like.

While the spread of Islam into Southeast Asia was mainly limited to the insular region, it was far from even. In the Philippines it was confined to the far south (specifically to Mindanao and surrounding complexes of islands) while the remainder became predominantly Christian. But this need not concern us here because it was mainly not a matter of ecology but rather of the Spanish blocking the spread of Islam to the north. It is therefore the other dimensions of the Islamization of insular Southeast Asia that have an interesting ecological basis involving, among other things, the pig.

While Indonesia has the largest Muslim population in the world, it also has sizable non-Muslim populations, including the Hindu Balinese and various indigenous peoples. Except for the Balinese, the situation is similar in Malaysia and in the southern Philippines. Islam is therefore primarily a religion of the coastal regions of the Malay Peninsula, Sumatra, Borneo, Sulawesi, and some of the other islands of the region. It is not limited to the coasts (most importantly in Java, the large population of which accounts for much of the numerical strength of Islam in Indonesia and Southeast Asia) but its greatest historical strengths have been in the coastal zone. This coastal strength, moreover, has usually been explained with reference to trade. Islam was brought to Southeast Asia primarily by Muslim traders from India and the Near East and spread first and most completely along the trade routes, especially that of the spice trade, one of the driving forces in the age of exploration and discovery. The tribal peoples of the interior of the islands of Indonesia and the Malay Peninsula generally did not convert to Islam. Today, although some have become Muslims, most have not. Many of these indigenous interior peoples have converted instead to various forms of Christianity, while some remain unconverted to any world religion.

This pattern may be explained in various ways. The interior peoples were not heavily exposed to Islam to begin with or inclined to convert if they were. Some of them were located in remote areas and had only indirect—if any—contact with the coastal peoples. Many of them were warlike and most were often at odds with the coastal Muslim peoples who tended to look down on them as primitive headhunters. Although some of the interior peoples were brought under the control of the coastal Muslim rulers or formed alliances with them, this seldom involved conversion to Islam. As European colonial rule, which also began in the coastal centers of trade, was gradually extended to the interior of various islands, so also was Christianity. Christian missionaries—who shared in the prestige of European colonial wealth and power, and who generally offered practical help in the form of medical clinics and schools as well as salvation—succeeded in converting some groups. However, this process was halting and uneven and remained only partial by the end of European rule. In Indonesia in the postcolonial period, conversion entered a new phase as the government began to press the unconverted interior groups to accept one or another of the monotheistic world religions. Most did so, at least nominally, but again the choice was mainly Christianity or some other non-Muslim option. In Malaysia the postcolonial situation was somewhat different, but the main direction of religious conversion among the interior indigenous peoples was to Christianity rather than Islam.

The question here is the role of food preferences and taboos in these developments. In Borneo (which I know best) the interior peoples are certainly pig lovers. The domestic pig is raised extensively by longhouse-dwelling horticultural peoples, and the wild pig is the favorite game animal of both these peoples and the hunting and gathering groups. Wild pigs can be a hazard to crops so hunting them perhaps has a double benefit in the case of cultivators. Further, the interior peoples in general do not have direct access to the fish and other rich marine fish and other resources that the coastal peoples do. This means (it could be argued) that conversion to Islam in the interior would result in considerably greater protein deprivation than on the coast. Today interior peoples are well aware of the food taboos of the various religions and make frequent reference to them in conversations about religion and conversion—indeed, discussions about religion in Borneo seem to be often about what you can and can't eat and drink. The tidal zone of Borneo was therefore probably more favorable to the spread of Islam in ecological terms than was the interior. However, the coastal and lower-river zones are also the regions in which contact and trade between Muslims and indigenous peoples have been most extensive, and therefore where Muslims have had the greatest opportunity to influence and convert them.

The spread of Islam would seem therefore to be not only a matter of protein, and it would be difficult to show just how important protein has been. In the interior the wild pig is not the only game animal. Further, the peoples of the interior are not only fond of pork and pig hunting; they are also very fond of alcohol. Wine or beer made from rice, palm sap, or other substances (now often replaced by locally distilled spirits) is extensively consumed during religious festivals and in relation to routine hospitality. Conversion to Islam means not only the abandonment of pork but also of alcohol, though in both instances lapses by Muslim converts are fondly noted by indigenous peoples.

RELIGION AND ENVIRONMENTALISM

In the 1980s and especially in the 1990s, various writers began to consider the environmental implications of religious beliefs and practices. The general idea was to understand how religion could support the conservation of resources, sustainable practices, and a general respect for the environment. The assumption was that, to the extent that particular societies had developed ecologically sound practices, these could be expected to have a religious basis.

Aside from the scholarly or research issues involved, proponents hope to demonstrate that conservation is rooted in the religious worldviews and values of indigenous and other traditionally oriented peoples, thereby lending further support to the environmentalist movement. Environmentalists are similarly encouraged to look beyond modern science as the only basis of sound environmental practices. It is held that traditional religious worldviews have often developed in the context of long-term adaptations to the environment and therefore provide well-established wisdom and conservation ethics. Hunting societies have developed deep and pervasive beliefs about the spiritual affinity of humans and animals and are therefore inclined to conserve game and to kill animals only out of necessity. Gathering and simple cultivating societies may revere and protect certain trees and are inclined toward sustainable practices. Even advanced agricultural practices in traditional societies may be based on religious beliefs.

Religion Promotes Sound Environmental Practices

The anthropologist Eugene Anderson makes such assertions in his book *Ecologies of the Heart* (1996). He notes, for example, that Polynesian peoples have frequently used religious taboos to protect resources. Overfished reefs, orchards of unripe fruit, and overharvested wild plants and animals may be put under taboo by chiefs until they are ready to be utilized again. The Polynesians, like the Chinese, also have sacred groves that preserve types of forest that would otherwise become extinct (Anderson 1996: 11).

Anderson notes that governments (as in Tokugawa Japan) have explicitly used traditional religion to promote environmental conservation. However, most of his examples involve instances in which religious beliefs and ritual practices are unknowingly used to support wise environmental practices. He explores such claims in case studies of the Chinese, the indigenous groups of the Northwest Coast of North America (everyone's favorite ecological example), and the Maya of Yucatan. The Chinese example involves feng shui, the doctrine and practice of locating and orienting tombs, houses, and other buildings according to traditional mystical beliefs. While modern, educated Chinese disavow such beliefs and practices as outmoded superstition, ordinary villagers and townsmen continue to invoke feng shui to explain things, including why architectural projects fail.

Anderson's analysis is again a functionalist one: whatever the truth or falsity of the beliefs on which it is based, the practice of feng shui has useful, adaptive consequences. He recounts that he discovered the practical wisdom of feng shui in Hong Kong when a building under construction collapsed. The construction project had been undertaken on a hillside that was too steep to support the foundation that had been constructed. This at least is how a scientifically oriented engineer would explain what happened. However, the ordinary local folk knew that the project was architecturally unwise because there was a dragon living in the hill and the excavation had cut through its pulse.[1]

While based on folk beliefs about supernatural dragons, tigers, and various other good and bad influences, Anderson argues, feng shui thus encourages sound engineering practices. Villages built according to traditional feng shui standards are located above flood level while those constructed in the more recent period in Taiwan without making such calculations are prone to flooding. Feng shui also encourages the planting of trees around the periphery of villages, the concentrating of graves away from houses and agricultural lands and, in general, good city planning (Anderson 1996: 15–27).

Why don't the Chinese just base sound building practices on rational, practical knowledge? Why do they need feng shui to do the seemingly obvious? The answer is perhaps that the seemingly obvious is not necessarily all that obvious after all or that that religious prescriptions and proscriptions serve to support adaptively correct behavior in marginal or stressful situations. Tempted by land shortages to put a building or village in a bad location or to engage in mining in an inappropriate place, people may be deterred by a powerful belief in harmful supernaturally

Figure 4.1.   A house in northern Laos being moved to a more auspicious location.

mandated consequences of doing so. Such cultural reasons, Anderson suggests, may also help villagers resist efforts by the state to undertake unsound projects.

RELIGIOUS BELIEFS AND PRACTICES THAT DO NOT SUPPORT GOOD ENVIRONMENTAL HABITS

Along with the various interpretations noted above that make arguments and provide examples of how religion can be ecologically or environmentally useful, there are contrary claims. These argue that religious beliefs and practices can have a harmful, even a disastrous effect on patterns of adaptation and environmental activities.

Religion and the Ecological Indian

Native American practices are one prominent, and again controversial, recent example. The anthropologist Shepard Krech begins his book *The Ecological Indian* by noting that Native Americans have long been a prominent symbol of contemporary pro-environment values and practices. The belief that they live in harmony with nature (or at least did so in the past when they could) has been an important part of the view that people now have of Indian culture. The original Americans did not pollute the environment, destroy the forest, kill more animals or catch more fish than they needed for their survival, at least not until the white man came along. Such ecological practices were based on their religion, including a general reverence for Mother Earth and a belief in the sacredness and interconnectedness of all creatures. Whites have not only come to mainly accept this view but also in many instances helped to create it. It would have been in conflict with the older view of the potlatch as involving overconsumption and waste in quest of prestige but in harmony with the revisionist, ecological interpretation of Harris and others that traditional potlatching was adaptive and only postcontact potlatching was excessive.

Krech argues against the idea that Native Americans have been practitioners of sound ecology and environmentalism as conceived in modern Western terms. He does not make the completely opposite argument but holds that the record, insofar as it can be known, is complicated. For the period before the arrival of Europeans and their expansion and domination of the North American continent, information about indigenous ecological practices is limited, but it can be said that population numbers were low and therefore that human impact was slight in comparison to what happened later. The extinction of many large mammals coincided with the arrival of the first Native Americans at the end of the Pleistocene, but their role in this extinction is a matter of sharp dispute among experts. Moreover, there were few if any market forces at work that encouraged the indigenous inhabitants to hunt and trap animals not only to meet their own needs for food, hides, furs, and other materials, but also in order to trade or sell meat, hides, and pelts to others as well.

Everything began to change after the Europeans arrived. However, Krech disputes the view that Native American attitudes and practices regarding animals were changed from being ecologically benevolent to destructive. He thinks that the religious basis of Native American hunting, trapping, and fishing practices has been wrongly interpreted and that a closer look at what knowledgeable anthropologists have reported creates a very different picture from the modern popular environmentalist one:

> Similarly, it has become conventional wisdom that Indians who exterminated deer, beaver, and other animals whose pelts were sought by Europeans did so because they had been corrupted by Europeans into abandoning the traditional conservation measures based in intricate taboo systems. At the heart was the belief that sentient, animated animals would punish hunters who flouted the rules for proper behavior. (Krech 1999: 152)

Krech does not dispute the extent to which things changed after contact, but he does not think that Indian religious beliefs and practices did so to a great extent. Nor does he dispute the importance of indigenous Native American religious beliefs and practices involving animals, but he does argue that these have been distorted by those who hold views of the sort reflected in the quotation above.

While Indians had deep-seated and religiously based respect for the birds, animals, and fish that they killed to meet their needs, their beliefs and values did not necessarily promote conservation and may have had the opposite effect. Indian hunters, trappers, and fishermen believed that the creatures they killed had souls and therefore they had a kind of supernatural ability to avoid being caught or killed. Any creature that was killed was taken because it had given itself willingly. If the animal, bird, or fish had not intended to be killed, it would not have been possible for the hunter, trapper, or fisherman to kill it. It went even further than this to include the belief that not killing a creature if the opportunity arose meant a breach of the spiritual bond between the human and the creature. Krech (2005: 81) also emphasizes the common indigenous belief in reincarnation as a negative factor in conservation:

> In North America, the belief in reincarnation was widespread and it was antithetical to conservation . . . For example, the Northwest Coast Gitsan ritually treat each year's salmon with great care. They construct an elaborate cultural context for salmon modeled on human sentience and human social life. Yet all that is required to renew salmon, they say, is to return their bones to the water (Gottesfeld 1994). In the North, Inupiat and Caribou Inuit hunted without restraint large animals like caribou and mountain sheep with the aid of firearms, and musk oxen without them. Here too reincarnation is the rule. The Inupiat and Inuit believed that seals, belugas, caribou, musk oxen and other animals existed "in essentially unlimited supply" and that no link existed between the size of their kill and the availability of prey (Burch 1994: 165). The Yupik also understood animals and birds as "infinitely renewable" and unaffected directly by human predation. (Fienup-Riordan 1990)

The buffalo population is interesting for several reasons in light of its importance (especially in the plains) because of what happened (it went from incredible abundance to near extinction in a few decades) and because of the religious beliefs and practices involved.

Buffalo hunting and its success or failure was a matter of ritual as well as practical effort, and buffalo figured prominently in other ceremonial activities, including curing. Some groups believed that in the past buffalo had ascendancy over people. This had been reversed by a culture hero or trickster who taught men how to make and use bows and arrows. Some also believed that in the past humans could talk to buffalo, and they interacted with them in the same ways that that they did among themselves: they fought, intermarried and had sexual intercourse, and shared food with them, and so on. In Krech's phrase (1999: 146), the Plains Indians regarded the buffalo as "animated other-than-human persons."

Krech presents the consequences of such beliefs on hunting practices in a way that makes them seem a sort of paradox in terms of modern Western values and expectations. The importance of the identification of the Plains Indians with the buffalo would lead to the expectation that they would have treated them benevolently and killed them only to the minimum extent needed; in other words, they would have practiced conservation. In actuality, he argues, this was not so, and in some circumstances practices were more nearly the opposite. The fact that buffalo were believed to have intelligence, emotion, will, and an ability to communicate with one another that was comparable to that of humans meant that it was necessary to kill entirely whatever particular group of animals was being hunted, which could involve hunting on horseback or driving them over a cliff, into a bog, river, or enclosure. Killing them all was necessary because any survivors would be angry and would warn other buffalo about what had happened, making it more difficult approach them.

Krech also discusses a second way in which indigenous Plains Indian beliefs about the buffalo led to attitudes counter to modern Western ideas of conservation. This involved the notion that, while the buffalo were "animated other-than-human persons" in some respects, they had a mystical status as well. The buffalo could come and go but not only as living humans (normally) could to other places on the surface of the earth but also to another world. The buffalo, like many other creatures, had originally come from the underground, to which they could and did regularly return. When the buffalo disappeared for the year, it was believed they had gone to grasslands beneath lakes, which they entered and exited through caves, springs, and other openings in the earth, from which they would emerge the next year. This was a way of explaining the seasonal migration of the buffalo, but it could also explain their absence otherwise as well—and here we come to the issue of conservation. If the buffalo did not appear when they usually did or in their usual numbers (the movement of buffalo depending on weather and other environmental variables rather than only time), it was thought to be because all or some of them were still in their other home beneath the water.

Such a mystical view of the comings and goings of the buffalo put the Plains Indians at a disadvantage when it came to understanding what was really (and rapidly) happening to the once seemingly endless herds in the latter half of the nineteenth century. It did not encourage or even permit the realization of a relationship between overhunting (by either Indians or professional white hunters) and the decline and disappearance of the buffalo. Whether or not such a realization would have done any good is another matter. Krech stresses that the Indians tended to hold to the belief that the annihilation of the buffalo was impossible and that the herds would eventually return from their pastures beneath the lakes. Eventually they did realize something was terribly wrong. When the great Ghost Dance spread over western North America to reach its peak in the Plains in 1890, it promised the return of the buffalo as well as the ancestors.

Religion and the Decline and Collapse of Societies

In his recent book *Collapse: How Societies Choose to Fail or Succeed*, the geographer and environmentalist Jared Diamond focuses on religion in his discussion of adaptive failure. He has far less to say about religion than does Krech, in part because he does not have the same sort of information available. For some of the societies he writes about, such information could only be inferred. Nonetheless, he writes, "Religious values tend to be deeply held and hence frequent causes of disastrous behavior" (Diamond 2005: 432). He suggests at one point that the fundamentalist Christian belief in the imminent end of the world may be used to justify environmentally destructive practices on the grounds that they don't matter in the long run because there isn't going to be a long run. He cites American mining company executives as important people who tend to hold such beliefs (2005: 462).

Diamond's most spectacular examples are part of his explanation for the failure of the societies of Easter Island and Norse Greenland to survive. Much of the deforestation of Easter Island, which brought the total collapse of Polynesian culture and the end of human society on that small island, can be attributed to religious practices, he concludes. The forests were cut mainly to get logs that were needed to move the many large stone statues (*moai*) that were the objects of veneration. In the case of the Norse colonists in Greenland, who managed to occupy (by farming and hunting) a few small parts of the island for four hundred years before mysteriously disappearing, he argues that religion was also a major cause of the failure. For one thing, after becoming Christians (they converted to Christianity after their arrival), the Greenland Norse spent resources they could ill afford to build churches. In addition, Diamond suggests that Christianity made the Norse more conservative than they might have otherwise been in their attitudes toward the indigenous peoples. Over the several centuries they were there, as the climate became colder and farming became ever more difficult, the Norse became more dependent on hunting. However, their identity as Christian Europeans made them unwilling to have anything to do with the Inuit peoples or learn from them. The Inuit were well adapted to the region and highly skilled in hunting

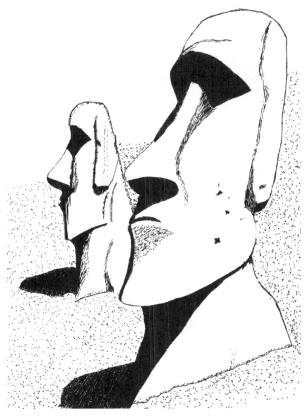

Figure 4.2. The famous large religious statues (*moai*) of Easter Island, which the geographer and environmentalist Jared Diamond holds responsible for the much of the deforestation, and therefore the ecological collapse, of the island.

sea mammals. Had the Norse not looked down on the Inuit as savage pagans and been willing to learn from them and adopt some of their ways they might have survived (Diamond 2005: 432).

It is difficult to know what to make of such specific examples, as it is also true of the ones noted earlier in support of the contention that religious beliefs and practices can serve to support useful ecological practices and environmental adaptation. In the case of Native Americans, Krech does not really claim that the religious beliefs he discusses were actually associated with the overexploitation of game animals, birds, or fish before European arrival for the simple reason that he does not cite any evidence of precontact overexploitation to begin with. In his discussion of the large animal extinctions at the end of the Pleistocene he concludes that indigenous hunting was probably only one of a number of causes. Nor does he seek to link Paleolithic hunting practices to the sort of religious beliefs that were in evidence 10,000 to 11,000 years later among Native American in the contact period.

In the case of Diamond, the possibility that the total deforestation that led to the collapse of Polynesian existence on Easter Island can be attributed in large part to religious motives needs to be set against the long-term successful adaptation of many other Polynesian societies. Why was religion an important negative factor on Easter Island but not in other Pacific Islands? Diamond points out that Easter Island had other things going against it, including its very small size, isolation, and far southern (in the Southern Hemisphere) position. But he is not prepared to say that the collapse would or would not have occurred even if all or any of these geographical conditions had been different. The building and moving of statues for religious purposes seem to have been the main thing, in his view.

The same question can be asked about the role of Christianity in the collapse of Norse Greenland. Diamond contrasts the unwillingness of the Norse to have anything to do with the Inuit, and therefore to learn from them or to adapt any of their practices, to the different attitudes and practices of the French in Canada. The French (at least those involved in the fur trade) established close ties with the various Indian groups with whom they traded and with whom they intermarried as well.

The comparison is interesting but it works against Diamond's claim that religion is a negative factor in adaptation. The French were also Catholic Christians; in which case why did religion not work in the same conservative way? If there were differences between the French and Norse versions of Roman Catholicism, Diamond does not mention them. It would seem therefore that other cultural differences between the French in Canada and the Norse in Greenland were more important than any differences there may have been in religion. The Norse had come to establish lives as farmers while the French (at least in many areas) had come to obtain furs, which meant getting along with the Indians and living close to and often with them. While the Norse had come as families and married among themselves, the French had often come as single men who married native women and established ethnically mixed communities, none of which appears to have been much inhibited by religious considerations.

THE PROBLEM OF REACHING CONCLUSIONS
ABOUT RELIGION AND ADAPTATION

Is there a general conclusion that can be reached about religion, ecological adaptation, and environmental practices? Perhaps not. It is possible to find examples in which religious beliefs and practices seem to have an underlying utilitarian motive or to serve to enhance environmentally sound practices. It is also possible to find examples that seem to counter these, and no one has evidently been able to show what the score would be if all of the instances could be totaled up. It does not even seem possible to offer limited generalizations for several reasons. For one thing, as stressed earlier, religion is not a single thing that that could have a single effect on other things. Further, the problem of evaluating religion, ecology, and the environment (beyond describing or explaining particular instances, which explanations are often themselves controversial) is partly that the number of instances is too large to come to terms with. And finally, there is also a logical or theoretical issue. Arguments that various religious beliefs and practices are ecologically adaptive or environmentally useful are basically versions of functionalism, and the criticisms of functionalism that led to its decline as a mode of analysis apply to these arguments as well. The only real criterion of functional adaptation is survival. If a group or society survives, it is functioning. It is therefore only in extreme instances, such as some of those discussed by Jared Diamond, that it is possible to see dysfunction, and even in such instances the reasons for failure may be too numerous to evaluate.

NOTE

1. A similar story is told by a Chinese community in northwestern Borneo. On the edge of the sleepy little Chinese market town of Bau in western Sarawak there is a beautiful small lake and park used for picnicking. The area also has gold deposits, which had attracted the Chinese more than a century and a half ago. As the price of gold rose in the 1990s, interest in mining was revived and a company decided to drain the lake to recover the ore known to lie beneath it. Consequently the local water table and ground level dropped, causing damage to buildings in the area. This confirmed the local expectation that there would be trouble. There is a dragon living in the lake and dragons, while not inherently malevolent (in this area the dragons also chase away the rain and bring an end to the winter monsoon and the destructive flooding it sometimes brings) are not to be trifled with. Eventually mining was finished, the lake was restored, and the architectural problems ended.

REFERENCES AND FURTHER READING

Anderson, E. N. 1996. *Ecologies of the Heart: Emotion, Belief, and the Environment.* New York: Oxford University Press.

Benedict, Ruth. [1934] 1960. *Patterns of Culture.* New York: Mentor.

Diamond, Jared. 2005. *Collapse: How Societies Choose to Fail or Succeed.* New York: Viking.

Douglas, Mary. [1966] 1984. *Purity and Danger: An Analysis of the Concepts of Pollution and Taboo*. London: ARK Paperbacks.

Harris, Marvin. 1978. *Cows, Pigs, Wars, and Witches: The Riddles of Culture*. New York: Random House.

———. 1985. *Good to Eat: Riddles of Culture*. New York: Simon & Schuster.

Krech, Shepard, III. 1999. *The Ecological Indian: Myth and History*. New York: Norton.

———. 2005. "Reflections on Conservation, Sustainability, and Environmentalism in Indigenous North America." *American Anthropologist* 107(1): 78–86.

Lansing, Stephen J. 1991. *Priests and Programmers: Technologies of Power in the Engineered Landscape of Bali*. Princeton: Princeton University Press.

Moore, Omar Khayam. 1965. "Divination: A New Perspective." In *Reader in Comparative Religion*, edited by William A. Lessa and Evon Z. Vogt, pp. 377–81. 2nd ed. New York: Harper & Row.

Rappaport, Roy A. 1967. "Ritual Regulations of Environmental Regulations among a New Guinea People." *Ethnology* 6: 17–30.

———. 1968. *Pigs for the Ancestors: Ritual in the Ecology of a New Guinea People*. New Haven: Yale University Press.

Reynolds, V., and R. E. S. Tanner. 1983. *The Biology of Religion*. London: Longman.

Simoons, Frederick J. 1994. *Eat Not This Flesh: Food Avoidances from Prehistory to the Present*. Madison: The University of Wisconsin Press.

5

⚜

Natural Symbols

In this chapter we are concerned with natural symbols (Douglas 1973). The notion of natural symbol refers to something that occurs in nature rather than being constructed. However, it also refers to something that humans have in common or tend to incorporate into their religion or culture in one way or another, and therefore that recurs in many places. This does not mean, however, that such symbols will necessarily have the same meanings or even similar meanings everywhere they occur.

WHAT ARE NATURAL SYMBOLS?

Do natural symbols really exist in this sense, or are all religious symbols only understandable within their particular historical and cultural context? This subject is controversial. For some anthropologists, the very notion of natural symbols is an oxymoron—a contradiction in terms. Symbols (even if they are natural things like mountains) are cultural and culture is learned and therefore infinitely variable—or so it might be put. Mary Douglas (1973: 11), for example, writes that

> A cross-cultural, pan-human pattern of symbols must be an impossibility. For one thing each symbolic system develops autonomously according to its own rules. For another, cultural environments add their difference. For another, the social structures add another range of variation. The more closely we inspect the conditions of human interaction, the more unrewarding if not ridiculous the quest for natural symbols appears.

Here the sophisticated reader will suspect that when a writer such as Douglas begins by saying that some proposition must be an impossibility, that is exactly what is about to be argued. In this instance she goes on to assert that, following the Durkheimian or *L'Année sociologique* of French sociologists, natural symbols do occur, in the sense that cross-cultural similarities in social structure give rise to similarities in classification systems. Her concern is specifically with the human body as a natural symbol and her argument is that the body tends to be regarded in religious ways that reflect and symbolize the social structure. The body can serve as an expression of social control (a rigidly controlling society will have strict controls over the uses and functions of the body). It also serves as a model or metaphor for communication and organization (a group or a society will often have a "head" as well as a "body" as in a "body politic"). In more distinctively religious terms attitudes toward the body express values about the purpose of life.

But the body and its various parts and organs are only one possible natural symbol, and Douglas's sociological interpretation is only one way that such symbols have been explained. Interest in widely recurring natural symbols is actually old in anthropology and comparative religion. The nature-myth school (discussed in chapter 6) held that religion came about as humans were awed by the great features and forces of nature and began to regard them as divinities. Such ideas were eventually discarded in anthropology in favor of the notion that religion began with the belief in souls, ghosts, and spirits. However, there can be no question that the major features and forces of nature are in some sense natural symbols. People have always incorporated features of their environment into their religious beliefs, and if the features are widespread so also are the symbols.

Mountains, especially the highest peaks in an area, have significance in many places as the abode of gods or spirits or as the location of the lands of the dead or as the sites of sacred events. And it is difficult not to suppose that mountains or mountaintops tend to be sacred or have mystical significance at least in part because they are closest points to the heavens above. Conversely, the sacred or magical associations of caves may be partly a matter of their mysterious depths, their strange geological formations, and their natural darkness and danger. But it may also be partly that caves appear to be natural portals to the underworld (a three-part universe consisting of an upper world of one sort of spirits or divinities, a lower world of another kind of supernatural creatures, and a middle world of humans being a very common cosmology). Rivers often figure in natural and supernatural cosmology as boundaries between one sort of realm and another, as routes to the land of the dead or the world of the gods, or as dwelling places of spirits, gods, or other supernatural characters, or as all of these things.

Fire and smoke (or incense) occur in religious beliefs and practices in so many ways that it is hard to know where to begin or how to explain them. This illustrates the point that a natural symbol does not have only one meaning or use, even within a single religious tradition, let alone in different ones. Fire can be an instrument of torture and destruction (as in hellfire), but it can also be sacred, a means by which human souls are released to be reborn in new bodies or move to the place of the dead, a way of conveying material goods to ancestors, and so on. It has been suggested that fire may be the oldest religious symbol. Perhaps it would be possible to come up with a single principle that could explain all of the different meanings and religious uses of fire, but this would have to be so abstract that it would have little meaning.

It is not always easy to decide if something is a natural symbol and, if so, how important it is as such. Directions are a good example. Directions tend to be widely important in belief and ritual, but are they a natural attribute of the environment or a cultural construction that developed over time? The directions of east and west derive from the path of sun throughout the day and it may be the rising and the setting of the sun that are important and the real natural symbol. The directions of north and south seem less important, at least in religious terms. Further, other notions of direction may overshadow direction in the sense of the cardinal points. In Borneo east and west as based on the path of the sun does have some of the significance indicated above, but north and south are not very important or meaningful. And even the solar directions seem to be overshadowed by an entirely different natural principle of direction—upriver and downriver. These directions, which have various important spiritual as well as practical meaning, can be in any direction of the compass (and frequently are) as rivers twist or meander even over very short distances. In general upriver is good, the direction of life and purity and superiority, while downriver is the direction of death, pollution, and inferiority.

With a few exceptions (fire and direction), the great features and forces of the environment mentioned above have not occasioned much comparative or theoretical interest in the anthropology of religion, at least since the lapse of the nature-myth school. Probably this is in part simply because the significance of the sun, moon, stars, mountains, caves, rivers, and so forth seems too obvious to warrant much comparative analysis. The interest in natural symbolism has rather involved things that are, while widespread, in some ways anomalous or at least not entirely obvious. Some of the elements of nature that have been discussed (and in some cases explained) in recent decades as the raw material or source of some religious symbolism include certain types of animals, colors, sounds, the human body and certain of its parts, left- and right-handedness or "laterality." But before turning to these, it is necessary to note several other qualifications.

To begin with, phrases like "widely recurring" or "cross-culturally common" are vague, but they are not meant to be assertions of universality—something found in the religion of every society everywhere. Also, there is the question of why natural symbols that recur widely do so or of how they have come to be so. One possibility is that people in different places kept creating them in the sense of incorporating them into their religions symbolism, mythology, or cosmology independently of one another. The other is that the symbols have spread from some central point to others. The latter process is referred to as diffusion and was at one time developed into an important explanation of how things came to be. The role of diffusion in religious change cannot be denied for it is well-known to have occurred (and to be occurring) in the case of the spread of the world religions. The possible role of diffusion in religious change, with or without the physical movement of people, may also be an interesting question in relation to complexes of religious beliefs and practices such as shamanism, even though this must have generally occurred in the distant past and without leaving direct evidence. But it does not seem like a very useful question to ask in the case of natural symbols, for there is little way of knowing if these diffused or were independently noticed and incorporated into religious belief and practice over and over. Moreover (and more importantly) they would have to seem important or appeal to different peoples either way.

ANIMALS

Of all the possible types of natural symbols, animals—including birds, reptiles, and insects as well as mammals—are perhaps most important. Animals of one sort or another play a significant role in the religions of all peoples, although not in the same way nor to the same extent; nor, of course, are the same ones involved in all instances. In addition to real animals there are also creatures of notable and widespread religious significance that exist only as mythological or believed-in supernatural beings, and therefore are not exactly or completely "natural." However, such creatures always have some natural, zoomorphic characteristics, though not necessarily of only one animal. In the case of the dragon, probably the most important and widespread of the mythical creatures, for example, most of its physical characteristics are reptilian. Animals figure in religious belief and practice in various ways, including the following:

- As *gods*, *deities*, or cult creatures from which help is sought or to which offerings are made. The term zoomorphic or theriomorphic refers to animal or animal-like attributes. Hybrid deities combine human and animal characteristics, as does the Hindu god Ganesha, who has the body of a man and the head of an elephant, the ancient Greek Minotaur (human body, head of a bull), or the ever-popular mermaid. However, in the case of images there can be a problem in just what is being depicted—a deity with a combination of human and animal features or a human wearing a mask of an animal (a problem in interpreting some of the images in the cave paintings of the European Paleolithic).

- As *totems* or creatures after which kin or other groups are named or with which they associate themselves, though not necessarily involving veneration or offerings. Totemism was once considered by some scholars to have been the original form of religion.
- As *were animals*, or creatures that can take either human or animal form. In the West the best known such creature is the werewolf while in Indonesia and Malaysia in Southeast Asia the main were-animal is the tiger.
- As *guardian animals* or *familiar spirits* in animal form, or any animal with supernatural power with which a person has a particular relationship.
- As *omen* creatures or messengers from the gods or the spirit world who are sent to give warnings or to inform humans that a course of action may or may not be followed, or that may be summoned or consulted by humans (often experts) as a form of divination. (In Borneo small birds are the main messengers or avatars of the gods.)
- As *tricksters*, or creatures (often otherwise relatively small and vulnerable) of either extraordinary intelligence or stupidity (or often a combination of the two) combined with supernatural powers; in some instances tricksters are topics of amusing or ribald folktales while in others they may also have major roles in mythology as culture heroes and creators.
- As objects of *taboo*. Animals that are taboo should not be killed or eaten, either normally or under any circumstances. Such restrictions can include both totemic animals special to members of particular groups as well as others that are forbidden to everyone. Taboos may also differ according to gender and other categories of social status. There may also be individual taboos.

Why Animals Are Important as Symbols

Several lines of interpretation have been applied to explaining which sorts of animals have been incorporated into religious beliefs and practices in one way or another, and why, including (1) functionalist, utilitarian, or materialist interpretations; (2) emotionalist explanations; and (3) structuralist interpretations.

Functionalist, Utilitarian, or Materialist Interpretations—Or, Animals Are
Good to Eat (Or Not to Eat, or to Protect, or to Be Protected From, etc.)

Utilitarian or functionalist explanations of the religious importance of animals are very old in anthropology. According to Malinowski's (1948: 20–21)
version of this approach, humans emphasize animals and to some extent
plants in religious terms because of their importance as sources of food and
other essential materials. Other versions of this line of explanation were
noted in the previous chapter, specifically the argument made by some
scholars that making an animal into a totem or placing it under a taboo can
protect it from undue exploitation, reserve its use for activities that are of
greatest importance for survival, or otherwise protect people by preventing
them from doing things they should not be doing. Harris's arguments
about the cow and the pig are the most notable examples of this line of argument but it often appeals to ecologically oriented anthropologists in general. Such arguments are, as also noted, versions of classic functionalism,
which holds that actions, practices, or traditions can have unintended but
useful or adaptive consequences and that the main job of the social scientist is to figure these out. Animal cults therefore help to reduce anxiety by
creating the illusion of control over important animals through ritual and
by creating bonds of solidarity and identification between humans and animals through totemic practices and the imposition of taboo restrictions on
the killing or eating of various animals (Lévi-Strauss 1962: 56–58).

Emotionalist Interpretations—Or, Dangerous Animals Are Good
to Fear and to Venerate

This sort of explanation holds that humans are inclined to venerate creatures (and sometimes other things such as volcanoes or fire) that are
powerful, ferocious, or otherwise dangerous and that therefore inspire
strong emotions, especially fear and anxiety. The proposition that fear
often underlies animal deities and cults works fairly well in the case of
larger, carnivorous animals, especially ones that are capable and sometimes inclined to kill and eat humans. The tiger, the lion, the jaguar, the
crocodile, and the grizzly or brown bear are good examples. The discredited belief that Neanderthals had cave bear cults also reflects such
thinking. The argument works especially well in the case of snakes (discussed below) because snakes are the animal most commonly incorporated as a religious symbol (or so it has been claimed) and because the
varieties of snakes chosen are usually the dangerous ones. The argument does not work well with birds (also discussed below), which are
also widely significant as religious symbols but which are not, with a
few possible exceptions, dangerous to humans.

Structuralist Interpretations—Or, Animals Are Good to Think

Lévi-Strauss (1962) concluded in his study of totemism that animals are "good to think." The significance of animals in human religious belief and practice is a matter of classification, of cultural principles of logic and mental categories, rather than utilitarian value. The argument has also been applied mainly to animals as totems and as objects of taboo. Lévi-Strauss rejected the functionalist or materialist approaches of Malinowski and others in favor of what he referred to as structuralism. The basic idea is that human thought is organized according to principles of classification that were based especially on binary opposition.

Structuralism was developed further in the 1960s and 1970s by Mary Douglas, Edmund Leach, and others. Leach attempted to show, for example, that food taboos operated in the same way or according to the same principles as those involving incest avoidance and marriage. Both Leach and Douglas were drawn to the Old Testament, especially to Leviticus and the other early scriptures that presented the basic tenets of Judeo-Christian myth and tribal law. Both scholars argued that various animals are singled out and regarded as sacred or tabooed as food because they are anomalous or reflect contrary or overlapping categories. Douglas (1984: 54–55) argued that according to the scriptures the pig was an abomination to the Jews because it was, like some of the other forbidden foods, an anomaly, in this case in terms of its anatomy and behavior. While the pig has a cloven hoof (like cattle, goats, and sheep), it does not chew the cud (as do cattle, goats, and sheep). The Lele, a central African people among whom Douglas had conducted fieldwork, had a somewhat similar reason for regarding the pangolin, or scaly anteater, as a sacred animal. In this case, while the pangolin is a mammal that lives on the land and climbs trees, it has scales like a fish, a creature of the water (1984: 168–69).

As do functionalist interpretations of religious rules about animals, the structuralist approach works well in some instances; and not only about food taboos but also about magical and religious beliefs in general. It is not hard to think of examples of the sacred that involve anomaly—in Christianity, for example, beginning with the central doctrine of the Virgin Birth. Indeed, miracles are by definition anomalous events. Among the Malays the anomalous combination of rain falling while the sun is shining has supernatural significance, as also does twilight, which overlaps day and night. Such ideas appear to be widespread.

Anomaly, and therefore structuralism, as an explanation has its limits, however. Some of what humans designate or create as sacred or taboo can be seen as being anomalous in one way, but it is also not difficult to think of things that are not. What anomaly, overlapping set of categories, or contradiction, for example, explains the sacredness of cattle in Hinduism

or in some African societies? And why are anomalies identified or regarded as interesting or troubling by only some peoples? Why, for example, were peoples outside the Middle Eastern religions unaware of or un-
concerned about the fact that while pigs have cloven hoofs they do not
chew their cud? Or, from the opposite perspective, what about the seemingly anomalous animals that have not been designated as sacred or
taboo? For example, bats would seem to be obviously anomalous in that
they are the only furry mammals that fly. However, while important in
folklore, bats (unlike birds) are seldom deified, except in Mesoamerica.
This also happens to be the only region of the world in which vampire
bats occur. This suggests that the mystical significance of bats is based not
so much on their seemingly anomalous nature as a flying furry animal, as
on the blood drinking habits of vampire bats in particular. Nor do flight-
less birds, another fairly obvious anomaly, seem to have attracted much
attention as sacred creatures in any of the areas where they exist. Indeed,
some of these were hunted to extinction because of their vulnerability.

Snakes

According to the extensive study of Balaji Mundkur (1983), snakes occur
more frequently and widely in the religious symbolism of the world—as
divinities, cult icons, and as other kinds of mythical creatures—than any
other type of animal.[1] The serpent as symbol occurs in all areas inhabited
by humans and, through diffusion or human migration, extends beyond
the actual range of snakes (which is already very extensive) to include the
culture of the Inuit (Eskimo). Snakes are even more common and important in religious symbolism if it is assumed that dragons are mythical versions of serpents or are based on them rather than other types of reptiles.
But serpents as such have an important role in the religions of all of the
primary civilizations in both the New and the Old Worlds. In pre-
Columbian Mesoamerica the affix "coatl" or "serpent" occurs in names of
eight major deities (Mundkur 1983: 143).

As is true of other symbols, snakes as motifs are represented in varying
degrees of abstraction. These range from highly realistic depictions of particular varieties to wavy or zigzag lines that could be of any snake and
that are sometimes also interpreted as moving water or lightning. At an
even further degree of abstraction, the forked tongue is also used as a motif. Serpentine features are sometimes combined with human characteristics and sometimes with those of other animals. The Celtic god of war had
the body of a snake and the head of a ram. Deities comprising snake and
bird combinations were common in Pre-Columbian Mesoamerica.

To say that they are important does not mean that snakes are always
worshiped as deities. While serpents often occur as deities in ancient and

indigenous or tribal religions, they have other roles in most of the existing world religions. In the Judeo-Christian tradition the serpent is best known in association with the temptation of Adam and Eve and their expulsion from the Garden of Eden, although serpents occur commonly in the Old Testament as supernatural creatures in a range of contexts. In Islamic traditions, *jin* spirits often take the form of serpents. It would therefore be difficult to argue that snakes always have the same meaning, and Mundkur does not do so, although he does claim that some associations recur

Figure 5.1. An ancient statue of the Buddha meditating while sitting on the coiled body of a seven-headed *naga* serpent, Angkor, Cambodia. The gold foil and the remains of incense sticks show ongoing veneration.

widely. These associations tend to be of several types, all of which derive from one or another natural characteristic.

To begin with, there are the meanings of the sort familiar to Westerners—evil and treachery. Such notions, as well as jealousy, are also common in China and Japan, Mundkur points out. Snakes also have strong positive associations, though they are less apt to be familiar to Westerners. One of these is a widespread association with rain, flooding, fertility, and the sun. In the temperate or colder regions snakes emerge from hibernation when the sun warms the earth. The connection with flooding is that snakes often appear as they seek refuge on higher ground when waters rise. Floods are often destructive but they are also recognized as a source of fertility, a notion that was extended to snakes. The latter notion is also linked to or reinforced by phallic associations of the shape and movement of the snake. Mythical equations of the snake and the penis are common as are references to the sexual penetration and impregnation of women by serpents. Mundkur, however, argues that psychoanalytical interpretations of serpents as phallic symbols are overdone, that snakes often have feminine rather than masculine associations, and that the primary basis of religious preoccupation lies elsewhere.

The final common meaning of the snake is as a symbol of immortality. This idea seems to be linked to the observation that snakes shed their skins, which has been seen as an alternative to death, or as symbolizing reincarnation. For example, in the well-known ethnographic film *Dead Birds* (by Robert Gardner) about the Dani in the New Guinea highlands, warfare is said to be explained by a myth about a race between a snake and a bird. If the snake had won men would, like snakes, have eternal life and would have presumably also lived in peace. But instead the bird won, and ever since men have had to die, and therefore to also kill one another.

While all of the meanings of snakes may be said to exemplify power in one way or another, Mundkur thinks that the most important one is fear. This is based especially on the ability of the venomous varieties to strike suddenly and, with little or no warning, inflict pain and death. This raises the question of how common or important the poisonous serpents are in terms of religious symbolism in contrast to the nonpoisonous ones. The serpent motifs and designs that have been present in religious iconography across the world for thousands of years are often too generalized or abstract to be able to identify in specific terms. But where it is possible to identify the kinds of snakes venerated as deities, or otherwise singled out for religious attention, they are usually poisonous varieties. These include especially the cobra in Egypt, India, and Southeast Asia, and the rattlesnake in Mesoamerica and elsewhere in North America. It is true that these two kinds of poisonous serpents stand apart from equally or more poisonous and dangerous varieties by other spectacular characteristics:

the flattened hood and raised upper body of the cobra and the whirring rattle of the coiled rattlesnake. Along this same line, Mundkur points out that humans are impressed by the distinctive ways that snakes move and by the often striking designs and colors of snake skin, although this seems to be a secondary consideration (the cobra, for example, is not very impressive in terms of skin color or pattern).

Not all religiously significant snakes are poisonous, but those that are not also tend to be dangerously powerful. Of the nonvenomous serpents that can be identified in the religious imagery of the past or are known in present-day ethnographic terms, only the larger pythons (which are venerated in Africa and in South America) are common. These animals also have the ability and the inclination to kill humans, although it is perhaps their ability to swallow large animals whole that makes them objects of religious awe.

Even where they are explicitly venerated, snakes are also feared and reviled. Their more positive associations notwithstanding, fear and revulsion are at the root of the religious fascination with serpents. Poisonous snakes fall into the general category of dangerous animals that are widely mythologized and venerated, but they have a special place within that category. "This is a consequence of the sheer abundance of reptiles in the tropics and, seasonally, in the temperate regions and their occupation of ecological niches unavailable to most large beasts of prey usually regarded as dangerous" (Mundkur 1983: 41). The large carnivorous mammals (including the bear, wolf, lion, tiger, jaguar, and leopard) are more restricted in their geographic range than snakes. Such animals need more living room, have thinner populations, and do not generally invade human living space as frequently as do serpents.

The human religious fascination with serpents therefore involves a universal fear that is not matched by that of any other creature. Moreover, Mundkur argues, this fear has an innate basis that is rooted in the evolution of primates.

> Unlike almost all other animals, serpents, in varying degrees, provoke certain characteristically intuitive, irrational, phobic responses in human and non-human primates alike; that, in this respect, the distinctiveness of man as a "logic"-employing, symbol-devising species is blurred; and that the serpent's power to fascinate certain primates is dependent on the latter's autonomic nervous systems to the mere sight of reptilian sinuous movement. (Mundkur 1983: 6)

Birds

As with the argument about the sacredness of seemingly anomalous creatures, the thesis that powerful and dangerous animals are often natural symbols does not work in the case of all such mammals and reptiles; nor is it true that animals are deified or otherwise incorporated into religious belief and practice in close proportion to the actual death and suffering they inflict on humans. While poisonous insects (especially spiders, centipedes, scorpions, and bees) are reportedly responsible for more human death and illness than reptiles or mammals, they have only a limited place in religious symbolism. The spider occurs as a trickster animal in West Africa and among Native Americans of the Plains, while Spider Woman is a divinity among some Southwestern groups. In some places the scorpion has been deified, most notably in ancient Egypt, where however it was less significant than the harmless scarab or dung beetle (Mundkur 1983: 118).

It is probably true to say that humans have particular inclinations to focus religious attention on animals that are dangerous to them. However, this has little relevance in the case of birds that, along with serpents, are the animals that have the widest and most prominent role in religious imagery. The birds of prey are by far the most prominent, but these pose no direct threat to humans. Their widespread significance has been explained in other ways. One of these is that, if birds of prey pose no threat to humans, they do to other, smaller creatures, including snakes, to which they are often opposed in terms of cosmology (as in the Dani story noted above). The ability of hawks and eagles to fly at great heights and some hawks to dive at great speed has also been noted. So has soaring, which is practiced not only by the daytime raptors but also by vultures which are also sometimes venerated (e.g., by indigenous Amazon peoples), and which have solar associations. The abilities of the owls to see and to fly silently through forest and field and to hunt at night makes for fairly obvious associations with the unseen world of spirits and death, of which they are widespread harbingers.

While the birds of prey have widespread significance as religious symbols, birds in general often have upper-worldly associations, in contrast to serpents and other reptiles that are linked to the lower world. Mundkur, who writes at length about animal icons in general in his book, suggests that, while they are the main rivals of snakes, there is little about birds except flight that accounts for their widespread religious significance. Aside from the seeming difficulty of proving that birds are less symbolically significant to humans in general, this claim is questionable in several ways. For one thing, if part of the general importance of snakes is that they are so widespread, then it needs to be noted that the range of birds considerably exceeds that of snakes. And while flight, with its heavenly associations, is perhaps the main thing, bird plumage, which is widely used in ritual as in other contexts, is probably also important. In some (perhaps many) instances plumage itself has upper-world mean-

Figure 5.2.   Dayak crucifix with a hornbill bird (the main symbol of the upper world) at the top, northern Borneo, east Malaysia. Photo by Lim Yu Seng, reproduced with the permission of the Sarawak Museum, Kuching, Sarawak, Malaysia.

ings. This is the case, for example, among some Amazon indigenous groups among whom persons adorn themselves with down from the King Vulture as part of the preparation for ascending to the sky world. Nor can the calls of birds, that make them among the most vocal of all animals, be of little importance. Especially in forest settings birds sometimes can be heard and not seen. In Borneo augury is often a matter of only hearing the calls of the omen birds.

COLORS

The literature on colors as widely recurring symbols in myth and ritual is less explicit or emphatic than that of some other things. In addition, there is again the problem of separating the distinctly religious from the general use or practical significance of color. Black, white, and red appear to recur commonly in ritual contexts, but they do so in other contexts as well. The beginning point for a discussion of recurring ritual or sacred colors should therefore probably be Berlin and Kay's (1969) classic study of what they call basic color terms. This work shows that colors around the world are perceived and labeled in far more similar ways than linguists and anthropologists had previously supposed. Berlin and Kay found that all peoples seem to classify colors in from two to eleven primary categories using terms that can be readily translated from one language to another. If people have the minimum of two color categories these are always "black" and "white," the former including all darker shades, the latter all the lighter ones. If people have three categories of color they are always black and white plus red; and additional colors are always added in the same exact manner. Their study also showed that the number of color categories recognized by a society is a matter of technological evolution: the technologically simpler the society, the fewer the categories of color; the more technologically developed, the greater the number.

Berlin and Kay's study does not address the issue of whether colors have similar cross-cultural meanings or ritual uses. It does appear that the three most fundamental of all the color categories—black, white, and red—have widespread religious significance. But if so, this may be for several possible reasons. One possibility is that humans have been inclined to attach the greatest ritual significance to the colors that are most basically encoded in the human mind. Another is that the most basic color categories acquired religious meanings at an early phase in human cultural evolution and have retained these meanings over time.

It is this latter argument that Victor Turner (1966) makes in his analysis of color symbolism among the Ndembu and some other peoples in the world. The Ndembu are a small-scale society of central Africa whose indigenous ritual processes and symbolism Turner studied in great detail in the 1950s. In his account of their color symbolism he begins by taking note of the theoretical emphasis given in the 1960s to binary oppositions, especially lateral or left-right categories (discussed below). Turner acknowledged that lateral or "handedness" symbolism could be found among the Ndembu as well, and noted that efforts had been made to reduce African color symbolism to two ritual categories of black and white. He claimed, however, that Ndembu color categories are fundamentally and irreducibly tripartite; red did not represent a synthesis of black and white or white of black and red, and so on. Nor are any of the three colors secondary to any other. These three colors each tend to have multiple meanings, but they are often similar; white has one series of meanings, black another series, and red yet another. Nor are the colors strongly associated with gender. While red is associated with maleness in some contexts, it is associated with femaleness in others. The primary association of the color red is blood. While blood is linked to the male activities of hunting and warfare, it is also linked to the female ones of menstruation and childbirth. The same is true of white: female milk on the one hand and male seminal fluid on the other. More generally, blood is associated with life and power and white with purity, goodness, and the sun and moon. Both red and white stand in opposition to black, which is associated with night, fainting, death, and sorcery, although in some contexts (dark soil, river mud, rain clouds) black is linked with fertility. The Ndembu explain the three colors as parts of a river that comes from god. Other things in the environment are valued in part and used in rituals because they have these colors.

Following his analysis of Ndembu color categories, Turner makes wider comparisons, first among similar societies in Africa and then elsewhere. In the African instances he cites, the same red, black, and white ritual colors recur and mainly with the same meanings. Black is an exception in that among some groups it has a more positive value than among the Ndembu. The Bushmen (now San or !Kung) of the Kalahari, for example, highly value a lustrous black powder made from pounded specularite (specular iron) and regard it as having magical powers. As an explanation of why black is valued in some places and not others, he suggests that it is apt to be an auspicious color in arid regions where black clouds bring the rains that mean the end of drought and deprivation, and an inauspicious one in humid places where water is not in short supply.

In terms of broader comparisons, Turner notes that red, black, and white are also the ritual colors of the aboriginal peoples of the interior of the Malay Peninsula (as is also the case in the interior of Borneo). These groups, who use the three colors for body painting, generally regard white as auspicious. This is also the case among Australian indigenous peoples who use the three colors in rock art as well as for body painting. There white symbolizes water and is often painted on faces, while red is equated with blood and strength. Among the Cherokee of North America white represents peace and happiness, red means success, and black implies death. The Cherokee also link the colors to directions (white with the south, red with the north, and black with the west) and to spirits (white and red ones being good, black ones bad).

From these far-flung ethnographic examples, Turner turns to the ancient world, specifically to the Hindu Upanishads. In these sacred texts the three colors are associated with the elements—red equals fire, white is water, and black is the original earth. When food is eaten it becomes different substances according to color; the black part becomes feces, the red becomes flesh, and the white becomes brains and mind. The same thing occurs with drink. In this case black becomes urine, red is transformed into blood, and white is turned into life force, presumably semen and milk.

Turner concludes that the color triad often has explicit reference to the fluids, secretions, and waste substances of the human body—especially of red to blood—though in all instances the meanings of the colors are complex. He suggests that the three colors are among the earliest symbols produced by humans because the bodily processes with which they are associated are all (though presumably some more than others) associated with heightened states of emotional awareness. Some of the bodily processes are also linked to, and therefore symbolic of, the most elementary and important of all social relationships, including those of mother and child and husband and wife—not to mention the more general association of blood with kinship. Because of these elementary associations, red, white, and black color symbolism is primordial and does not need to be explained on the basis of diffusion.

The situation is very different with color symbolism that extends beyond the basic triad. Colors such as saffron, yellow, gold, blue, green, purple, and so on, which are ritually (and otherwise) important in various places, do need to be explained as a matter of diffusion. While colors other than black, white, and red are more culturally relative than universal, some natural (or quasi-natural) links seem basic. Green, obviously associated with plant life, could be expected to have particular significance in arid areas where the vegetation is often scarce (and where human life has long been tied to limited areas of cropland and pasture). Green, along with white (that symbolizes purity and cleanliness), is the main color of Islam.

The ritual significance of color is not only a matter of recognition or classification but also of availability. It therefore may be of some significance that black, red, and white pigments are relatively easy to obtain or produce in most environments in contrast to ones such as blue, yellow, or green (not counting the use of natural things that have these colors, such as leaves or feathers, both of which are also widely used in rituals). This is especially true if red is taken to include orange and white to be also light shades of gray.

Reddish pigments are most commonly obtained in the form of ocher—clay tinted with iron oxides. Ocher is abundant in many places in the world and also has been widely reported in archaeological sites, including Paleolithic ones. Pure black in the form of soot or charcoal is readily available from the use of fire and can be used with or without the addition of oil or grease for body paint, rock art, or other purposes, including tattooing (the use of colors other than black in tattooing is modern, although the actual appearance of tattoos created by injecting black pigment varies somewhat according to skin color but is generally a dark blue).

Clay in the form of kaolin is a source of white pigment in some areas, though it is less common than ocher. The more thorough burning of wood or bone produces light gray ash, while the burning of shell produces nearly pure white lime. Such lime has important ritual uses throughout Southeast Asia and beyond. When chewed with green betel leaf and pinkish gray areca nut, lime produces blood-red spittle, which eventually turns the teeth black. In addition to being widely chewed for their mild physical effects, packets of these three ingredients (usually referred to as betel nut) have important ritual uses, especially in betrothal and wedding ceremonies and as offerings to spirits.

Finally, it is hard not to suppose that in humid tropical environments, apart from the relative ease of making them, part of the significance of black, white, and red is that they are relatively rare in an environment overwhelmingly dominated by varying shades of green and brown. Black is probably nearly everywhere associated with night, although not necessarily with death and evil, as it is in the West. White is more complicated, being the color of purity in the West and in many other places, but also of death and ghostliness in East Asia. Red is probably everywhere associated with blood, although this may not be the reason it is so highly valued in some places.

LATERAL SYMBOLISM: LEFT- AND RIGHT-HANDEDNESS

The widespread ritual and social significance of right and left was first systematically explored by the French anthropologist Robert Hertz in a long article published in 1909, "The Pre-eminence of the Right Hand: A Study in Religious Polarity."[2] Hertz began with the common belief that right-handedness is natural and asserted that the only real evidence for this is its link to the greater development of the left sphere of the brain. He quoted Broca's claim that "we are right handed because we are left brained" (Hertz 1973: 4). While acknowledging the link, he argued that the direction of causality remained unproved and suggested that it could be equally possible that "we are left brained because we are right handed." The animals most closely related to humans (the primates), he went on, are ambidextrous. As for humans, the evidence was that about two people in a hundred were naturally left-handed, and a considerably larger number right-handed, but most people were by heredity neither left- nor right-handed and could use either hand.

Hertz drew especially on information on the Maori but went on to argue that the significance of handedness was pervasive in human society. In small-scale societies it was a matter of ritual and religion, while in modern ones lateral symbolism was more secular but nonetheless important. Everywhere notions of sacredness and profanity surrounded handedness. The right hand is pure, the left impure. These notions, in turn, were associated with a broader dualism that pervaded primitive society—light and dark, day and night, male and female, high and low, sky and earth, life and death, purity and pollution, and so on.

Handedness was also associated with directions, Hertz noted. The right was associated with east or south and the left with north or west. However, he disputed the assertion of some observers that right and left symbolism derived from natural directions. The idea here is that the worshiper looks to the east (the direction of the rising sun) in prayer and ceremony, which puts the south to the right and the north to the left. This means also that the right is the direction of sunshine and warmth while the left is that of darkness and cold. The problem with this, he pointed out in a footnote, is that such natural associations only work in the Northern Hemisphere (and the symbolism of right and left is not reversed in the Southern Hemisphere).

Hertz died at a young age in World War I and his paper, written in French, did not become widely influential in English-language anthropology until published in translation many years later. It eventually led some anthropologists to examine and write about left-right symbolism among various groups throughout the world.[3] Nearly all of the ethnographic examples supported Hertz's claims about the general ritual and social importance of handedness and about the pervasiveness of the preference for the right hand, although not necessarily about the prevalence of dualistic classification in all realms of life.

Hertz's claim that human habits and ritual practices, rather than natural heredity, are responsible for the pervasiveness of right-handedness in human populations has not been fully sustained. Since Hertz wrote at the beginning of the twentieth century a great deal more research has been done on handedness and left and right brain functions, involving humans, other primates, and other animals. Many more things are now known, including the association of language with the left hemisphere of the brain and therefore, by extension in some sense, with right-handedness (Springer and Deutsch 1998). Other mammals and even birds develop "pawednesss" or "footedness" in reaching or hitting but do not appear to have an innate preference for left or right. The evidence of primates that Hertz alluded to is not conclusive but tends not to support his contention. Chimpanzees, at least, tend to be right-handed, though not to the extent of humans. Physical anthropological and archaeological studies, including the examination of flake and use patterns on ancient stone tools, are controversial but suggest that human right-handedness is old enough in evolutionary terms to predate the development of the religious and cultural preferences that Hertz noted. Such evidence suggests the pervasiveness of right-handedness has an innate basis (McManus 2002), although one that is strongly reinforced by cross-cultural preferences. That would mean that right and left are natural symbols in the fullest sense of the term.

PERCUSSION SOUNDS

In another effort to find and explain recurrent symbolism used in religion and ritual, Rodney Needham (1979) suggests that sounds made by percussion have a special significance in efforts to communicate with supernatural beings. Percussion sounds range from those that can be made without an instrument (such as hand clapping or body slapping) to those made by striking one relatively hard or resonant object with another, to ones made by the use of highly complex instruments. While the latter are distinctly or fully cultural, the former, to the extent that they are cross-culturally pervasive or common, can be said to be natural. Since drums, gongs, and bells are of course human artifacts, the sounds they produce are not exactly natural. However, the sounds such instruments produce more nearly parallel natural ones than do those produced by any other type of musical instrument.

Needham therefore focuses particular attention on the drum, the gong, and the bell. His point of departure is the drum, specifically its recurrent mention in the ethnographic literature as the instrument used by the shaman to summon or make contact with the spirits. In searching for evidence and explanation, he came upon an obscure ethnological paper on the origins of the drum and the bell by Maria Dworakowska, who asserted that while the bell was commonly thought to be exclusively an instrument of music and signaling (between humans), this was erroneous. In fact, the bell plays a role similar to the drum among many peoples, as does the gong. Dworakowska suggested that the three instruments represented an evolutionary sequence that began with the drum and ended with the bell of western Europe. The suggestion that the drum is a continuation of the coffin log may or may not be correct, but the main point is that there is a close connection between the drum and the dead. The drum, the gong, the bell, and cognate instruments are all part of the cult of the dead (Needham 1979: 313; citing and quoting Dworakowska 1938).

Needham also cites the suggestion made by Ernest Crawley in 1912 that the music of the drum is more closely connected with the whole range of human emotion than that of any other instrument. Needham suggests that the sounds produced by drums (and some gongs) and bells produce their effect on the emotions by reverberating and impacting the body like thunder or cannon fire. They produce effects ranging from an agonizing disruption of the organism to subliminal thrills, effects that suggest otherworldly connections. Drums and other percussion instruments are not the only way of producing such effects, but they are, or can be, a technologically simple (and therefore presumably early and widespread) means of doing so. Drums (and in some places gongs) are also widely used, often in association with dancing, to achieve trance states, an important and elementary channel of communication with the spirit world.

To all of this Needhan adds the suggestion that percussion has another fundamental use in religious ceremonies and other events. Percussion is associated with a wide range of ritualized situations including birth, initiation, marriage, sacrifice, war, healing, and death. In such activities, he suggests, percussion signals transition from one stage to another. He closes with an affirmation of seeking comparative explanations of human phenomena that transcend conventional explanations, and cites Turner's analysis for color symbolism as another example of what can be done.

THE HEAD AND ITS PARTS

Our last example of alleged natural symbolism takes us back to where we began—to the human body, in particular, the head. It also involves a very different line of interpretation than the one advocated by Mary Douglas in her analysis of the body as a symbol of different forms of social organization. The head itself consists of various parts including the mouth, nose, eyes, and ears. But those that figure most importantly in what follows are, in addition to the entire head itself, the skull, brains, scalp, and hair; the face is also involved but is less important than might be supposed. Here the perhaps obvious point could be made that while a thing itself can be a symbol its various parts can also be symbols in themselves.

Hair

Hair is the topic of one of the most provocative of the efforts by British social anthropologists to identify and explain cross-culturally recurrent or natural symbols—Edmund Leach's (1958) analysis of hair symbolism.

Leach took his departure from a book on hair symbolism by Charles Berg, a psychoanalyst. Berg based his book on therapeutic work with his own patients, who were often preoccupied with hair, but he also made use of ethnographic and historical material. He began with the easily accepted assumption that in most societies, including modern Western ones, hairdressing is a matter of ritualistic elaboration. His explanation of this particular attention to hair is that it is a universal symbol of the genital organs. Hair cutting and shaving are a form of symbolic castration—"symbolic" in this case meaning "unconscious." There is also an association between hair and feces, but most broadly hair is used as a symbol for sexually aggressive drives of all kinds. Therefore, in shaving and hair cutting people deal with aggressive impulses by directing them against their hair.

Leach disputed the psychoanalytic interpretation but noted abundant comparative evidence that hair symbolism everywhere involves both sexuality and aggression. His main argument is that this symbolism is mainly overt rather than unconscious. He cited a long-standing anthropological awareness of hair cutting or head shaving as a part of mourning ceremonies. He also noted a similar connection between head-hunting and the fertility of crops among Southeast Asian tribal groups. Both sorts of explicit symbolic notions were also manifestations of the less overt belief that the head or the hair is the locus of the soul or soul stuff or magical energy of some sort. Generally speaking, in ritual situations long hair equals unrestrained sexuality, short hair or partially shaved head or tightly bound hair equals restricted sexuality while a closely shaven head indicates celibacy. There are usually differences between male and female practices and shaving, cutting, or binding are not the only things that are done to hair. There is also the uncut, matted, and totally neglected hair of the Indian (South Asian) religious ascetic that symbolizes the complete denial of sexuality. Leach also suggested that a fuller understanding of the religious significance of hair also has to consider the covering of the head with hats or other things.

From the perspective of religion, Leach noted that the most important thing about hair is its widespread magical or sacred significance. He asserted that this is not necessarily a matter of sexuality but his examples suggest that it frequently is. The most interesting is the depiction of the Buddha in statues and other images. While Buddhist monks shave their heads (symbolizing celibacy), the Buddha is shown with tightly curled hair that Leach interprets as intended to symbolize his fertilizing power. In the earliest artistic depictions, the Buddha is shown along classical Greek lines with a natural head and hair but surrounded by a halo. The halo, moreover, while generally interpreted in Christian iconography as a golden circle indicating angelic goodness, probably originated as a ring of fire indicating magical or divine power.

The Skull, Head-Hunting, and Scalping

Leach's analysis of hair symbolism was followed by reaction, argument, and further research. The psychological anthropologist Gananath Obeyesekere (1981) examined Leach's arguments at length in a book-length study of hair symbolism among religious ascetics in Sri Lanka; however, Obeyesekere confined his analysis to the Indic Hindu-Buddhist tradition. Then without mentioning Leach, the American anthropologist La Barre

(1985) took the issue in a different direction. He argued that what was important was the head. It was cross-culturally important because of what was thought to be inside of it. He also examined head-hunting, which Leach had mentioned but did not explore, as a worldwide practice and attempted to trace the cult of the head back in time to the Paleolithic. Because hunting was at the heart of Paleolithic culture, humans were familiar with the anatomy of animals, including the framework of the bones and their contents, although their understanding of how the different parts of the body worked was limited. While it might be assumed that early humans would have supposed that blood was the main life force, La Barre argued that they actually regarded bones and marrow, along with the spinal cord and brain, as the most crucial part of humans and other animals. A cult of bones is, therefore, the oldest manifestation of religion in prehistory.

The basic idea is what La Barre terms *muelos* (from the Greek) or "marrow," a notion previously explored by the historian Richard Onians (1951) in his study of the origins of European thought about the mind, body, and

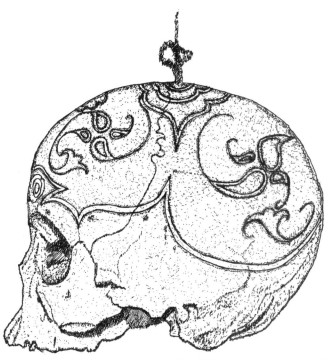

Figure 5.3.   A Bidayuh Dayak engraved trophy skull from northwestern Borneo (east) Malaysia.

soul. *Muelos* was thought to be the life force of the body and of fertility and the source of semen in men. While various bones contain *muelos*, the largest amount by far is stored in the head. The notion also includes the belief that the supply of *muelos* in the head is directly connected to the male genitalia by way of the spinal column. This idea remained in vogue in Europe until the Renaissance, as shown in a drawing by Leonardo da Vinci and several passages from Shakespeare.

It is the notion that the skull is the main repository of *muelos* that makes the head so important in ritual terms. The head is conceived to be the repository of the soul because it is the main repository of *muelos*. Therefore *muelos* is the "soul stuff" that Leach and others have spoken of in relation to the head without an explanation of just what it was conceived to be or why it was there rather than somewhere else in the body—in the heart, for example.

The Paleolithic *muelos* notion also includes the belief that a person, and by extension the village or tribe, has only a finite amount. Each emission of semen represents a loss of a man's and his society's total store of *muelos*. Another belief, however, is that it is possible to obtain and consume the *muelos* of others literally or physically through cannibalism. The direct transfer of semen from one male to another can also accomplish it. (As in the ritual homosexuality of some New Guinea societies in which older men donate semen to male adolescents so that they can mature.) *Muelos* can also be captured, it is widely believed, by cutting off the head of someone, including an enemy in battle or a victim of human sacrifice, and incorporating the head as a ritual object, thereby acquiring its spiritual power. In this instance, the transfer of *muelos* is connected with magic and is regarded as enhancing the fertility (agricultural as well as human) of a community in general rather than an individual in particular. This explains, La Barre suggests, the custom of requiring or encouraging a young man to take the head of an enemy (and thereby acquiring his spiritual essence) before marrying and therefore beginning to expend his and his community's limited store of *muelos* in sexual intercourse.

The practice of head-hunting is the most important indirect evidence in favor of the widespread ritual importance of the head. La Barre (1985: 13–28) argues that head-hunting, based on a cult of skulls, is worldwide in terms of prehistoric, protohistoric, and ethnographic evidence. His range of examples is somewhat limited, though broad enough to include Europe, Polynesia, New Zealand, Melanesia, insular and mainland Southeast Asia, and North and South America. For Europe he cites evidence that head-hunting for the purpose of brain eating survived into the Bronze Age and in some instances at least into historic times.

The New World evidence of head-hunting and skull cults is complicated because head-hunting has tended to be overshadowed in some regions by human sacrifice and scalping. In North America, head taking was less common than scalping, at least in the historic period for which most information exists. By the early twentieth century, however, the argument had been advanced that scalping had spread as an innovation resulting from European influence. According to La Barre, French and English colonists paid bounties to whites as well as Indians to whom they were allied to kill Indians they regarded as enemies or otherwise wanted to be rid of. Initially the Europeans paid for heads but came to prefer scalps. The change also suited the Indians insofar as dried scalps were much lighter than heads and therefore more could be carried, especially given the weight of guns and ammunition that also came into use in the colonial period (James Mooney, as quoted in La Barre 1985: 58).[4]

The evidence that the human head is a powerful natural symbol seems overwhelming. However, that the symbolism of the head is based on the notion of what La Barre calls the *muelos* superstition seems less well supported, at least by direct evidence. The only ethnographic evidence La Barre cites in which informants have explicitly described what could be called *muelos*, involves Indian Hindus. According to the psychiatrist-anthropologist Morris Carstairs (1967: 84),

> Everyone agreed on one point, that the semen is ultimately stored in a reservoir in the head, whose capacity is twenty *tolas* (6–8 ounces). Semen of good quality is rich and viscous, like the cream of unadulterated milk. A man who possess a store of such good semen becomes a "superman."

Further, while false from the perspective of modern scientific knowledge, this is not exactly a supernatural idea or one associated with ritual practices involving the capture of the spiritual essence of other persons.

Conversely, if we approach the problem from the opposite direction of head-hunting we seem to lack direct evidence that practitioners necessarily think of the head in terms of the *muelos* notion. Southeast Asia and especially Borneo is the locus classicus of head-hunting as far as the more recent ethnographic and historical literature is concerned. Yet scholars disagree about the cultural motives underlying the practice or maintain that it is now difficult to find what the motives were at the time when head-hunting was in full practice. It is the specific religious or ritual motives that are disputed or unclear. For example, in an Iban myth explaining the origin of head-hunting, Lang, the god of war, took a head and split it open. It was filled with rice seed (Freeman 1979: 236). Head-hunting among the Iban and other groups does seem to be clearly linked to notions of fertility, a *muelos*-like idea as La Barre notes. At the same time, the Iban term for trophy heads is *antu pala*, for which the literal translation is ghost (or spirit) head. The trophy head among the Iban, and also among the Bidayuh of northwestern Borneo, is conceived of and treated as a ghost or spirit of the person or the repository of the spirit. In the rituals of head-hunting, heads were treated as captured persons who were welcomed into the longhouse. Skulls kept in houses are still occasionally offered food, drink, and betel nut.[5]

The Eye

No discussion of the importance of the head as a natural symbol, as standing for the person, or as containing the soul or spiritual power or energy of a person would be complete without also making reference to the eye. The eyes of the heads taken and kept as trophies and ritual objects of mystical power sooner or later disappear. But the dark sockets that remain and seem to stare are probably the most striking features of the skull.

The eyes have great importance as a symbol of beauty, character, personality, and behavior. The eye frequently serves as a sign of mystical or magical power, as when Chinese fishermen paint eyes on boats or Southeast Asian headhunters embellish or restore trophy skulls with cowry shell inserts for eyes (the wide appeal of cowry shells as objects of value and decoration rests in part on their opening slit on the bottom both to the eye and to the vulva). People in many places depict monsters, spirits, demons, or other supernatural creatures by distorting natural eye forms in one way or another, but especially by enlarging them (also fundamental to the appeal of Mickey Mouse, Donald Duck, and other modern cartoon characters). And it is not a large step from viewing the eye as a means for seeing and knowing in both ordinary and extraordinary ways to regarding it as having the power to affect others, which it can and does do in various important real ways. Staring, gazing, and eye contact are all fundamental forms of human signaling behavior that, while undoubtedly subject to cultural elaboration and variation, are of universal significance. Staring or gazing at (or "eyeing") another person can mean attachment, attraction, dominance, or aggression (or varying combinations of these), and eye contact is a potent form of signaling behavior and communication, not only among humans but primates and some other mammals as well. Staring at an object also tends to mean the display of one or another of a few strong emotions including attraction, desire, or dread. Evolutionary anthropologists point out that all of this is due in part to the development of a large, visible white area of the eye that makes eye movement, gaze direction, and therefore signaling more obvious and potent than it is even in other higher primates among which such a white area is lacking (Tomasello 2007).

In the realm of religion perhaps the most cross-culturally common manifestation of eye symbolism is the belief in the evil eye—the notion that certain individuals have the ability to harm others simply by casting their gaze on them. According to this belief, while such persons may cause deliberate harm, in some instances the damage may occur without intent. Children are thought to be especially vulnerable. In some places evil eye notions are part of the larger complex of witchcraft beliefs (Dundes 1981).

Anthropologists and folklorists have found evil-eye beliefs to be frequent among villagers in eastern and southern Europe and in India, among other places. Such notions have also been reported to be common among Semitic populations—Jews and Arabs of Europe, North Africa, and the Middle East. In addition, immigrants from Old World communities brought evil eye notions to the New World, including the United States and Canada, where they are today mainly regarded by others who know about them—the children and grandchildren of such immigrants—as amusing Old World folk superstitions. For those who actively hold such beliefs, however, they are a serious matter to be prevented or countered with appropriate ritual procedures. (One such common action is to spit quickly when exposed to the look of someone who has or might have the power of the evil eye.) The suggestion that evil eye beliefs and behavior reflect a tendency to be fearful or signs of jealousy or envy on the part of others is compatible with other dimensions of what is well-known about eye symbolism. The belief that witches can cause harm through their gaze or have red or staring eyes is common (Mair 1969: 43).

NATURAL SYMBOLS AND NATURAL RELIGION

As we have seen in this chapter, there appear to be natural or widely recurring symbols, although, as with the head, they cannot be well explained in all respects. Do such symbols then combine to form natural or recurrent religions? Here Douglas's point about the unlikelihood of finding widespread cross-cultural commonalities seems to be valid. Some efforts have been made to develop evolutionary typologies or schemes of religion which, by definition, involve putting the religious beliefs, practices, and organizations of separate societies into a set of classes, although this is not to say that they are assumed to be identical in their features. Several decades ago the prominent sociologist of religion Robert Bellah (1965) developed such an evolutionary scheme consisting of several types of religion that were also supposed to be stages of development. It attracted interest for a while in anthropology but eventually lost influence. It might be reasonable to think that beneath all of their diversity the religions of humankind are all the same because the fundamental needs, desires, and problems of humans are basically the same. For example, all the world religions seem to have one feature in common that sets them apart from other kinds of religions—formal systems of morality based on either the proposition that gods or divinities care about how humans treat one another and will reward or punish them accordingly, or that there exists an impersonal and cosmic law of karma according to which humans will also be rewarded or punished for their conduct, including their behavior toward one another. But in other respects, different fundamental features mark the world religions. The most basic of these features concern time and human fate. In the Eastern religions cosmic time is circular and endlessly repetitive while in the Western ones it is linear and finite as far as human life on earth is concerned. Even the Eastern and Western versions of religion and morality work differently. Beyond the matter of divine judgment versus karma, the Eastern religions include the treatment of animals in the scope of morality in a way that the Western religions do not.

There is an even greater problem with evolutionary schemes at the opposite end—that of earliest forms of religion. The problem is that we know very little about such religion, at least as total systems of religious belief and practice. In chapter 4 we considered some of the things that are known, inferred, or guessed about early religion. But this does not add up to much in terms of the total religions of a society of the sort that an ethnographer studying a living society could find. Along with grave goods and other artifacts, the spectacular cave art of southwestern Upper Paleolithic Europe seems to provide vivid clues about early religion but there seems to be little agreement about what such paintings reveal beyond brilliant skill, a serious, presumably sacred purpose, and a preoccupation with animals and various stylistic themes. And then there is the rest of the world that was occupied by humans during the Upper Paleolithic, which is to say much of the Old World of Europe, Asia, and Africa, as well as Australia and Melanesia. Evidence of early religion in these regions outside of southwestern Europe is considerably more meager. As already noted, evolutionary schemes based on ethnography, travel, and other recent accounts of living peoples propose radically different opinions about whether the earliest religious beliefs were animism (or preanimism) or monotheism.

But while it does not seem possible to identify whole natural or systems of religious belief and practice, it does seem possible to go beyond various symbols to what might be called recurrent complexes. This is the focus of the next several chapters, beginning with myth and ritual.

NOTES

1. In English, unlike in many other languages, there are two words for the same creature; that is, "serpent" as well as "snake." Mundkur (1983: 2) notes early in his

book that, while the difference may be dim in popular usage, the two terms have different connotations. The term "snake" is the native term and the more commonly used. The word "serpent" by contrast is considered alien and is sometimes reserved for poisonous or larger species. "A snake is merely the zoological entity, but 'serpent,' as we shall see opens up vast metaphorical possibilities."

2. The original article was subsequently combined with another seminal one by Hertz on death rituals (first published in 1907) and published in English in 1960 as a volume entitled *Death and the Right Hand*.

3. *Right and Left: Essays on Symbolic Classification*, edited by Rodney Needham.

4. Such a possibility seems more plausible if scalping was already practiced among some groups as an alternative to head taking. This is the argument that La Barre makes. The hair and scalp were associated with much the same beliefs and practices as the head itself, and scalping and head-hunting were both found in some regions including ancient Europe. The shrunken heads of the Jívaro and other groups are actually scalps, La Barre points out, because the skull itself was discarded. In Borneo, Dayak groups practiced head-hunting rather than scalping, and some preserved skulls with the skin and hair intact by smoking while others kept only the skull. However, human hair from heads that had been taken was widely used to decorate war shields and swords.

5. In some places skulls are still given offerings and credited with consciousness and emotion. When several years ago (in 1998) I went to see several skulls that had been incised with elaborate designs in a Bidayuh village in western Sarawak, an old man who looked after them went into the enclosure where they were kept before me; I heard him talking to the skulls and afterward asked him what he had said. He replied that he had told the skulls not to be alarmed, that nothing bad was going to happen. Among the Bidayuh, stories are told of skulls that make noises or throw themselves down and roll around to warn of the approach of robbers and enemies. Skulls are also believed to mysteriously disappear from one location and appear in another. In other words, in some instances, skulls are more than simply repositories of soul stuff; they embody actual souls or spirits and are treated accordingly.

REFERENCES AND FURTHER READING

Bellah, Robert. 1965. "Religious Evolution." In *Reader in Comparative Religion*, edited by William A. Lessa and Evon Z. Vogt, pp. 73–87. New York: Harper & Row.

Berlin, Brent, and Paul Kay. 1969. *Basic Color Terms: Their Universality and Evolution*. Berkeley: University of California Press.

Boyer, Pascal. 1994. *The Naturalness of Religious Ideas: A Cognitive Theory of Religion*. Berkeley: University of California Press.

Carstairs, G. Morris. [1957] 1967. *The Twice Born: A Study of High-Caste Hindus*. Bloomington: Indiana University Press.

Douglas, Mary. [1966] 1984. *Purity and Danger: An Analysis of the Concepts of Pollution and Taboo*. London: ARK Paperbacks.

———. 1973. *Natural Symbols: Exploration in Cosmology*. New York: Vintage.

Dundes, Alan. 1981. "Wet and Dry, the Evil Eye." In *The Evil Eye: A Casebook*, edited by Alan Dundes, pp. 257–312. New York: Garland.

Freeman, Derek. 1979. "Severed Heads That Germinate." In *Fantasy and Symbol: Studies in Anthropological Interpretation*, edited by R. H. Hook and George Devereux, pp. 233–46. London: Academic.

Hertz, Robert. [1907] 1960. *Death and the Right Hand*. Glencoe, Ill.: Free Press.

———. [1909] 1973. "The Pre-eminence of the Right Hand: A Study in Religious Polarity." In *Right and Left: Essays on Dualistic Classification*, edited Rodney Needham, pp. 1–31. Chicago: University of Chicago Press.

Hook, R. H., and George Devereux, eds. 1979. *Fantasy and Symbol: Studies in Anthropological Interpretation*. London: Academic.

La Barre, Weston. 1985. *Muelos: A Stone Age Superstition about Sexuality*. New York: Columbia University Press.

Leach, Edmund R. 1958. "Magical Hair." *Journal of the Royal Anthropological Institute* 88: 147–64.

Lévi-Strauss, Claude. 1962. *Totemism*. Boston: Beacon.

Mair, Lucy. 1969. *Witchcraft*. New York: McGraw-Hill.

Malinowski, Bronislaw. [1925] 1948. *Magic, Science, and Religion and Other Essays*. Garden City, N.Y.: Doubleday Anchor.

McManus, I. C. 2002. *Right Hand, Left Hand: The Origins of Asymmetry in Brains, Bodies, Atoms, and Cultures*. Cambridge: Harvard University Press.

Mundkur, Balaji. 1983. *The Cult of the Serpent: An Interdisciplinary Survey of Its Manifestations and Origins*. Albany: State University or New York Press.

Needham, Rodney, ed. 1973. *Right and Left: Essays on Symbolic Classification*. Chicago: University of Chicago Press.

———. 1979. "Percussion and Transition." In *Reader in Comparative Religion*, edited by William A. Lessa and Evon Z. Vogt, pp. 311–17. 4th ed. New York: Harper & Row.

Obeyesekere, Gananath. 1981. *Medusa's Hair: An Essay on Personal Symbols and Religious Experience*. Chicago: University of Chicago Press.

Onians, Richard B. 1951. *The Origins of European Thought*. Cambridge: Cambridge University Press.

Springer, Sally P., and Georg Deutsch. 1998. *Left Brain, Right Brain: Perspectives on Cognitive Neuroscience*. New York: Freeman.

Tomasello, Michael. 2007. "For Human Eyes Only." *New York Times*, January 12.

Turner, Victor W. 1966. "Color Classification in Ndembu Ritual: A Problem in Primitive Classification." In *Anthropological Approaches to the Study of Religion*, edited by Michael Banton, pp. 47–84. London: Tavistock.

6

⚜

Myth and Ritual,
Old and New

In the last chapter we asked if there are natural or recurring symbols in religion and considered various beliefs, images, and practices that had been discussed in these terms by anthropologists and others. In this chapter we shall be asking similar questions about myth. Here attention has been focused on two central protagonists in myth—the hero and the trickster. But it will be necessary to begin by discussing other matters, including what myths are in the first place, and then how they have been studied and interpreted over time. In this regard, a central question since the nineteenth century has been whether it is possible to understand myths apart from their context, especially their relationship to ritual. We shall conclude by looking at some present-day urban myths and then rumor myths, also in comparative terms.

The term "myth" comes from the Greek *mythos* and originally meant the stories of the ancient gods and heroes of Greece and Rome, to which were soon added those of India, Europe, and elsewhere. While the term is still used in this way, it has acquired other meanings as well. Most importantly, at least since the middle of the nineteenth century myth has had the common meaning of a false story or particular belief that is widely accepted but wrong. Myth in this ordinary sense has nothing to do with religion in particular. While all or most myth in the classic sense falls within the domain of religion, myth used in the more common way does so only in so far as it has a supernatural dimension.

In scholarly and literary terms, mythology is a large and complex topic. It has been the concern of historians, psychologists, folklorists, and scholars of language, literature, drama, and comparative religion, among others.

The study of myth therefore goes far beyond anthropology, although since the late nineteenth century anthropologists have had a prominent role in its study. This role has involved both the collection and analysis of information on the mythology of peoples around the world—the ethnography of myth—and the explanation of the nature and uses of myth in comparative and theoretical terms—the ethnology of myth.

WHAT MORE EXACTLY IS MYTH?

Anthropologists and most other scholars would probably agree that myth in the classic sense has a number of characteristics. To elaborate on several recent efforts to specify these (Bowie 2006: 268–69; Segal 2004: 4–6) here is a brief list:

1. It is a story rather than a statement of belief or doctrine.
2. It includes personalities that may be human, animal, or supernatural, or a combination of these, who do things or to whom things happen.
3. It is a story that is not just known but believed and is regarded as important or sacred.
4. It has no known author or authors; myth is different in this way from religious revelation or prophecy, to which it may otherwise be similar.
5. It involves events or activities that are in some way extraordinary, "larger than life," if not necessarily supernatural.

Beyond such characteristics there is likely to be less agreement. Depending in part on their academic discipline, scholars tend to take either a broad or a narrow approach to myth. Among scholars who seek to deal with myth in general comparative terms, folklorists have tended to advocate the most exact definition. According to this view, myth is a form of folk narrative, and more specifically part of a larger category of stories or tales that are transmitted orally (or at least originally were; some myths were written down thousands of years ago and are only known in their written versions). For folklorists, myth is defined in contrast to legends, on the one hand, and to folktales, on the other, although further distinctions may also be made. In the strictest folkloric interpretation, myths are sacred accounts about how the world and humans were created in their present forms. According to this view also, the phrase "creation myth," which is in wide use, is redundant. In the case of the classic myths of ancient Greece and Rome, for example, those that simply involve the doings of the gods but don't really concern the creation of anything would not, strictly speaking, qualify as myth. Indeed, the folklorist Alan Dundes (1996: 148–49), who advocates a very narrow or "strict constructionist" definition of myth as sacred creation stories, specifically asserts that the tale of Oedipus—the best known of all of the tales of Greek mythology—is not a myth! Because nothing gets created, it is rather a legend. Or, if we apply such an exact definition of myth to the Judeo-Christian Bible, for example, only some sections would seem to fit closely. The accounts of Genesis, including the creation of the world and its inhabitants and the expulsion of the first humans from the Garden of Eden, are certainly myth in the strictest sense. The story of Moses would also certainly be included in that Moses not only lived a life involving extraordinary achievements and miracles but also delivered the Ten Commandments that Jews and Christians appear to regard as the main basis of their law and morality. Much else in the Bible, including the entire New Testament, would seem to belong to another category—legend—as would also accounts of miracles and saints.

Legends are also accounts that are regarded as true but differ from myths in that they concern events or persons set in the more recent past. They may or may not be religious or sacred in nature and, even if they are, they may or may not be important or include outright miracles. The concept of legend suffers from the same tendency to be popularly regarded as a story that has been made up or at least embellished, as when the incident of chopping down the cherry tree and admitting it was added into the story of George Washington. Those who believe in important legends would generally prefer they be regarded as history—something that it is assumed really happened.

Folktales in turn differ from both myth and legend. They are said to be "timeless" rather than set at the beginning of time or more recently. Sometimes the time is "once, long ago" or "once upon a time," or simply "once," and so on. Folktales are told to amuse, although they may also be intended to instruct or to subtly criticize or to mock pretension and hypocrisy (as in The Emperor's New Clothes). They are not supposed to be believed as literally true and are told in a way that often includes a beginning formula that is intended to signal that what is to be said is not to be taken as an account of something that has actually happened. In some genres, however, the intent may be to fool the listener or to create uncertainty about whether what has been told is truth or fiction. Compared to myths or religious legends, folktales are not regarded as important, except perhaps for their value as folk culture by modern nationalists.

In contrast to folklorists, anthropologists generally adhere to a broad view of myth; they tend to think that it is not possible to make clear, cross-culturally valid distinctions among myths, legends, and folktales—or that it is not necessarily useful to try to do so. For one thing, there is the issue of ethnocentrism or Euro-centrism. The threefold scheme of myth, legend, and folktale grew out of the study of European traditions (Dundes credits the brothers Grimm with originating it two hundred years ago). The question is therefore how well it holds up beyond European or Western society.[1] Finally, anthropologists show some inclination to go beyond the sort of narratives defined in terms of the five characteristics noted above to include urban legends and what may be called "rumor myths," some examples of which will be discussed at the end of this chapter.

THEORIES, APPROACHES, AND EXPLANATIONS OF MYTH

The comparative study of mythology developed rapidly in the nineteenth century as ethnological information on the beliefs of indigenous peoples across the world continued to accumulate, and as linguists went beyond the Greek and Roman Classics to the study of Sanskrit (the ancestral Indo-European language of India) and other ancient languages and literatures. As anthropology and folklore developed, the mythology of nonliterate, indigenous peoples was added to that existing in written traditions, with consequences that continue to resonate. By the end of the nineteenth century, an important division developed about myth that continues until today: whether myths can be usefully studied, analyzed, and compared on their own or whether they can only be understood in relation to their cultural and social and historical context, above all in relation to ritual. Those who adhere to the first position continue to do what scholars of myth have done since the ancient Greeks and can therefore be referred to simply as mythologists. They include in their ranks Otto Rank and Carl Jung. This is the approach to myth that is familiar to the public through the works of popular writers, above all Joseph Campbell. Those who adhere to the second position are the myth-ritualists who descend from Robertson Smith.

By the latter part of the nineteenth century the most important version of the mythological position was that of the nature-myth school, also commonly known as the solar myth school—the latter in reference to its best-known English language version. The nature-myth approach was basically German and focused especially on Indo-European religions. The general thesis was that the gods and heroes of the ancient myths were, in actuality, personified versions of natural phenomena, including the sun and moon, followed by the stars, great rivers, the dawn, the spring, and other awesome things. The approach was brought to England and developed there by Max Müller, who was a scholar of Sanskrit. Müller was a proponent of the solar myth version of the school and interested especially in the gods of ancient India and of the Classical world of Greece and Rome, although he supposed that his interpretation was valid for the myths of all peoples. The main idea was that myths were composed in a sort of code that had to be deciphered in order to learn the underlying meaning, which would usually turn out to have something to do with the sun. Eventually Andrew Lang and other critics showed that such interpretations were far-fetched or absurd. For one thing, there is the question of why, if the sun were openly deified in many places in the world, it was necessary to refer to it in terms of metaphor and allegory. As the folklorist Richard Dorson (1965) put it, the solar myth school eventually went into an eclipse from which it never emerged.

William Robertson Smith and Myth-Ritualism

By the end of the nineteenth century the mythological approach came under attack by William Robertson Smith, a biblical scholar and professor of Arabic at Cambridge University. Smith launched what became myth-ritualism not as a grand theory but as a modest, mainly negative assertion about a basic contrast between ancient religions and modern or present-day Christianity. While mythologists in the late nineteenth century debated the correct way to interpret the meaning of myths and their symbols, Smith raised the more fundamental issue of whether myth mattered much in the first place. He did so in a series of lectures on the religion of the ancient Semites (first published in 1889 as *Lectures on the Religion of the Semites*), an assault on prevailing idealistic and intellectualist interpretations of religion at a time that Müller's influence was at a peak. Because of the enduring importance of his views, his general statement is worth quoting at length:

> Thus the study of religion has meant mainly the study of Christian beliefs, and instruction in religion has habitually begun with the creed, religious duties being presented to the learner as flowing from the dogmatic truths he is taught to accept. All this seems so much a matter of course that, when we approach some strange or antique religion, we naturally assume that here also our first business is to search for a creed, and find in it a key to ritual and practice. But the antique religions had for the most part no creed; they consisted entirely of institutions and practices. No doubt men will not habitually follow certain practices without attaching a meaning to them; but as a rule we find that while the practice was rigorously fixed, the meaning attached to it was extremely vague, and the same rite was explained by different people in different ways, without any question of orthodoxy or heterodoxy arising in consequence.
>
> In all the antique religions, mythology takes the place of dogma; that is the sacred lore of priests and people, so far as it does not consist of mere rules for the performance of religious acts, assumes the form of stories about the gods; and these stories afford the only explanation that is offered about the precepts of religion and the prescribed rules of ritual. *But strictly speaking, this mythology was no essential part of ancient religion, for it had no sacred sanction and*

no binding force on the worshippers [emphasis added]. The myths connected with individual sanctuaries and ceremonies were merely part of the apparatus of the worship; they served to excite the fancy and sustain the interest of the worshipper; but he was often offered a choice of several accounts of the same thing, and, provided that he fulfilled the ritual with accuracy, no one cared what he believed about its origin.

This being so, it follows that mythology ought not take the prominent place that is too often assigned to it in the scientific study of the ancient faiths. So far as myths consist of explanations of ritual, their value is altogether secondary, and it may be affirmed with confidence that in almost every case the myth was derived from the ritual and not the ritual from the myth; for the ritual was fixed and the myth was variable; the ritual was obligatory and faith in the myth was at the discretion of the worshipper. (Smith 1901: 16–17)

Following these and other statements about the secondary and derivative nature of myth, Smith went on to acknowledge that myth became more important in the later stages of the ancient religions. This was not a natural or general evolutionary development but rather a consequence of the special struggle of the ancient religions with skepticism, on the one hand, and Christianity, on the other. Competition forced the adherents of the ancient religions to search for ideas of a more modern cast, and this included developing allegorical interpretations of their myths. But such allegorical approaches (which continue to be popular) are "the falsest of the false guides to the old religions" (1901: 19).

The effect of such criticism on the mythologists is debatable, but James Frazer among others took the idea up and developed it in the *Golden Bough*. Here the crucial idea was that the most important rituals of the ancient world concerned the fertility of crops, the passage of the seasons, and the renewal of life in general. The most important mythical figure was that of the divine king whose life, death, and resurrection were necessary to these processes. The early part of the twentieth century was the heyday of efforts to find such rituals of fertility linked to myths of divine kings who had to die and be reborn in the ancient world of Egypt, Mesopotamia, Greece, and Rome. Such efforts were associated especially with Cambridge University.

Today, the term "myth-ritualism" is used broadly to include any interpretation that posits a close relationship between myth and ritual, without necessarily assuming that ritual comes first or is of greater importance (Segal 2004: 61). At least as a general principle, it is difficult to demonstrate that myth always comes from ritual and has no importance apart from it. That is, our knowledge of modern belief and practice suggests that the connection between myth and ritual is easier to demonstrate from the perspective of ritual than it is from myth. For example, the rituals of

Christmas celebrate the story of the miraculous birth of Christ and those of Easter his crucifixion, death, resurrection, and ascension. All Americans probably know that the ritual of Thanksgiving is based on the myth (or legend if you like) that the Pilgrims who survived until their first harvest had a feast with the Indians who had helped them in celebration of their deliverance. Jews and Muslims are similarly familiar with the sacred narratives on which their major rituals are based.

But viewed from the perspective of myth, the connection between myth and ritual seems more difficult to establish. Not all myths appear to have attached rituals, at least ones that are known to many people. One possible explanation of myths without rituals is that they have continued to exist because of writing. The myths once associated with rituals survived after the rituals disappeared because the myths were written down; otherwise they would be gone as well. This could be true of the mythology of the Old Testament as well as that of ancient Greece and Rome and of anywhere else that writing has been in existence since there were rituals to go along with the myths. The old rituals in these instances were already dead, or at least they had been turned into something else. What then of myth and ritual in traditionally nonliterate societies? Here was an opportunity for fieldwork-oriented anthropologists studying living religions to make a contribution to the debate.

Malinowski seized this opportunity as a part of his larger analysis of religion, magic, and science in the Trobriand Islands in Melanesia. Malinowski wrote about myth and ritual in various places throughout his corpus of Trobriand ethnography and theoretical papers, but addressed the issues most fully in an essay titled "Myth in Primitive Psychology" (originally a lecture given in honor of James Frazer, then published as a book in 1926, and later in *Magic, Science, and Religion and Other Essays*). Malinowski's (1948: 96–148) position on myth differed from Robertson Smith's in one important way. As we have seen, Smith sought to downplay both the significance and the independence of myth and belief in the ancient religions. In contrast, Malinowski went to great lengths to stress the importance of myth in relation to Trobriand religion, magic, and culture generally. Otherwise, he was very much a myth-ritualist in making clear that Trobriand myth made little sense except in relation to ongoing Trobriand practices of religion and magic. He believed that the purpose of myth was not so much to explain things as to serve as a charter, specifically a charter for the present. Trobriand myths were continuously changing or readapted in relation to ongoing ritual practices and political and social dynamics.

In the United States, Clyde Kluckhohn somewhat later (1942) published a general review of the myth-ritual controversy as it involved indigenous, preliterate societies. Kluckhohn's discussion was broadly oriented but had special reference to the Navaho and other Native American societies of the American Southwest. His position can be summarized by saying that he too found support for a moderate version of the myth-ritual argument. On the one hand, there were groups such the African Bushmen who had many myths but few rituals. On the other, there were those peoples, such as the Eskimo, in which all myth seemed to be associated with rituals of one sort or another. Kluckhohn also found mixed cases in which some myths were acted out in ritual while others were not. In the case of the Navaho and other Southwestern peoples, all ritual was supported by myth and there was a strong tendency for the two to coalesce into a single complex of belief and practice. However, much traditional secular behavior (such as the different ways that men and women are supposed to sit) was also supported by myth. Myth provides an explanation for ritual, but while some rituals are supported by single myths others are justified by a variety of myths. In general, Kluckhohn found myth and ritual to be interdependent rather than a matter of one determining the other. Further, myth and ritual were sometimes borrowed from other groups. And at least some myth among the Southwestern groups and other Native Americans is known to have originated independently of ritual in dreams or visions.

Lévi-Strauss and the Structural Study of Myth

For the first half of the twentieth century anthropologists and mythologists mainly went their separate ways, the anthropologists adhering to some version of myth-ritualism and functionalism and the mythologists proceeding on the assumption that myths could be studied as literature, narrative, or historical text, that is, on their own terms as meaningful, recurring stories. Then Claude Lévi-Strauss changed all of that. With his impeccable anthropological credentials and a commitment to an anthropological approach to myth, Lévi-Strauss proceeded to analyze and explain myth as a thing in itself, as a fundamental and irreducible pattern of human thought, culture, and language. For several decades in the second half of the twentieth century he completely dominated anthropological interpretations of mythology. The long-standing anthropological commitment to studying myth in relation to ritual in particular and to its social and cultural context in particular was largely forgotten. Lévi-Strauss's principal innovation in the analysis and explanation of myth is referred to as structuralism. His inspiration derived from linguistics, specifically from the so-called Prague school and the work of Roman Jacobson in particular. The point of his analysis was to reveal the structure of myth (and everything else in culture).

A French anthropologist and an intellectual heir of Marcel Mauss and Emile Durkheim, Lévi-Strauss began his career with fieldwork among the Indians of the Amazon and then expanded his interest to include North American Indians, especially those of the Northwest Coast. He began by writing an important comparative study of marriage and kinship around the world that established his reputation as a first-rate and original thinker who had mastered one of the most complex and esoteric subjects dealt with by anthropologists. This book was followed by others on the nature of elementary human thought (translated from the French as *The Savage Mind*) and totemism (*Totemism*), the latter an attack on a concept and venerable topic that largely destroyed both. He also early on published a more personal philosophical account of his fieldwork and experiences in the Brazilian Amazon (published in English both under the title of *A World on the Wane* and *Tristes Tropiques*) that was read far beyond anthropology and established his reputation as a leading Western intellectual and literary master. Two volumes of his essays were translated and published under the title *Structuralism*.

Following these diverse, wide-ranging works he turned to detailed comparative studies of mythology and related topics. Focusing on the mythology of the Indian peoples of the Amazon and South America, these studies took the form of a four-volume collection (published in English as *Introduction to a Science of Mythology*). These volumes contain his fullest exposition of his comparative approach. However, the simplest and clearest statements of his theory and method are to be found in his earlier writings, as the myth that seems to remain the favorite among the great many he has analyzed, "The Story of Asdiwal" (Lévi-Strauss 1967).

Originally collected in four versions by Franz Boas between 1896 and 1916, the myth is Tshimshian, one of the northern Native American peoples of the Northwest Coast of North America. In his account of the myth, Lévi-Strauss tells us nothing about the ritual context of the myth, or even if it was told in association with a ritual or simply as a story recounted for amusement. He begins by summarizing the basic ethnography of the Tshimshian because this is important to his analysis. The Tshimshian lived along the lower Skeena River and the seacoast. Their economy centered on fishing and collecting. They moved seasonally between their winter villages on the coast and their summer fishing villages along the river. In social organization, they were organized into four matrilineal clans and three hereditary social strata.

The story, in brief, is as follows: Asdiwal, the protagonist of the myth, is a miraculous child, the son of a mortal woman and a supernatural omen bird who at birth gives him various magical objects, including a bow and snowshoes. When he grows up, he follows a white bear into the sky. The

bear turns out to be Evening Star, the daughter of the Sun, who allows Asdiwal to marry her after he performs a series of impossible tasks with his
magical equipment. They return to earth where they live until Asdiwal is
unfaithful, at which point his wife leaves him and returns to the sky. Asdiwal follows and she kills him with a thunderbolt, but his father-in-law
the Sun brings him back to life and they live together in the sky for a time.
Then Asdiwal returns to earth and marries a Tshimshian woman. With his
wife and her brothers he moves north to the Nass River. He challenges his
brothers-in-law to a hunting contest and wins because of his magic bow.
His brothers-in-law are angered and take his wife and abandon Asdiwal,
who eventually marries another woman with four brothers and has a son.
He again challenges his brothers-in-law to a hunting contest, this time involving sea lions, again wins and makes them angry. They leave him without food or fire on a barren reef but his bird-father saves him and a mouse
takes him to the underground home of the sea lions. Here he heals the sea
lions he has shot and asks them in return to get him home, which they do.
There his wife helps him kill her brothers, but eventually Asdiwal becomes homesick and returns one last time to the Skeena valley. When winter comes he goes hunting in the mountains but, having forgotten his
magic snowshoes, he becomes immobile and turns into stone.

Lévi-Strauss analyzes the myth by showing that it is structured by four
sets of codes, one geographical, another economic, another social, and the
last cosmological. The events of the myth each concern one or another of
the codes, or sometimes all at once. Marriage involves geographical
movement, economy (fishing), and movement between earth and sky, as
well as family and kinship. Lévi-Strauss argues that the myth depicts con-
tradictions in Tshimshian society, which it then seeks to resolve in various
ways. Ultimately, then, myth reflects the structure of human thought.

THE PROTAGONISTS OF MYTH

For many scholars as well as ordinary readers, mythology comes alive
when attention is focused on the central characters or protagonists, not on
abstract arguments about the primacy of belief or ritual in religion or on
the underlying structural characteristics of mythical thought. As already
noted, myths can concern many kinds of beings, including ordinary humans, animals, spirits, and gods, as well as various combinations of these.
Scholars have focused particular attention, however, on two types of characters that recur across cultural boundaries: the hero and the trickster. The
first became well-known from classic and European mythology, the second mainly from studies of Native American, African, and other non-
Western myth and folklore.

The Hero

The term "hero" has two meanings, a popular, everyday one (a person of extraordinary achievements requiring courage who saves the day) and a more specialized one applied especially to a mythical protagonist. British anthropologist and folklorist Lord Raglan (Fitzroy Richard Somerset Raglan) has analyzed the mythical hero as a cross-cultural type. Raglan's general view of myth places him in the myth-ritual school of interpretation. In fact, Raglan holds to a very strong version of myth-ritualism: all myths, including those of hero figures, arise from rituals rather than from efforts to explain the world or from psychological needs. There is a problem here in that myths seem to exist by themselves and have been frequently treated as if they do. In Raglan's case, this also seems to be so; in spite of the importance he attributes to ritual as the basis of myth, it is myth that he mainly talks about. The problem is that, especially where classical antiquity or ancient Europe is concerned, a lot more is known about the myths than about the rituals they presumably went with. Raglan advances the explanation that over time, at least in societies that develop writing, myths are written down and thereby take on a life of their own. They become folklore and then history, or in some instances literature and drama, and such changes obscure their original role in ritual.

In the case of mythical heroes, Raglan argues further that the common euhemerist supposition that mythical heroes may be based on real-life persons is wrong.[2] Although the latter certainly exist as well, they are quite different than the heroes of myth. At an early point in his book *The Hero* he discusses in some detail several well-known instances from England in which mythical heroes have been mistakenly explained as having some basis in the lives of real men. His examples include Robin Hood and Arthur.

Robin Hood is especially interesting because of what he later became in folklore and literature, not to mention Hollywood. Raglan notes that the general tendency among scholars as well as the general public in England has been to suppose that Robin Hood is based on a once real (or historical) person whose character and doings were embellished over time as his story was passed down through the generations—a legend. He was accordingly changed from a real or once living hero into a legendary one. Raglan argues that there is no evidence in favor of this possibility and a good deal against it. The alleged incidents of Robin Hood's career are analogous to those of many other heroes of tradition, especially William Tell, who is generally acknowledged to be wholly mythical (Raglan 1975: 53). There is abundant evidence, Raglan argues, in many parts of England and Scotland that Robin Hood is the name given to the principal character in the May Day dramatic performances and revels, that is, in a ritual context. Therefore, Raglan argues, Robin Hood was originally worshiped as a god in association with a fertility festival that later became May Day. He returns to Robin Hood later in his analysis of the general features of the hero.

Raglan became interested in the comparative characteristics of mythical heroes as a result of studying the myth of Oedipus and then finding many analogies in other Greek myths. He then undertook a study in which he began by listing twenty-two characteristics that together form a pattern or set. This set of characteristics is as follows.

(1) The hero's mother is a royal virgin; (2) His father is a king and (3) Often a near-relative of his mother; but (4) The circumstances of his conception are unusual, and (5) He is also reputed to be the son of a god; (6) At birth an attempt is made, usually by his father or his maternal grandfather, to kill him, but (7) He is spirited away, and (8) Reared by foster parents in a far country; (9) We are told nothing of his childhood, but (10) On reaching manhood he returns or goes to his future kingdom; (11) After a victory over the king and/or a giant, dragon or wild beast; (12) He marries a princess, often the daughter of his predecessor, and (13) Becomes king; (14) For a time he reigns uneventfully, and (15) Prescribes laws, but (16) Later he loses favor with the gods and/or his subjects, and (17) Is driven from the city, after which (18) He meets with a mysterious death, (19) Often at the top of a hill; (20) His children, if any, do not succeed him. (21) His body is not buried, but nevertheless (22) He has one or more holy sepulchers.

After listing the twenty-two characteristics of the hero pattern, Raglan analyzes a series of hero myths to see how well each fits the pattern. Each hero myth is summarized briefly and scored. This is done by noting the presence of an element of the pattern and assigning a point in each case, and then adding up the score. No hero myth makes a perfect score of twenty-two points, but one achieves twenty-one. The high-scoring myth is, not surprisingly, that of Oedipus, the most famous of all of the classical Greek myths. His analysis of Oedipus is as follows:

His mother, Jocasta, is (1) a princess, and his father is (2) King Laius, who, like her, is (3) of the line of Cadmus. He has sworn to have no connection with her, but (4) does so when drunk, probably (5) in the character of Dionysos. Laius tries to kill Oedipus at birth but, (7) he is spirited away, and (8) reared by the King of Corinth. (9) We hear nothing of his childhood, but (10) on reaching manhood he returns to Thebes, after gaining victories over his father and the Sphinx. He (12) marries Jocasta, and (13) becomes king. For some years he reigns uneventfully, but (16) later comes to be regarded as the cause of a plague, and (17) is deposed and driven into exile. He meets with (18) a mysterious death at (19) a place near Athens called the Steep Pavement. He is succeeded by (20) Creon, through whom he was deposed, and though (21) the place of his burial is uncertain, he has (22) several holy sepulchers. (Raglan 1975: 175)

Following that of Oedipus (who lacks only the characteristic of having been a lawgiver), twenty-one other hero myths are summarized and scored. Of these, ten more are Greek (those of Theseus, Heracles, Perseus, Jason, Bellerophon, Pelops, Asclepios, Dionysos, Apollo, and Zeus), all of whom earn at least twelve points and most fifteen or more, and one is Roman (Romulus, whose story has eighteen of the twenty-two characteristics of the complete hero). Of the others, three come from the Old Testament, including the highly important lawgiver Moses (who scores an impressive twenty points) as well as Joseph (a modest twelve points) and Elijah (only nine points), and three are from England or Great Britain, including Llew Llawgyffes (Celtic and found to earn seventeen points), Arthur (also Celtic and given nineteen points) and Robin Hood, who is described and scored as follows:

> His father is a Saxon yeoman, but he is also (5) reputed to be the son of a great noble. We hear nothing of his youth, but on reaching manhood he leads a life of debauchery until compelled to fly (10) to Sherwood, where he marries Maid Marian, the Queen of the May, and becomes King of the May and ruler of the forest. For a long time he reigns, and (15) prescribes the laws of archery, but eventually illness overtakes him, and he (17) has to leave the forest and (18) meets a mysterious death in (19) an upper room. He (20) has no children. The place of his death and burial are (21) variously given, but (22) miracles were performed at his tomb at Kirkley, in Yorkshire. We can give him thirteen points. (Raglan 1975: 184)

From the perspective of logic and method, Raglan's study is not beyond criticism. He examines a series of myths, discovers a pattern, and then tests it against the same set of myths in which he has already found it, plus some others in which he also finds it, rather than against a larger set of myths or a sample of myths selected by a different criteria (such as all known Greek myths or all known Greek and Roman myths, or all of the hero prophet stories of the Old Testament). This process involves circular logic or a tautology.

If Raglan's summaries and scoring are accepted, he demonstrates an impressive pattern in ancient Greek myths, and one that seems to have certain parallels elsewhere, including several in the Old Testament as well as Celtic and Saxon ones in Great Britain. Raglan also includes a few other examples, including the Germanic myth of Siegfried, whose mother was a princess and whose father was a king. His two other more distant cases include one from Africa. This is Nyakang, a king of the Shiluk of the Upper Nile, whose mother was a crocodile princess, and whose life and death have some of the other usual heroic characteristics—fourteen points worth according to Raglan. The other one is from Java in insular Southeast Asia.

It seems reasonable to conclude from this analysis that the myths show that the ancient Greeks and some other peoples, including the Jews and various ancient northern European peoples, tended to be fascinated and/or horrified by such things as virgin birth or unusual conception involving royalty and commoners (or animals), fathers slain by sons returning from mysterious adolescence in distant places, and mother-son incestuous marriage leading ultimately to calamity. Sigmund Freud thought that the myth of Oedipus was the key to understanding human psychological development and made it the centerpiece of his theory and therapy of psychoanalysis.

This being so, how do Raglan's twenty-two characteristics of the mythical hero relate to his general proposition that heroes in their original form could not be separated from rituals? His answer is that the incidents of the hero's life fall clearly into three groups: those connected with the hero's birth, those linked to his accession to the throne, and those associated with his death. This suggests that each phase of the hero's life corresponds with the three main rites of passage: those carried out at birth, at initiation, and at death. Such an association, however, seems to be entirely conjecture. Nothing seems to be known of the actual rituals to which, Raglan argues, the various hero myths were linked. While the myths survived because they were written down or turned into folktales, information about the rituals did not survive.

The Trickster

The other important mythological protagonist is the trickster. In *The Trickster: A Study in American Mythology*, American anthropologist Paul Radin is mainly concerned with Native American tricksters. But he does make broader comparisons and includes commentaries by two other scholars that concern tricksters in Greek myth and elsewhere. Radin begins by pointing out that the trickster is a primordial mythical character—one that appears to have persisted with little change over a very long period.

> We encounter [the trickster] among the ancient Greeks, the Chinese, the Japanese and in the Semitic world [to which could be added the Polynesians and the Southeast Asians and doubtless other peoples as well]. Many of the Trickster's traits were perpetuated in figure of the medieval jester, and have survived up to the present in Punch-and-Judy plays and in the clown. (Radin 1956: ix)

What exactly is a trickster? A simple answer would be any sort of mythical or supernatural creature that is believed to play tricks. As found in what Radin takes to be its most archaic form among North American Indians, the reality is more complicated:

> Trickster is at one and the same time creator and destroyer, giver and negator, he who dupes others and who is always duped himself. He wills nothing consciously. At all times he is constrained to behave as he does from impulses over which he has no control. He knows neither good nor evil yet he is responsible for both. He possesses not values, moral or social, is at the mercy of his passions and appetites, yet through his actions all values come into being. (1956: ix)

The literature on tricksters elsewhere in the world presents an even more complicated picture than does Radin's account of the Native American version. As we shall see, their humorous nature notwithstanding, Native American trickster tales are myths in the most exact sense. This is less obviously so in some other instances. For anyone who insists on a clear distinction between myth and folktale or between a trickster and certain other sorts of mythical creatures, the comparative situation presents problems and ambiguities. This may be so because the descriptions that have been provided are not as accurate or full as they could be or because the various kinds of beings described as tricksters differ in important ways.

According to Radin (1956: 155), the Native American trickster is a creator or culture hero. The overwhelming majority of the trickster myth cycles in North America give an account of either the creation of the world or of some dimension of its transformation. Put differently, the trickster is among other things a demiurge (a creator divinity), and trickster tales are etiological myths. Tricksters also accomplish other culture hero types of things such as liberating the sun, capturing daylight, or stealing fire from the other world, all of which benefit humans, though inadvertently.

Tricksters outside of Native American mythology are not necessarily culture heroes. Prometheus, the ancient Greek trickster who stole fire from the gods, is an example of one who was, but others are harder to find. Asian trickster stories, for example, do not appear to contain creation themes. The apparent absence of creation themes from trickster stories would make them seem more like folktales, at least from a strict constructionist folklore perspective, especially since they are assumed to be told for amusement.

In North America, Old Man in the Plains is an anthropomorphic (having human form) trickster. Most other tricksters are theriomorphs or hybrids, which take the form of animals or of human-animal combinations. After trickery, an animal form is probably the most distinctive characteristic of the mythical tricksters. Like divinities, spirits, or other supernatural beings in general, tricksters appear to have at least some human or anthropomorphic characteristics along with their theriomorphic ones, in order to make them seem like plausible agents.

Tricksters always appear to be relatively small animals rather than large, ferocious ones, but beyond this they are difficult to generalize about. In Native American mythology, trickster animals vary according to region and include small to medium-size mammals, birds, and the spider. In the Northwest, tricksters take the form of the Raven, the Mink, and the Blue Jay. In much of the rest of the Far West the Coyote is the main animal, while in the Plains it is the spider. In the Eastern Woodlands tricksters include the hare and the Whisky Jack (a bird). Outside of Native North America the list is similar. Several of the same creatures, including the hare, the spider, and the fox, appear in different places.

Radin downplays the animal side of the trickster among Native Americans, reasoning that the particular characteristics of the various animals that have been selected are not important. As tricksters, all have the same basic behavioral and mental characteristics (greediness and a strong appetite for food and sex, and a combination of cleverness and stupidity) and several of the same physical ones (a very large penis and large intestines, both wrapped around the outside of the body). Some of the characteristics of the various animals are part of the picture (Raven flies and Coyote travels on the ground), but otherwise one kind of animal is interchangeable with another. In the stories tricksters interact frequently with humans as well as with deities and other animals. This further reduces the importance of particular animal characteristics as opposed to the common trickster ones.

Finally, there is the question of the context of Native American trickster myths. This is again the major weakness of Radin's account and of the other literature. Radin is evidently not a myth-ritualist, for he says nothing about the ritual occasions at which trickster myths were (or may have been) told. Nor, beyond providing ethnological information on which animals are tricksters in which areas, does he say much about context at all. One possibility is that the Native American trickster stories are more like folktales (told primarily for amusement), even though they concern origins and transformations and not merely adventures or misadventures. Another possibility is (also again) that the stories survived after the rituals disappeared, or that those who collected the tales did so without much concern for their ritual uses or other context.

Trickster Animals in Japan

As a contrast to the trickster animals of Native North America, let us consider those of Japan. Japanese mythology includes various animals with supernatural powers (Dorson 1962). Of these, the two that most clearly fit the trickster model are the Fox or Kitsune and the Badger (actually the False Badger or Raccoon Dog) or Tanuki. Both are known as "witch animals." Both of the real animals live throughout much of Japan in close association with humans and both are conventional trickster animals in being rather small. However, although there are some further parallels, these trickster animals are also somewhat different from those of either North America or Africa. Unlike the North American trickster animals described by Radin, Kitsune and Tanuki are not interchangeable. The two differ not only as animals but also as types of tricksters, although both play tricks on humans, among other things. And the different roles or aspects of the two tricksters in Japan is bound up with the

Figure 6.1. Statue of Tanuki, one of the two main trickster animals in Japan. Lacking the more sinister traditional characteristics of the fox (though Tanuki is not to be trifled with), he is today regarded as an amusing figure that has been extensively incorporated into modern cartoons and kitsch. Tanuki statues are popular as garden adornments and as welcoming figures for houses and shops.

complexity or layering of Japanese religion, with Buddhism on the one hand and Shinto on the other.

Tanuki is the more conventional trickster. Known at least as far back as the thirteenth century, Tanuki has the usual trickster combination of cleverness and stupidity. He also has the usual overdeveloped trickster appetites, in this case for alcohol as well for food and sex, all of which are shown in his popular image. Small ceramic statues of Tanuki, which are popular household objects, show him standing upright like a human, with as a large, protruding belly and a jug of wine over his shoulder. The large stomach and the wine jug show his fondness for eating and drinking, but the large round belly is also used as a drum. Tanuki beats on his distended belly with his paws, making a booming sound that carries across the mountains at night. He is also highly sexed. This is similar to the Native American trickster, but with the difference that Tanuki is endowed not with a very long penis but a huge pair of testicles that reach the ground when he is standing upright.

One of his tricks involves putting his head between his legs and pressing his mustaches and mouth together so they resemble a woman's genitals, thereby attracting a man to attempt to have sexual intercourse with him. Playing a trick on a man by pretending to be a woman who wants to have sex is also in keeping with a pattern of symbolic inversion. The Japanese are presumably fond of jokes and stories about him because he represents something close to the opposite of proper Japanese character and behavior. Tanuki symbolism and humor also involve Buddhism. People sometimes dress Tanuki like a Buddhist priest, and another of Tanuki's tricks is to dress in robes and go begging like a monk.

Compared to Tanuki, the Fox is a less conventional, more complicated sort of trickster. For one thing, the Fox is simply clever, rather than both clever and stupid. Nor does he have the overdeveloped appetites of Tanuki. In terms of the several religious traditions of Japan, Kitsune is associated with Shintoism rather than Buddhism. Here the Fox is a messenger who reminds villagers of the need to make donations to the rice god. And finally the Fox plays a role not usually characteristic of tricksters, that of a demon animal who can take possession of a human's personality and thereby cause sickness or other harm. As creatures that can take possession, foxes are also thought to be involved in sorcery. They may be owned by individuals or families and used to attack other persons or to gain wealth or power. Possession and sorcery are established by a spirit medium who holds a ceremony in which the Fox-possessed victim is questioned and, if possible, the Fox spirit is persuaded to leave. The Fox that is involved in possession and sorcery is described as having distinctive physical characteristics that distinguish it from ordinary foxes. According to Carman Blacker (1975: 51–52), author of a book on Japanese shamanism, "the creature described does not in the least resemble a fox or a dog, but rather a small weasel or a large shrew."

While associated with possession and sorcery, the Fox is also a conventional trickster who gets even with anyone who causes him harm. This can be found in a story collected and published by the folklorist Richard Dorson (1962: 128–29). Here is a condensed version: On his way to town, a man name Santaro passes several foxes lying in the sun near a persimmon tree. He decides to play a joke on them and sneaks up and then shouts loudly. The foxes jump high in the air and then run away. Santaro is pleased and amused because he has shown that while foxes are supposed to foresee the future this is not really so—they are nothing but animals. He proceeds to town where he tells everyone he meets what he has done, heaping ridicule on the foxes. After buying some fish he starts for home, but soon night falls and he looks around and sees a light in the distance. It is the house of an old woman who agrees to his request for lodging but then leaves, telling him to look after the house. Santaro becomes uneasy as the fire burns down and the woman does not return. Then he notices an object in the corner that begins to glow. He looks more closely and sees that it is the body of a dead man that then begins to stand up. Santaro is stricken with terror and flees but is pursued by the dead man, who has his arms outstretched and is making sounds with his wide-open mouth. Santaro fears that he may be caught and climbs a big tree nearby. The dead man does not see this and keeps going. Santaro spends the night in the tree, relieved but wishing that morning would come. When it becomes light, he sees that he is in a persimmon tree and climbs higher in order to pick some fruit. But the branch breaks and he falls into the river next to the tree. He is chilled but not hurt. Then he becomes aware that he is crawling around the spot where he had frightened the foxes the previous morning. And the fish he bought in town are of course gone.

MYTH AND GENDER

For the past several decades the gender issue has been present in the study of mythology. As the reader will probably have noted by now, the mythical protagonists discussed so far have all been male. All twenty-two of Raglan's myths are about males. Although women also appear in at least some of these stories (and perhaps would in all of them if the full version were given), they are never the main character. The gender of the trickster also seems to be mainly or always male; or to put it differently, if gender is mentioned at all it is male. Of those instances noted above, the Native American trickster, given the emphasis on his genital equipment and its uses, is most emphatically male. The gender of the Japanese Fox trickster in the story recounted above seems irrelevant, but the Badger trickster is crucially and again emphatically male.

Why is there not more sexual balance in mythology? Many Native American groups were matrilineal but none appear to have had female tricksters. The issue of females as heroes (or heroines but this term seems to now be out of favor) has been raised by several scholars. The history of religion scholar Wendy Doniger has done so in a series of books. Mary Douglas, who has not generally made a point of writing about religion from the perspective of women or gender, chooses to deal with Little Red Riding Hood in an essay about myth (discussed below). And in a recently published book (*The Anthropology of Religion*) the British anthropologist Fiona Bowie makes a number of interesting observations about gender in mythology. Taking mythology very broadly to include literature, films, and other nonreligious forms, she writes that

> While heroes can in theory be of either sex and of any age, they are predominantly young males (Luke Skywalker in *Star Wars*, Frodo Baggins in *The Lord of the Rings*). Adult men may also feature as heroes, or share the role with a younger protagonist (as Aragorn shares the hero role with Frodo Baggins). Where the hero is female she is almost always pre-pubescent (*Alice in Wonderland*, Dorothy in *The Wizard of Oz*, or Lucy in C. S. Lewis's *The Lion, the Witch and the Wardrobe*). It is as if the hero role is inimical to mature femininity.
> . . . Where women do embark on a heroic journey they often do so in disguise. They need to find some strategy to deny or detract attention from their sex (as with Joan of Arc, who dressed and lived as a man), or they may stress their harmless female nature so as to divert attention from their actions (as many women mystical writers did, including the twelfth-century Rhineland abbes Hildegard of Bingen. Virginity or celibacy may be stressed (as with Queen Elizabeth I of England, the "Virgin Queen"), rejecting or surmounting accepted female role models. As women are seldom authorized to teach or hold positions of authority, they commonly need to wait until they are post-menopausal, or use the authority of visions or claims to supernatural guidance in order to bestow the boon or share the wisdom that they have won on their journey . . . A woman in myth is more likely to be cast in the role of goddess or temptress, wise woman or witch, than hero of the tale. (Bowie 2006: 289–90)

CONTEMPORARY URBAN MYTH

The traditional folkloric approach to defining myth narrowly has been further modified with the interest that has developed over the past several decades in what are referred to as urban myths or urban legends. "Urban" in this case refers more to "modern" or "contemporary" than to "city." There is no reason to suppose that such stories are any less likely to circulate in towns, suburbs, or villages than in cities. Again, nothing gets created.

The Mouse in the Coke Bottle, a well-known early example of the genre, is a simple story about someone opening a bottle of Coke and drinking part of a dead mouse, becoming ill, and then discovering why by pouring out the remainder of the drink. Other urban legends that have a supernatural edge seem closer to myth, such as the classic tale of the Vanishing Hitchhiker, the title of Jan Brunvand's popular book on urban legends. Someone picks up a hitchhiker who mysteriously vanishes after being let out. In a Malay version of this story, which I first heard in Kelantan, Malaysia, in the 1980s, a man is driving a car (or riding a bicycle or trishaw, or driving a truck or taxi) along a lonely road at night and sees a beautiful woman by the side of the road signaling him to stop. The woman gets in and later, as she gets out (usually near a graveyard), he notices a large hole in her back under her hair. He then realizes that he has picked up a *langsuir*, the horrible ghost of a woman who has died in childbirth. In other versions of such encounters, the driver learns the real identity of the mysterious women when he attempts to have sexual intercourse with her.

Rumor Myths

Although interesting as examples of modern oral traditions, such tales hardly seem important enough or to have other qualities that would allow them to be called myths in the strict sense even if they have strong supernatural content. Some anthropologists, however, have taken a version of such stories to be an important form of contemporary mythmaking. Although there is no agreed-on term for them, such stories might be called rumor myths because they concern not merely isolated, creepy but interesting incidents of the vanishing hitchhiker or mouse in the Coke bottle sort but ongoing and repetitive activities. Rumor myths have several themes. One is that they (at least those that are told in poor or developing country settings) often concern great differences in wealth or power and exploitation, usually of indigenous or local people by Westerners and/or the local rich or corrupt government officials. A second is that the stories involve anxiety about strangers or foreigners, often Westerners. A third is that advanced technology is often concerned in one way or another. A fourth and final theme that is sometimes present involves a reversal of assumption about who is apt to do what to whom.

A recent example involving the second and third themes comes from Iraq. During the early phase of the Iraq war, the news media reported that use of night vision goggles by American troops led to the rumor that they enabled the user to see through clothing and look at the naked bodies of Iraqi women—a story that may seem amusing when circulated in a modern Western society but a more alarming matter in a Muslim society where female modesty is a serious concern.

In her essay on the story of Little Red Riding Hood, Douglas provides another example involving cannibalism myths in modern Africa that involves the first, second, and fourth of the themes noted above:

> In Central Africa to this day there are traditional myths about child-eating ogres, some male, some female. There are also contemporary myths, widely believed, about white men who go around at night in lorries picking up any little black children they can find and taking them off to be butchered and eaten. If anyone questions the validity of the myth, they are given what seems to be compelling circumstantial evidence. Go to any European hotel and see for yourself the vast quantities of meat served there regularly, grilled or stewed or in sausages. How else but by cooking their fellow humans can such an extravagant carnivorous cuisine be maintained? (Douglas 1996: 37)

Another example, (involving the first three themes) is that of organ stealing, provided by the American medical anthropologist Nancy Scheper-Hughs (2002). These are stories about people being kidnapped and having various body parts (kidneys and coronas in particular) removed and sold to those who are rich enough to buy them, especially Westerners. These stories circulate in various places where an export trade in organs exists (a trade that has been generated by modern, Western-based, medical technology of organ transplantation). Although such stories occur in some areas of Europe (Russia, Poland, Italy), they are concentrated in Brazil and in other regions of Latin America, Africa, and Asia. In all of these instances it is mainly the poor who tell and believe the stories, a reflection of their anxiety about such things happening to them.

To those who have written about them, such rumor myths are significant because they exist at the margins between myth and history, between what actually happens and what is imagined or "constructed," between fact and fantasy. If you can create goggles that enable you to see at night or machines that let you see into bodies, then why not also goggles that let you see people's bodies through their clothing? Obviously the claims of some rumor myths are more plausible than of others. The story that Europeans in Africa have an abundant meat supply because African children are the source does not seem likely to be true, except perhaps in a metaphorical sense. On the other hand, the rumors about organ stealing seem more plausible. Scheper-Hughs thinks so and reports firsthand knowledge of a woman in São Palo, Brazil, who had an operation to remove an ovarian cyst and learned later that one of her kidneys had also been unnecessarily taken out (and presumably sold) as well. And the practice of removing and selling the organs of convicted and executed prisoners in China has received wide media attention in recent years as a real occurrence.

Government Head-Hunting and Construction Sacrifice in Borneo

A final example of rumor myth, in this case from Borneo, falls somewhere between the two extremes of plausibility. This one concerns government-sponsored head-hunting, kidnapping, and construction sacrifice and involves all four of the themes. Such stories have been reported throughout Borneo, and to some extent from other islands in the region as well. As rumor myths go, this one is quite old. A version was first reported more than a hundred years ago by the anthropologist Alfred Haddon (1901) during European colonial rule. Other versions have continued into the postcolonial period to the present.

The basic rumor myth goes as follows: Mysterious agents of the government (in northern Borneo generally known as *penyamun*) are abroad looking for human heads or victims for human sacrifice to provide offerings to be made at construction sites, especially ones involving steel and concrete bridges or, more recently, offshore drilling platforms—both involving technology beyond the traditional building practices of the indigenous peoples of the island. The general idea is that the offerings (newly acquired heads or whole victims) are to be placed beneath the foundation of the structure to help ensure that what is built will successfully stand. From the perspective of myth-ritualism we thus have a real myth in the sense that the beliefs are tied to a ritual, or at least a ritual (human sacrifice) which is supposed to take place. The myth takes the form of a rumor that suspicious strangers have been seen in the area, on foot, or more recently in unknown automobiles traveling on back roads at night with their lights out, and that people have gone missing. And the rumors are not just creepy stories told for amusement but as alarming news that is acted on. Strangers encountered in the forest are attacked, roadblocks are set up, and unfamiliar vehicles are stopped or sometimes shot at as they pass by—all occurrences I have read in local newspapers in Borneo. Unknown white men in rural areas are particular objects of suspicion.[3] In Sarawak the government takes the rumors seriously and attempts to dispel them, although since government building projects are supposed to be the reason that victims are required, there is a problem of credibility here: "Of course the government will deny it; they are the ones who are doing it."

So far as we know, *penyamun* rumor myths are false. No published account has acknowledged even the possibility that any colonial or postcolonial government in Borneo has ever practiced or permitted human sacrifice or the offering of fresh heads for a construction ritual or for any other purpose. Indeed, the attribution of head-hunting or human sacrifice to the government is interesting as an example of the theme of reversal. One of the relatively few changes that the colonial government in Sarawak sought to force on the Dayak populations was the elimination of warfare and head hunting. At the same time, this change was accomplished in a way that seemed to be evidence that the government only cared about eliminating head-hunting among some groups; that is, the rebels, who refused to accept government authority. This was because the main way of subduing the hostile groups was to use punitive expeditions consisting largely of Dayaks loyal to the government who were permitted to take heads in the course of their attacks. Another tactic the government used to help eliminate head-hunting also sent the message that the government was interested in obtaining heads. Since heads were considered essential for various native rituals, someone had the bright idea that the government could meet the ritual need by collecting skulls from enemy longhouses and loaning them out for ceremonies. This involved keeping the skulls in the government's upriver forts until they were needed.

NOTES

1. The folklorist and anthropologist William Bascom (1984) has probably made the best case for approaching stories and tales from around the world in terms of the standard categories of myth, legend, and folktale.

2. Euhemerism is a theory propounded by the third century B.C.E. Greek writer Euhemerus that myths are based on once living men and their activities.

3. The anthropologist Peter Metcalf (1996) reports being taken for a *penyamun* and shot at while walking in the forest doing ethnographic research in Sarawak.

REFERENCES AND FURTHER READING

Bascom, William. 1984. "The Forms of Folklore." In *Sacred Narrative: Readings in the Theory of Myth*, edited by Alan Dundes. Berkeley: University of California Press.

Beidelman, T. O. 1974. *W. Robertson Smith and the Sociological Study of Religion*. Chicago: University of Chicago Press.

Blacker, Carmen. 1975. *The Catalpa Bow: A Study of Shamanistic Practices in Japan*. London: George Allen & Unwin.

Bowie, Fiona. 2006. *The Anthropology of Religion: An Introduction*. Malden, Mass.: Blackwell.

Breasted, James Henry. 1934. *The Dawn of Conscience*. New York: Charles Scribner's Sons.

Brunvand, Jan Harold. 1981. *The Vanishing Hitchhiker: American Urban Legends and Their Meanings*. New York: Norton.

Dorson, Richard M. 1962. *Folk Legends of Japan*. Rutland, Vt.: Tuttle.

———. 1965. "The Eclipse of Solar Mythology." In *The Study of Folklore*, edited by Alan Dundes, pp. 57–83. Englewood Cliffs, N.J.: Prentice-Hall.

Douglas, Mary. 1996. "Children Consumed and Child Cannibals: Robertson Smith's Attack on the Science of Mythology." In *Myth and Method*, edited by Laurie Patton and Wendy Doniger, pp. 29–51. Charlottesville: University Press of Virginia.

Dundes, Alan. 1996. "Madness in Method Plus a Plea for Projective Inversion in Myth." In *Myth and Method*, edited by Laurie Patton and Wendy Doniger, pp. 147–59. Charlottesville: University Press of Virginia.

Dundes, Alan, ed. 1984. *Sacred Narrative: Readings in the Theory of Myth*. Berkeley: University of California Press.

Haddon, Alfred Court. 1901. *Headhunters Black, White, and Brown*. London: Methuen.

Kluckhohn, Clyde. 1942. "Myths and Rituals: A General Theory." *Harvard Theological Review*, 35: 45–79.

Leach, Edmund, ed. 1967. *The Structural Study of Myth and Totemism*. London: Tavistock.

Lévi-Strauss, Claude. 1963. *Structural Anthropology*. 2 vols. New York: Basic.

———. 1967. "The Story of Asdiwal." In *The Structural Study of Myth and Totemism*, edited by Edmund Leach, pp. 1–47. London: Tavistock.

Malinowski, Bronislaw. [1925] 1948. *Magic, Science, and Religion and Other Essays*, Garden City, N. Y.: Doubleday Anchor.

Metcalf, Peter. 1996. "Images of Headhunting." In *Headhunting in Southeast Asia*, edited by Janet Hoskins, pp. 249–90. Stanford, Calif.: Stanford University Press.

O'Flaherty, Wendy Doniger. 1980. *Women, Androgynes, and Other Mythical Beasts*. Chicago: University of Chicago Press.

Patton, Laurie L., and Wendy Doniger. 1996. *Myth and Method*. Charlottesville: University Press of Virginia.

Radin, Paul. 1956. *The Trickster: A Study in American Indian Mythology*. New York: Bell.

Raglan, Lord Fitzroy R. S. [1936] 1975. *The Hero: A Study in Tradition, Myth, and Drama*. Westport, Conn.: Greenwood.

Rickets, Mac Linscott. 1987. "Tricksters." In *The Encyclopedia of Religion*, edited by Mircea Eliade, pp. 167–70. New York: Macmillan.

Scheper-Hughes, Nancy. 2002. "Mind(ing) the Body: On the Trail of Organ-Stealing Rumors." In *Exotic No More: Anthropology on the Front Lines*, edited by Jeremy MacClancy, pp. 33–63. Chicago: University of Chicago Press.

Segal, Robert K. 1998. *The Myth and Ritual Theory: An Edited Anthology*. Oxford: Blackwell.

———. 2004. *Myth: A Very Short Introduction*. Oxford: Oxford University Press.

Smith, William Robertson. [1889] 1901. *Lectures on the Religion of the Semites*. London: Adam and Charles Black.

Strenski, Ivan. 1992. *Malinowski and the Work of Myth*. Princeton: Princeton University Press.

7

❧

Ritual and Belief

Ritual is a less well-known, more specialized subject than myth. In addition to being a classic interest in anthropology, myth has long been studied by scholars of language and folklore, not to mention various psychologists including Freud, Jung, and Rank. Mythology has a popular and scholarly identity that makes it a discipline in itself. This cannot be said of ritual. In anthropology, no scholar of ritual has had the rank or influence that Lévi-Strauss achieved in relation to the study of myth.

Yet ritual is a core topic in the anthropology of religion, not just one of many things that has to be discussed. As noted earlier, the common modern Western (certainly American) assumption that a person can be religious in the sense of believing or having faith without practicing rituals. We do not necessarily have to agree with Raglan and some other adherents of the myth-ritual school that it is only ritual that really matters, and that throughout history and among most people outside of the modern West, religion has largely been about down-to-earth matters such as getting the rain to fall, the crops to grow, the animals to increase, the sick to recover, the enemies to become weak, and the souls of the deceased to leave the village and get to the land of the dead. We do need to go beyond the common Western view that religion is only or mainly a matter of belief or meaning. Most anthropologists who work on religion in broad, comparative terms would probably agree that belief and ritual go together and that neither can be well understood without the other.

In this chapter we shall consider ritual by moving from the general to the particular. We shall begin by considering the most elementary

145

dimensions of ritual, and then move to those rituals that have received the greatest attention from anthropologists and that have been best explained, which are those associated with the changes from one stage of life to another. We shall end by considering the least optional of all the life crises rituals—those involving death.

THE NATURE OF RITUAL

Just what do we mean by ritual? The terms "ritual" and "ceremony" can be and often are used interchangeably, although scholars prefer "ritual" while "ceremony" is more common in popular discourse. "Rite" is another term for ritual, but it is less commonly used and while in the past a distinction between rite and ritual was sometimes made, this is now seldom done in anthropology. Finally, the term "ritual" has also to some extent suffered the same linguistic fate as myth—used to refer to something that is not what it purports to be, in this case an empty gesture, a formal pattern of behavior followed for the sake of precedent or for some deceptive reason and not really necessary from a practical perspective (e.g., "the whole thing was nothing but a ritual").

What scholars and researchers call ritual behavior is not limited to humans. It occurs among animals in greeting, courtship, and mating patterns and in dominance and submission behavior. Such rituals are mainly signaling devices that elicit appropriate counterresponses in other animals of the same species or group. Where some ritual displays have no evident communicative purpose, they seem most likely to be emotional outlets or tension reduction devices, probably for fear or anxiety or confusion. The spectacular "rain dances" of the chimps at Gombe stream observed by Jane Goodall are probably the best known example, but there are others as well. Finally, as already noted, the evident fact that nonhuman animals have ritual but not "belief" has led to the supposition that religion began as ritual rather than belief (Wallace 1966: 224).

Ritual among humans is not limited to religion. The term can refer to any fixed or stereotyped practice, behavioral pattern, or embellishment that has no evident instrumental purpose beyond communication or symbolization. Shaking hands is a simple example. It has been suggested that once men coming together may have clasped hands to prevent either from seizing a weapon and attacking the other. But if so, few would now think of the joining of right hands as anything other than a greeting gesture of acknowledgment, friendship, or respect or agreement. Table manners would be a more complicated example of secular ritual behavior.

A final general characteristic of ritual is that it has both positive and negative dimensions. The positive dimensions consist of things that are to be done—actions to be carried out, words to be spoken, and offerings to be made—because they are required for some purpose. The negative dimensions of ritual include the things that must not be done. These are usually referred to as *taboos* (from the Polynesian *tabu*) or rules of avoidance, prohibition, or restriction. However, we are speaking here of taboo regarding a particular ritual state or setting, not as a general rule of conduct, such as the incest taboo or the Jewish or Muslim taboo on eating pork. Ritual taboos are rather those things that are not supposed to be done in relation to some particular activity, time, or place—for example, by women during menstruation or by husbands during their wives' pregnancy.

RELIGIOUS RITUAL

In the broadest sense, ritual can be said to refer simply to customary religious behavior, action, or activity, in contrast to belief, faith, or assumption. It is one thing to have faith or believe in God as a part of your conscious thoughts but another to act on it in some way. If you profess your beliefs or faith out loud (even if very softly or rapidly so what you say is inaudible to anyone else), you can be said to be engaging in ritual action.

But religious ritual has other characteristics too. To begin with, it usually involves a more or less fixed pattern or sequence of actions and utterances, the success of which is thought to depend to some extent on the correctness of procedure. Some rituals are carried out to an exact standard in terms of what is said and done, and in the coordination of one act to another. Examples can be found in most religious traditions, including the celebration of mass in the Catholic Church or the five required daily prayers in Islam. In some instances the failure to follow ritual procedures correctly—to do and say the right things at the right time and in the right order—is thought to not merely negate the value of process but to be dangerous. When I made inquiries in Borneo about why some ritual or other was no longer being performed, I was often told that it was because there was uncertainty about how some things were supposed to be done or the correct words to be used, and that it would be better not to do it at all than to do it incorrectly. The spirits that had been summoned might be confused and angered if they were not dealt with in the right manner or given the right offerings, and cause serious trouble as a result. This is partly why religious ritual is often conducted—or at least led or supervised—by specialists. And further it is why, once systems of writing or recording developed, calendars became highly important as determinants of when rituals were to be held or, to put it slightly differently, calendars were developed in the first place for ritual purposes. The emphasis on precision is part of what is meant when we say that something is done "ritualistically."

Finally, some rituals involve fairly discrete or clearly bounded activities such as saying prayers, making an offering, or burning incense or lighting a candle at an altar. Much ritual, however, occurs within a larger context or involves a sequence or cycle of activity. While a church service, for example, can be seen as a single religious event or ritual, it also includes a series of ritual activities. This is also true of festivals, celebrations, or holidays (or holy days) and pilgrimages.

Positive and Negative Dimensions of Ritual

In Western religious practices the negative dimensions of ritual have generally diminished or disappeared as religion has been modernized (and in a sense secularized), although many readers may be aware of the ban on eating meat on Friday that was a part of Roman Catholic ritual proscriptions until fairly recently. But in more traditionally oriented places, indigenous religions, and some of the world religions, restrictions or prohibitions remain an important dimension of ritual life. Ritual taboos may focus on individuals, households, or entire villages, depending on the occasion. In the case of the world religions such taboos may include everyone.

Religious ritual probably does not ever consist of only proscriptions. The Muslim fasting month provides a good example. This is the month of Ramadan, the month of year as determined by the Muslim lunar calendar, which means that its occurrence will gradually move in relation to the solar year or the seasons. The entire month may be considered as a ritual period during which all adults are required adhere to a series of restrictions—to abstain from food and drink from dawn to sundown, with a few exceptions (including those who are ill or injured, and travelers who would suffer hardship). The fasting month is likely to be considered by most non-Muslims as a period of negative ritual requirements, but this is not so. Religious celebrations including meals and prayers are also held in the evening or into the night, and good deeds are believed to count for more than during other times.

Funerary rituals are another good example. The traditional purpose of funerals (to which we shall return) is in many places twofold: to dispose of human remains by burial or cremation or in some other way, and at the same time to move the spirit of the deceased from the place of death and the living and to send it on its way to the other world, the place of the dead. All of these activities plus others form the positive side of the funerary ritual (or rituals). The negative side includes the proscriptions and restrictions we refer to as mourning. Among indigenous peoples of Southeast Asia these negative ritual practices often include closing the village to outsiders or at least to those not closely related to the deceased, or of restricting or prohibiting all entry or exit. Mourning rituals also usually involve particular restrictions placed on family or household members, especially the husband or wife of the deceased.

SOME COMMON FORMS OF RELIGIOUS RITUAL ACTIVITY

Here is a list of elementary ritual acts or activities. It is not necessarily complete, and some of the activities are simpler or more elementary than others. It involves ritual activities at which I have been present, sometimes on numerous occasions in various places.

Elementary Ritual Actions

1. Prayers. Verbal expressions or formulas (spoken, sung, or chanted) addressed to spirit beings, often accompanied by appropriate gestures or postures and sometimes by music. Prayers may be expressions of devotion and loyalty, on the one hand, or pleas or requests for assistance, on the other, or a combination of both.

2. Spells. Verbal formulas intended to have some mystical or magical causal effect on spirits, animals, humans, or other things. The distinction between prayer and spell can be ambiguous, but prayers involve supplication while spells are efforts at manipulation; also, while prayers can be free form or fixed, spells are formulaic.

Figure 7.1. A young woman earns merit by making a ritual offering of rice to Buddhist monks on their early morning round of begging in Pakse, southern Laos. Although Laos is an officially communist country, Buddhism continues to flourish.

3. Offerings. Food, drink, flowers, and other physical or symbolic gifts, the burning of candles (a gift of light) or incense or tobacco, as tribute to spiritual beings, either as routine devotions, in association with requests for assistance, or in payment of vows made previously.

4. Sacrifice. Offerings that usually involve killing a living creature and often pouring its blood on the ground or on persons, or smearing it on statues, altars, parts of buildings or other objects; sometimes the offering of blood is drawn without killing. The sacrificial animal is usually killed by stabbing or cutting, drawing its blood being an essential part of the process.

5. Divination or augury. Efforts to learn the future, find a lost object or a desired thing such as water in the ground, choose a course of action or a correct path, or avoid disaster by mystical means such as manipulating objects or substances, letters or numbers, listening to the calls or observing the flight of birds, or calculating the position of heavenly bodies.

6. Communion. The sharing of food or drink (or in some circumstances sex) by a group of people, in part at least for a mystical or religious purpose.

7. Trance. An altered state of consciousness, begun while awake and usually deliberately sought and achieved through various techniques, believed to bring extraordinary modes of perception and communication, and sometimes insensitivity to ordinary stimulation or physical pain, on the one hand, and extraordinary feats of strength or resistance, on the other.

8. Spirit mediumship or deliberate possession. To invite or permit a spirit or god to enter into one's body or self, to take control of one's voice or actions, usually but not necessarily associated with trance. Rituals of spirit mediumship are often dramatic activities and sometimes include amusing and obscene dialogue or action as well as more solemn ones. Curing or exorcism is one common purpose of spirit mediumship and another is to enable the living to communicate with the spirits of the dead.

9. Exorcism. Efforts to discover and then drive out a malevolent or unwanted spirit that has taken control of a someone's body or mind, or that is causing confusion, sickness, or pain. Exorcism is often accomplished by invoking more powerful spirits to help defeat or dislodge the malevolent one. Therefore rituals of exorcism are often combined with those of spirit mediumship.

More Complex Ritual Activity

Beyond the fairly limited and discrete forms noted above, ritual activity can be more varied and complex. Much of what is called ritual may be drawn out over hours, days, months, or even years and consists of some of the core acts noted above as well as other activities, including travel, visiting, penance, deprivation, seclusion, punishment or mutilation, wailing and displays of sorrow, grief or happiness, feasting and drinking, greeting and socializing, gift giving, music and dancing, contests of skill and strength, gambling, animal fights, dramatic presentations, sexual license, joking, horseplay, and mockery. Rituals are commonly classified according to their purpose but also according to other criteria.

SOME COMMON TYPES OF RITUAL

Curing. Ritual activities aimed at helping someone recover from illness or affliction, including ones (such as prayer) that supplement physical treatment as well as ones that consist entirely of mystical or religious actions, such as spirit possession or exorcism.

Subsistence. All ritual activities intended to maintain or enhance the subsistence activities, including those intended to promote the fertility and protection of crops or to enable hunters to find game or fishermen to catch fish; sometimes part of a seasonal cycle beginning with planting and ending with a harvest celebration.

Calendrical. Rituals held for any purpose on a regular basis, for example, on a particular date every year.

Rites of passage. Rituals held in relation to the major transitions in life, including birth, puberty, marriage, and death.

Pilgrimage. A ritual journey to a sacred place in order to request supernatural aid, fulfill a vow, accumulate merit, meet a requirement, express devotion, or several or all of these.

Ritual and Time

Rituals are sometimes referred to according to whether or not they are held at regular points in time. Broadly speaking, calendrical rituals are held at particular times of the year, such as Christmas or Easter, as opposed to noncalendrical ones such as weddings, which can be held whenever people want to hold them, though many peoples do so during particular seasons, or funerals, which are held when the need arises, except in the case of secondary mortuary rituals (discussed below) which may also be concentrated in certain seasons.

THE STRUCTURE OF RITUAL ACCORDING TO ARNOLD VAN GENNEP

The most satisfactory approach to explaining ritual has concerned the structure of rites of passage. The crucial scholar here was Arnold van Gennep. Born in Germany to a Dutch father and a French mother, van

Gennep lived mainly in France and studied and wrote in the same French tradition of comparative armchair scholarship as Mauss, Durkheim, and Hertz. Van Gennep's interpretation of ritual was set out in his *Les rites de passage*. First published in French in 1909, this study was not issued in an English translation until 1960, after which its influence spread much more widely. It is now considered to be among the core works in the anthropology of religion.

Although concerned especially with the nature of life transition rituals, van Gennep's approach was more broadly focused to include all ritual activity that involved passage or transition from one status or period to another. This included, for example, the rituals of travel, especially pilgrimage, house building, and the changes of seasons and years, as well as of birth, coming-of-age, marriage, and death. Like the works of other French anthropologists in the first decades of the twentieth century, though not to any significant extent based on personal firsthand or fieldwork research, van Gennep's study seems ahead of its time.

The most basic idea in *Les rites de passage* is not merely that all societies ritualize transitions in the life cycle and other things but that they do so in similar ways—at least if you take a structuralist point of view and look beneath the surface variations to the underlying commonalities. So viewed, all rituals of transition have a beginning, a middle, and an end. The beginning is a rite of separation and the end is a rite of incorporation or reincorporation, while the middle stage is liminal or transitional.

JOURNEYS AND BOUNDARIES

Van Gennep thought the basic idea of ritual transition is best understood by looking at territorial passage or travel, especially at travel as it used to be. Crossing frontiers has a magico-religious dimension in many places. Today, he noted, traveling from one country to another in Europe is often abrupt as one country directly touches another, but in the past it was common for countries to be separated by strips or zones of neutral ground. In classical antiquity, especially in Greece, such zones were used as marketplaces or battlefields. Among tribal peoples such neutral zones are often deserts, marshes, or, most often, forests, where everyone has the right to travel and hunt. Moreover, people on both sides regard this between zone as sacred, and this makes anyone who passes through it also, for a time, sacred as well. "Whoever passes from one to the other finds himself physically and magico-religiously in a special situation for a certain length of time" (van Gennep 1960: 18). This same thing applies to all of the ceremonies that accompany the transition from one social and magico-religious position to another.

Pilgrimage

The importance van Gennep places on travel as a key to understanding rites of passage brings us first to pilgrimage. A simple definition of pilgrimage that appears to cover the ground fairly well is this: A pilgrimage is a nonroutine ritual journey to a sacred site or shrine to acquire supernatural aid, fulfill a vow, pay penance, accumulate merit, meet a requirement, express devotion, or several or all of these. Put most simply, a pilgrimage is a special journey to a sacred place for a religious purpose.

Ritual visits to sacred sites are probably found in all types of religions. The vision quests of Native Americans could be regarded as a form of pilgrimage to the extent that they involved visits to particular mountaintops or other sacred places. Visits to sacred sites are well-known features of the religious practices of Australian aborigines and can probably be found among hunter-gatherers elsewhere as well. However, the extent that long-distance journeys are undertaken exclusively or mainly in order to visit sacred sites (as opposed to incorporating such visits into a more general round of nomadic movement involving hunting and gathering, ritual and social visiting, and other ceremonial activities) is another matter. Many peoples, including food producers as well as hunter-gatherers, are not in a position to undertake long-distance journeys for ritual purposes. Such travel is all the more difficult and unlikely if it involves entering into or crossing hostile territory.

For such reasons, pilgrimage in the narrow sense is probably most characteristic of the world religions. It is certainly among these that pilgrimage as defined above is best known and most often exemplified. Here van Gennep's formulations of the ritual significance of crossing boundaries and the sacredness of strangers on journeys comes most completely into play. Robertson Smith (1901: 80, 109, 276) noted that pilgrimage activities began in the Arabian Peninsula and elsewhere among Semitic peoples in ancient times but developed more fully later on. However:

> It is only under Islam that the pilgrimage becomes a bond of religious fellowship, whereas in the times of heathenism it was the correct usage that the different tribes, before they broke up from the feast, should engage in a rivalry of self-exultation and mutual abuse, which sent them home with all of their old jealousies freshly inflamed. (1901: 276–77)

Pilgrimage sites are sometimes classed as local, regional, and international in regard to the areas from which they attract pilgrims. Pilgrimage sites are often referred to as shrines, which may be anything but are often the place where a miracle is believed to have occurred, or a saint or other religious leader to have been born or to be buried. Almost by definition, a pilgrimage site is believed to be a place of miracles or mystical power;

sometimes a grave comes to be regarded as that of a saint only after it is noticed that supernatural things have begun to happen to humans or animals in contact with it or in the vicinity of it.

Although the culmination of a pilgrimage consists of the activities carried out in relation to the shrine (or shrines), including the final approach, the entire journey is a ritual activity. Once the pilgrims begin, they are in a sacred *liminal* state. This is often signified by special dress designed to cover what ordinary clothing reveals in the way of place of origin, ethnicity, class status, or wealth. In the view of Victor and Edith Turner (1978), participants experience pilgrimage as *communitas*, or unstructured, egalitarian bonds of commonality and mutual goodwill, and this is part of the attraction. However, the positive side of pilgrimage and sacred sites does not generally extend beyond a particular religious community, for exam-

Figure 7.2. A newly returned Malay Muslim pilgrim in an Arab head covering standing with his proud son at the train station in Pasir Mas, Kelantan, west Malaysia. His status forever changed, he will always be referred to with the honorific title of Haji.

ple, to the members of a different world religion that may also regard the pilgrimage site as sacred for the same or a different reason.

Anthropology came late to the study of pilgrimage. The study of Christian pilgrimage by the Turners, and the first major anthropological work on the topic, was published only in 1978. There are several possible reasons this line of research and analysis took so long to emerge. As noted above, fully developed pilgrimage is not really characteristic of the religious traditions of indigenous, small-scale societies. In addition, pilgrimage is an activity that by definition is played out in more than one place, and anthropological research traditionally is based on work in a particular location. Finally, pilgrimage is a ritual activity that can pose problems from the perspective of the traditional methodological practice of participant observation—more so perhaps than some other types of ritual activity. For example, the main Muslim pilgrimage sites are closed to non-Muslims. However, the problems of researching and writing about pilgrimage are usually not insurmountable, and by now there have been many anthropological studies involving various places around the world.

RITES OF PASSAGE

Life transition rituals are often said to form a cycle, especially in the case of those societies that assume human souls are reincarnated.

Pregnancy and Childbirth

Van Gennep points out that rituals of pregnancy and childbirth form a whole but at the same time differ according to the perspective of the mother and the child. From the perspective of the mother, the process begins with the recognition of pregnancy. This often involves rites that separate the pregnant woman from her normal routines and relationships, which sometimes means actual physical separation and seclusion. Once separated, the woman is in a liminal state that generally involves various kinds of taboos, including ones involving sex, diet, and in some instances other normal activities of marriage such as cooking. Often the rituals and restrictions of pregnancy are extended to the husband as well. All rites become more complicated in the case of abnormalities. The birth of twins is special, often requiring particular rituals, and sometimes is regarded as a disaster. At least in the case of normal birth, the liminal state ends with childbirth, or rather with ceremonies held sometime later that serve to reincorporate the woman into society and therefore lift the restrictions of pregnancy.

From the perspective of the child, birth involves separation from the body of the mother and the establishment of a new social being. The cutting of the umbilical cord is therefore a symbolic or ritual act as well as a practical one. The cord and placenta commonly become important ritual material linked to soul of the child and treated accordingly if variously— sometimes buried somewhere in the house or, conversely, in a hidden place outside; sometimes in one place for a boy and another for a girl (among the Hmong, for example, under the threshold in the case of a boy and under the hearth or beneath a bed platform in the case of a girl). Again, there is a liminal period between birth and incorporation, during which the child is not yet a real or complete person. The death of a child during this period often is treated differently from that of one that has been ritually incorporated, for the transition to life is incomplete. The rituals that are held following birth can include ones of separation as well as incorporation. Van Gennep suggests that hair-cutting or head-shaving ceremonies found in many places are, like the cutting of the umbilical cord, rites of separation; so also are purification ceremonies such as the first bath. As for rites of incorporation, while various activities may be involved, those of naming are particularly important and widespread. Baptism, however, is both a rite of separation (because it involves purification) and of incorporation (because it involves naming) (van Gennep 1960: 62–63).

Coming-of-Age and Marriage

The rites of passage that follow those of pregnancy and birth involve puberty or coming-of-age, on the one hand, and marriage, on the other. Marriage as a rite of passage is relatively uncomplicated and can be dealt with quickly in terms of van Gennep's scheme. Marriage involves the transition from being single to being married, which also often involves the movement from one family household to another, and therefore both separation and reincorporation. The in-between or liminal state in this case is engagement or betrothal. Traditional wedding rituals may also display this three-stage process. In the case of Western weddings, the marriage sequence involves the separation of the bride and groom from their respective families followed by a transitional (also liminal) honeymoon and then their reincorporation into a household of their own. While not all societies ritualize marriage extensively, most do in one way or another, and in ways that fit with van Gennep's approach.

Rituals of initiation are more complicated than those of marriage. Van Gennep stresses that (even more than in the case of pregnancy and birth rituals) the relationship between the timing of puberty rituals (social puberty) and biological puberty is very loose. For girls, it is commonly supposed that puberty is marked exactly by menarche but in many societies this event as such is not noted or ritualized, and beyond this the physical changes that constitute biological puberty extend over a period of time. In some societies the crucial event that makes a girl into a woman is pregnancy and childbirth, not just physical development. For boys, there is no single event such as menarche, and the ritual activities of initiation take place at widely varying ages in different societies. Even within specific societies, boys and girls are often initiated at ages that differ by several years or more. The rituals of initiation consist of the usual sequence of separation, followed by a liminal period and then reincorporation. The sequence may be condensed into a brief period or drawn out over a period of years.

Van Gennep's treatment of coming-of-age initiation rituals probably overemphasizes their uniform importance in cross-cultural terms. What we seem to find in the world are three kinds of variation. First, there are differences from one place to another in terms of whether coming-of-age is given much attention at all; and, to the extent that it is, whether it is dealt with in rituals that are specifically concerned with it or that are concerned with other matters and simply serve as initiation. For example, especially in comparison with those of some areas such as Africa, Melanesia, and Australia, the peoples of Southeast Asia do not generally place much emphasis on coming-of-age ritual. And in some cases where rituals are held, they are not ones aimed specifically at the transition from childhood to adulthood. Among Malays, who are all Muslims, children begin to learn to read the Qur'an several years or so before adolescence and, in the case of boys, the completion of study is followed by circumcision, at which time they are considered to be adults in religious terms and expected to pray regularly, to attend Friday prayers at the mosque, and to fast. Thai Buddhist boys traditionally enter monasteries as novice monks about the time of puberty for some period up to several years, but men can do this at later points in their lives as well and often do.

As in the last example, a second sort of variation concerns the differences between what takes place for boys and girls in the way of puberty rituals (Child and Child 1993: 148–50). Coming-of-age initiation rituals are based on gender. That is, they do not involve turning children into adults but rather of making boys into men and girls into women. Boys are usually initiated by men and girls by women. Further, little may be done in the case of female rituals but a lot in the case of male ones. And finally, different things are apt to be done to boys as opposed to girls. It would certainly be expected that there would be differences if surgical alterations to the genitals were part of what takes place, but there are likely to be other differences as well. For example, removal and isolation from normal relations and activities, sometimes for several years, is a common procedure in coming-of-age ritual sequences for both boys and girls but handled differently. In the case of boys, removal often involves their complete removal from the village to the forest or bush, while for girls it commonly involves seclusion in a special place in or near the house. Further, boys are likely to be removed in groups whereas girls are apt be secluded individually.

A third variation concerns severity. Initiations can be mild or severe and in several different ways. One of these involves harsh physical treatment in the form of hazing, beating, the deprivation of food and water, and teasing and ridicule. Another concerns the things that are done to mark or mutilate the body of the initiate in the way of cutting, excision, scarring, and the like. Over the past several decades a great deal of attention and condemnation has been focused on the severe forms of female genital mutilation practiced in various African societies, especially in eastern Africa.

Is it possible to explain any or all of the three sorts of variation: why some societies emphasize rites of passage from childhood to adulthood to a much greater extent than do others, why there are great differences in what is done in the case of males and females, and why rituals of initiation involve a steep gradient of severity across societies? Over many decades anthropologists have conducted cross-cultural studies that have attempted to answer such questions. Alice Child and Irvin Child (1993: 148–60) have reviewed and discussed the results of these studies. They show that the answers have been sociological in some cases and psychological in others. For one thing, the overall emphasis on coming-of-age rites in a society tends to correlate with the importance of male solidarity and the extent of male dominance. Male puberty rites are apt to be emphasized and to involve harsh methods where male solidarity is stressed and organized. Male initiations separate boys from the world of women, in which they begin their lives and in which they spend much of their childhood. Male initiation procedures stress the development of adult male virtues, male solidarity, and often secret mythology and ritual procedures.

Women's initiation practices are usually not simply the reverse of those of men. In some regions, especially West Africa, women may be initiated into secret societies that enhance female solidarity and give women separate and important ritual roles. More often, female initiation rituals are present in societies with marked male solidarity and male dominance. In these situations the presence of female initiation is aimed not at creating adult female solidarity but rather at reducing or neutralizing the mystical harm that women are held to be capable of causing men, especially regarding pollution and sexuality. The extreme forms of female mutilation practiced in some African societies epitomize this pattern. These practices involve the excision of external genitalia associated with female sexual pleasure, the purpose of which is the reduction of the likelihood that women will be tempted to engage in premarital or extramarital sex that would wound the honor of their families and husbands.

As noted above, men as well as women are liable to initiation practices that involve genital mutilation. The male initiation practices found in Melanesia and Australia have attracted particular attention. In some groups in New Guinea these procedures have included homosexual activities between the initiates and adult men. In some societies in Australia as well as in New Guinea and elsewhere the initiation of males includes forms of genital mutilation that deliberately cause bleeding or that have the effect of making the male genitals appear and function somewhat like female ones. Ritual homosexuality has been explained on the basis that repeated infusions of semen are necessary not only to create fetuses in the wombs of women but also to change boys into men. Genital mutilation that induces bleeding or makes male genitals appear more like female ones has been explained as an effort by men to imitate or acquire the powers of women associated with menstruation and reproduction (Child and Child 1993: 156).

MORTUARY RITUAL

The ritual practices associated with death can be considered simply as a rite of passage and analyzed according to the same concepts applied to pregnancy and childbirth, and coming-of-age and marriage. In societies that believe in reincarnation, life and death are seen as forming a cycle. Van Gennep's notion of liminality, as we shall see, has a particularly important applicability to the beliefs and practices surrounding death in some places. At the same time, death is not simply just another life crisis. For one thing, as readers hardly need to be reminded, while not everyone undergoes pregnancy and childbirth rituals, nor coming-of-age or marital ones, death, if not the rituals that go with it, is not optional. Further, unlike the other transitional events of life, death may be sudden and unexpected— and some peoples, as we shall see below, are particularly horrified by forms of death that have such characteristics and deal with them in particular ritual ways. And finally, while anthropologists are fond of pointing out that public or overt expressions of grief are a matter of culture and vary greatly from one place to another, death always carries with it a greater emotional burden than any other life crisis.

Notions of the Soul and the Afterlife

Anthropologists and other scholars who work on religion in comparative terms would probably agree that all peoples have a belief in the soul as the spiritual dimension of a person that is separate from the body and that survives the body after death (which is not to say that all peoples in all societies hold such a belief). In fact, the soul is a problematic notion in several respects, and most anthropological and other scholarly discussions of concepts of the soul are abstractions and oversimplifications. The issue is not so much whether all people have some kind of a belief in an immortal soul but rather that many people believe that a person has more than one. Often the different souls are associated with different parts of the body and behave differently.

Cultural ideas of the fate of the soul that live on after death fall into two main categories. One of these involves beliefs in a residence in a land of the dead or another world, and the other that the soul is reborn into a new body to live another life in this world. Among the world religions, beliefs in reincarnation are held in those of the East while those of an afterlife in another world exist in those of the West. Nor are the two sorts of beliefs necessarily separate or mutually incompatible in indigenous religious traditions. They can be combined, as in the idea that that the soul goes to the land of the dead for a time but is sooner or later reincarnated into a newborn person.

Beliefs about the location of the land of the dead vary. In some instances it is an island, in others a mountaintop or inside a walled area; it may be underground or in the sky. It may be an invisible village close by that of the living, but more commonly it is far away. Especially in the case of people who travel by water in life, the journey is often supposed to be also over water, in which case the dead are commonly placed in boat-shaped coffins or provided with a miniature boat and oars. Whether by land or water, the journey is long and difficult. The dead are given instructions on how to get there and what they will encounter on the way, sometimes in the form of long death chants; they are sometimes provided with passwords and money or provisions. They may also be provided with guides (known as psychopomps, from the Greek *psychopompoi*).

The belief or assumption that the souls of the dead are sooner or later reborn into new lives in the world of the living is the main alternative to the belief that the soul goes to dwell permanently in the land of the dead. The belief in reincarnation or the transmigration of souls is a hallmark of Eastern religions where it is associated with the ritual practice of cremation. In Hinduism and Buddhism the doctrines of reincarnation are complex and abstract, most notably in holding that rebirth is based on the moral law of karma (that fate is a sum of good and bad acts done in all previous lives) and can therefore involve rebirth in hell, as an animal in this world, as a poor or a rich person, or in some level of heaven. Beliefs in reincarnation occur widely and may be just as ancient as the belief in a land of the dead. According to Åke Hultkrantz's overview of Native American religion:

> Belief in reincarnation is widespread all over America, reaching a climax among the Eskimos, where it also takes its most peculiar forms. The Eskimo

link reincarnation to the naming ceremony of the child. Some Algonkin tribes east of the Mississippi practice a remarkable adoption rite: an outsider, adopted by a family that has lost one of its members, takes over the name of the deceased and is regarded as the dead person reincarnated. (1979: 137)

Beliefs in reincarnation are also common (if not pervasive) in indigenous Australian religious traditions and can be found among indigenous (i.e., non-Buddhist) as well as Buddhist and Hindu peoples in Southeast Asia.

Notions of reincarnation in indigenous religious traditions differ from those of the Indic great traditions of Hinduism and Buddhism in that they are not tied to doctrines of karma or morality; they lack a belief that the sort or level of rebirth depends on the conduct of the past life or lives that pervade Indic doctrine. Conversely, indigenous peoples are apt to believe that souls are reincarnated into persons closely related to the deceased. For example, a deceased grandfather's soul is reborn into a grandchild or at least into someone of the same lineage or clan. In Australia a common notion is that after death, souls wait for opportunities to enter the bodies of suitable women in order to be reborn.

Bad Death

Beliefs and practices involved with death can be complicated by another consideration: by the significance of how a person dies, especially if it involves "bad death"—modes of dying that are apt to be regarded anywhere as awful in the sense of premature, unnatural, frightening, bloody, or painful, or involving the disfiguration or mutilation of the body. Bad death can include suicide, drowning, being killed by an animal, dying in childbirth, by violence, or sometimes by dreaded disease. Note that with the possible exception of suicide, these do not imply a moral lapse. In another sense, bad death is regarded as being dangerous or polluting for living people and is therefore handled in special ways.

These ideas appear to be widespread in the world. Writing about Native American mortuary beliefs and practices, Hultkrantz notes that "in many American religions a separate realm of the dead is assigned to women who have died in childbirth, to people struck by lightning, to suicides, drowning victims, and others whose death is unexpected or violent" (1979: 136). Similarly, van Gennep (1960: 50) reports that, among the Ostyak of Siberia, "the land of the dead has three entrances . . . one for the assassinated, the drowned, the suicides, etc., another for the sinners, and a third for those who have lived a normal life."[1]

Beliefs about problematic or troublesome deaths and their implications are widespread or pervasive in Southeast Asia among adherents of both world religions and indigenous ones. Here also there is the belief that where souls go to reside in the afterlife depends on the manner of death. This is a common notion in the interior of Borneo, for example (Metcalf 1982: 254–56; Rousseau 1998: 98). In addition, Southeast Asian peoples often ritually treat bad death in a special manner. Such practices are marked by fear and avoidance based on the belief that the soul of a person who has died in a bad way will become an especially dangerous spirit. In extreme instances, people who hold such beliefs will flee or abandon dwellings or even villages in which bad death has occurred, while in others the body may be quickly taken away and buried away from the village or outside of the cemetery; in yet others funeral ceremonies may be attenuated and special cleansing rituals held.[2]

FUNERALS AS RITES OF PASSAGE

The ritual activities carried out in relation to death are most commonly referred to as funerals. Anthropologists sometimes prefer "mortuary practices" because this phrase has a usefully broader focus. Funerals or funerary rituals refer to the ceremonies involved in the preparation of the corpse and its disposal plus the feasting, visiting, memorials, displays of grief, wakes, and so forth that go along with it. The notion of mortuary practices includes all of this plus the rituals of mourning that continue

Figure 7.3.   A Malay Muslim funeral procession, Kelantan, west Malaysia.

after the funeral. These involve spouses, family members and other kin and, in the case of kings or other great men, the nation.

Van Gennep stressed that, as with the rites of birth, it is necessary to consider mortuary practices from two different perspectives. In this case, the two perspectives involve the person who has died, on the one hand, and those who survive (especially the spouse, family, and kin of the deceased), on the other. From the perspective of the latter, death places those closely affected in a ritual state of mourning. This means they are put in some degree of isolation and in an impure sacred state. Mourning is also a transitional period for the survivors, one that they enter through rites of separation and exit through rites of reintegration. From the perspective of the deceased, the ritual procedures that are most important are those of separation from the world of the living and incorporation into the world of the dead. Van Gennep interprets such mortuary practices as the breaking up of a dead person's possessions, the killing of his or her animals, and the destruction of the house as ritual acts of separation, although these actions have also often been interpreted as efforts to send the possessions to the land of the dead along with the soul of the deceased.

TWO-STAGE MORTUARY PRACTICES

Of all mortuary practices known, those involving "secondary burial" are perhaps the most difficult to understand in terms of what we are apt to think that funerals are all about: the ritual disposal of the remains of the deceased and the separation of the soul from the living and its conveyance to the land or the dead or to be reborn into a new person. To begin with, as a matter of definition, the use of the term "secondary burial" is somewhat inappropriate in that what happens in the second stage does not necessarily involve reburial. Indeed, in Southeast Asia at least, reburial in the ground never seems to take place at all. Further, the reburial of human remains may be done for many practical reasons that have nothing to do with the full two-stage funeral practices with which we are concerned here, for example, to move a cemetery in order to make room for a new building or a road. What usually occurs is therefore more accurately termed "secondary treatment," which could include cremation or the placement of what remains of the bones in an aboveground receptacle of one sort or another. The term "secondary," however, is also somewhat misleading insofar as it implies "lesser," for the second ceremony is the larger and more elaborate one. An even broader and therefore more appropriate phrase would therefore be "two-stage mortuary practices."

Described in the simplest of terms, two-stage mortuary practices involve two funerals rather than one. These include an initial ceremony of disposal that is usually modest and often hurried, and a later and far larger one that usually includes the reburial or other reprocessing of the remains. Why should some people follow two-stage mortuary practices? What is the logic involved? One possibility is that once a death has occurred there is a desire or need to do something with the body quickly, but at the same time a desire or need to hold a large ceremony that requires the accumulation of resources and the gathering of people from far as well as near. In actuality, while such considerations may be involved, they are not the main one. The real or most crucial part of the explanation was formulated a century ago by the French anthropologist Robert Hertz (1960) on the basis of ethnographic evidence from Southeast Asia, especially Borneo, where two-stage mortuary practices until recently were common (Metcalf 1982; Schiller 1997). The explanation also fits perfectly with van Gennep's three-stage model of the sequence of ritual, especially his notion of liminality, which in this instance is the phase between physical death and the later point at which the soul goes to the afterlife or is reincarnated, or between the first and the second funerals.

The complete two-stage mortuary tradition includes the following elements:

1. An initial funeral is held and the remains are disposed, either by burial or storage in some receptacle above ground.
2. The remains stay where they have been placed until only (or mainly only) the skeleton is left, and further until resources for holding the final ceremony have been accumulated and the often lavish preparations completed.
3. The skeletal remains are then recovered, cleaned, and reburied or placed in a new container for permanent storage or cremated.
4. The second phase of the funeral involving the recovery and reprocessing of the remains is larger than the initial one and often has an air of celebration and festivity that is lacking at the first.

A crucial part of Hertz's explanation of two-stage mortuary practices is the belief that death is a drawn-out process rather than an instant occurrence. In the modern Western view life and death form a simple dichotomy: a person is either alive or dead; a persons is alive until breathing has stopped and other vital signs have ceased. Of course, advanced medical technology has complicated this and we are fascinated and troubled by states that are between life and death such as coma; consider the highly politicized national controversy over the cessation of life support for the long-comatose Terry Schiavo. We are also fascinated with vampires and zombies, but none of this alters our fundamentally dichotomous view of life and death.

In the case of two-stage mortuary practices, the belief is that death is only the beginning of a process that will continue months or more and not be completed until the second ceremony is held. Until the second ceremony, the soul of the dead person lingers about the grave or in the vicinity of the group, where it is a danger to the living. The final ceremony will be delayed until the resources for what Hertz called a "great feast" can be accumulated. In Southeast Asia this will involve animals to be sacrificed, rice and other food for feasting, and rice wine for drinking. The second ceremony must wait until the flesh of the body has disintegrated, leaving only the bones. Hertz concluded that the process of death was believed to mirror the transformation of the body. It was with the disappearance of everything but the bones that death is complete and the soul can be released for its journey to the land of the dead or to be reincarnated.

Two-stage mortuary practices have been claimed to be widespread. One researcher has asserted that they were at one time universal. In his book *The Buried Soul* the prehistorian Timothy Taylor (2002: 27) states that "for most of recent human history (roughly the last 35,000 years) funerary rites were twofold: the primary rites zoned off the freshly dead . . . the secondary rites . . . firmly and finally incorporating the deceased into the realm of the ancestors." Taylor explains neither how he came up with the number of 35,000 years (but presumably he means the beginning of the Upper Paleolithic) nor the generalization about universality. His analysis of the meaning and purpose of two-stage mortuary practices is based on Robert Hertz and the Southeast Asian ethnographic evidence combined with archaeological evidence of reburial from various places. This hardly seems to be convincing proof of universality.

Ethnographic and other evidence of two-stage mortuary practices does seem widespread, although nowhere do all peoples in a culture area follow such traditions. According to Peter Metcalf and Richard Huntington (1991: 35), outside of Borneo and Indonesia, "examples could be cited from Central Asia, North America, South America, Melanesia, and elsewhere. Reburial was part of the Jewish tradition and is still practiced in Greece." Australia could be added to this list. There is, however, the problem of deciding which traditions really fit Hertz's model. For example, Harold Driver's overview of Native American funeral practices includes this brief observation:

In a few areas memorial ceremonies were held some months or years after death. The Hurons, and some of their neighbors in northern parts of the Prairies and East, held an elaborate feast of the dead at intervals of twelve years. The corpses were retrieved from scaffolds and trees by their relatives and deposited in a huge community burial pit amid wailing, singing and speechmaking. (Driver 1961: 450)

As far as it goes, this seems to be a description of what Hertz is talking about. It does not, however, say anything concerning the beliefs and motives about the transformation of the soul that Hertz held to be at the heart of two-stage mortuary traditions.

Greek practices seem to fit less well. Greek villagers follow the custom of exhuming remains at some point after burial and then reinterring them (Alexiou 1974: 47–48). The purpose of the exhumation is to examine the condition of the bones in order to learn the fate of the soul: a clean white skeleton indicates the soul is in heaven while blackened bones or incomplete decomposition show that the soul has suffered the opposite fate (although priestly ritual intervention may still save the day). The practice, which is said to be a holdover from pre-Christian times, does involve ritualized reburial. But the purpose and meaning seem quite different from that of two-stage funeral traditions as described by Hertz and van Gennep. Nor is the exhumation and reburial accompanied by a great feast.

Two-Stage Mortuary Practices in the Central Highlands of Vietnam

In addition to the classic two-stage funeral practices that occur in Borneo and among some other Indonesian societies, there are other mortuary traditions in Southeast Asia that include major secondary ceremonies but do not involve the full two-stage pattern. Most notably perhaps, the indigenous peoples of the northern central highlands of Vietnam hold "tomb abandonment" ceremonies. These practices lack the actual exhumation and reinterment of remains but otherwise qualify as classic two-stage procedures. Some of the peoples who follow such traditions include the Giarai and Ede (Rhade), who are speakers of Austronesian languages that link them to the Indonesian peoples to the south; others, such as the Bahnar and the Mncng, speak variants of Mon-Khmer that do not. The tomb abandonment ceremonies held in the central highlands have attracted the attention of Vietnamese ethnologists in part because they are the largest and most important of the ritual activities followed by most of these groups. In addition, the ceremonies are the occasion for the creation and erection of often elaborate mortuary architecture and statues. Vietnamese scholars Nguyen Van Ku and Luu Hung (2003) have recently published a volume of photos of the ceremonies, the tombs, and the statues that includes a description of the mortuary sequence and the beliefs involved.

Although what takes place varies somewhat from one group to another, the general sequence is as follows. After death the body is placed in a coffin and buried in the village cemetery. This at least is the procedure with normal death. Persons dying in bad ways of the sort noted above (e.g., drowning, dying in childbirth, being killed by a tiger or in battle, or dying by suicide) are not buried in village cemeteries or accorded the two-stage treatment (Nguyen and Luu 2003: 50). For those who die in ways that allow the normal procedure, single burials are the norm but some groups will inter several members of a family together. A roof is erected over the grave and a stockade of logs or a fence is built around it. This begins the liminal phase, when the soul of the deceased is assumed to remain in or near the grave. Family members are in mourning and visit the grave regularly with offerings of food and drink for the soul. All of this continues for a year or so until the tomb abandonment ceremony is held. These ceremonies are commonly held in the dry season and require large-scale, village-wide preparations of food and drink, ritual materials, and work on the tomb and the statuary. The wealthier, more prominent, or more important the deceased, the bigger the ceremony will be. Guests come from the surrounding area and much farther in the case of an important funeral. For three days people eat and drink, animals are sacrificed and rituals are performed, drums and gongs are played. The activities include a dance of farewell in which everyone forms a circle and dances in single file slowly around the tomb to say good-bye to soul of the deceased. Although the bones of the dead are not excavated, the ceremony is a decisive point of transition. The soul is believed to leave the grave for good, the mourning period is ended, and the tomb is abandoned forever; the wooden roof, fence, and statues eventually decay and collapse.

The statues that are carved and erected for the tomb abandonment ceremony are diverse. They include carvings of birds, animals, and people, and those of people are clothed in modern as well as traditional dress, including military uniforms and western attire. Many are of people doing ordinary things, such as women pounding rice and men playing gongs. Some statues are intended to be amusing, others serious. Several traditional kinds of figures are particularly common and striking. One involves the so-called Hokker motif that is common in Southeast Asia. This is a carving of a squatting man or woman with elbows resting on knees and head resting on hands, in this case said to be showing a grieving mourner at the tomb. Others are of pregnant women and of men and women preparing to copulate or engaged in doing so. While the prominent place given to explicitly erotic statuary in a mortuary ceremony seems out of place, it is not. It is accounted for in two ways. When the meaning of these statues was first explained to me in a Bahnar village in Vietnam, it was suggested that their purpose was to provide an amusing distraction in an otherwise sad situation. While this may be so, the traditional meaning also includes fertility, for the female figures are usually carved with swollen stomachs, and fertility is in keeping with the belief that the souls of the dead will eventually return into one or another of their descendants.

NOTES

1. How a person dies is not believed to be the only criterion that can determine the place of residence in the afterlife. Sometimes different types of people are supposed to be sorted out as well; shamans are sometimes mentioned in this regard.

2. Some Southeast Asian peoples believe that bad death can be put to put to magical uses. In Malaysia the license plate numbers of vehicles involved in fatal accidents are regarded as likely sources of winning lottery numbers. Similarly, among Malays in the east coast peninsular Malaysian state of Kelantan people believe that oil rendered from the body of a murdered person (*minyat mati bunoh*) is a potent medicine for those who engage in sorcery.

REFERENCES AND FURTHER READING

Alexiou, Margaret. 1974. *The Ritual Lament in Greek Tradition*. Cambridge: Cambridge University Press.

Child, Alice B., and Irvin L. Child. 1993. *Religion and Magic in the Life of Traditional Peoples*. Englewood Cliffs, N.J.: Prentice-Hall.

Chung, Sue Fawn, and Pricilla Wegars, eds. 2005. *Chinese American Death Rituals: Respecting the Ancestors*. Walnut Creek, Calif.: AltaMira.

Crumrine, N. Ross, and Alan Morinis, eds. 1991. *Pilgrimage in Latin America*. New York: Greenwood.

Driver, Harold E. 1961. *Indians of North America*. Chicago: University of Chicago Press.

Dubisch, Jill. 1995. *In a Different Place: Pilgrimage, Gender, and Politics at a Greek Island Shrine*. Princeton: Princeton University Press.

Eade, John, and Michael J. Sallnow, eds. 1991. *Contesting the Sacred: The Anthropology of Christian Pilgrimage*. London: Routledge.

Eickelman, Dale. 1990. *Muslim Travelers: Pilgrimage, Migration, and the Religious Imagination*. Berkeley: University of California Press.

Hertz, Robert. [1907] 1960. *Death and the Right Hand*. Glencoe, Ill.: Free Press.

Hudson, Alfred B. 1966. "Death Ceremonies of the Padju Epat Ma'anyan Dayaks." *Sarawak Museum Journal* 13: 341–416.

Hultkrantz, Åke. [1967] 1979. *The Religions of the American Indians*. Berkeley: University of California Press.

Metcalf, Peter. 1982. *A Borneo Journey into Death: Berawan Eschatology from Its Rituals*. Philadelphia: University of Pennsylvania Press.

Metcalf, Peter, and Richard Huntington. [1979] 1991. *Celebrations of Death: The Anthropology of Mortuary Ritual*. Cambridge: Cambridge University Press.

Nguyen Van Ku and Luu Hung. 2003. *Funeral Houses in the Central Highlands of Vietnam*. Hanoi: Gioi Publishers.

Rousseau, Jérôme. 1998. *Kayan Religion: Ritual Life and Religious Reform in Central Borneo*. Leiden: KITLV Press.

Sallnow, Michael J. 1987. *Pilgrimage in the Andes: Regional Cults in Cusco*. Washington, D.C.: Smithsonian Institution Press.

Schiller, Anne. 1997. *Small Sacrifices: Religious Change, and Cultural Identity among the Ngaju of Indonesia*. New York: Oxford University Press.

Smith, William Robertson. [1889] 1901. *Lectures on the Religion of the Semites*. London: Adam and Charles Black.

Symonds, Patricia V. 2004. *Calling in the Soul: Gender and the Cycle of Life in a Hmong Village*. Seattle: University of Washington Press.

Taylor, Timothy. 2002. *The Buried Soul: How Humans Invented Death*. Boston: Beacon.

Turner, Victor W. 1969. *The Ritual Process: Structure and Anti-Structure*. Chicago: Aldine.

Turner, Victor, and Edith L. B. Turner. 1978. *Image and Pilgrimage in Christian Culture*. New York: Columbia University Press.

van Gennep, Arnold. [1909] 1960. *The Rites of Passage*. Chicago: University of Chicago Press.

Wallace, Anthony F. C. 1966. *Religion: An Anthropological View*. New York: Random House.

8

⋞∕∂

Witchcraft and Sorcery: Past and Present, Far and Near

Although there is no unanimity regarding the exact scholarly meaning of witchcraft and sorcery, these terms are widely taken to involve beliefs that some persons are capable of destroying, harming, or controlling others through mystical or supernatural means. Anthropologists assume that witchcraft and sorcery are things attributed to people who will seldom freely admit to them and who do not see themselves and their beliefs and practices in this way. Many anthropologists have gone further and assumed that witchcraft involves beliefs (about witches and what witches can do) that are impossible; therefore all that can ever be studied are rumors, gossip and accusation, and the things done to discover and deal with suspected witches or sorcerers. Bear in mind also that when anthropologists speak of witches they have in mind real persons who are believed to have a supernatural dimension to their personality, rather than beings that are simply believed to be spirits or demons.

A further problem with discussing witchcraft and sorcery has arisen recently. The assumption that witches and witchcraft are necessarily conceived to be evil has been challenged by modern-day practitioners who identify themselves as witches, Wiccans, pagans, neo-pagans, or magicians, who practice more or less openly and who deny they are doing harm, supernaturally or otherwise, to others or themselves. As a result, some anthropologists have sought to broaden the traditional definition of witchcraft to include not only the beliefs and processes noted above but also those of the modern self-proclaimed practitioners of witchcraft or ancient religion. In any case, at the level of explanation, witchcraft in all forms has been interpreted in the same range of social, psychological, symbolic, and other ways that have been applied to religious beliefs and practices in general.[1]

In this chapter we shall consider witchcraft and sorcery from the perspective of three separate but related topics or projects. These include first the ethnographic study of such beliefs and practices in traditional and modernizing small-scale societies or in local peasant communities. The locus classicus of such studies has been Africa, but they have involved other regions of the world as well. Most of these studies have concerned developing or Third World peoples. The cumulative effect therefore is to give the impression that traditional witchcraft and sorcery are limited to such populations, at least in the present. However, at least one important study of witchcraft has been published that concerns traditional malevolent mystical beliefs and practices among Western European populations. This is Jeanne Favret-Saada's *Deadly Words: Witchcraft in the Bocage* (1981).

The second project has involved the study of witchcraft in Europe and its colonies in the late medieval and early modern period (roughly the fifteenth through the seventeenth centuries) in association with what is usually referred to as the witchcraze or the great witch hunt. The witchcraze— the large-scale, fanatical search for and vicious persecution of alleged witches—has been mainly left to historians. However, anthropologists such as Alan Macfarlane (1970) have done specific historical studies, while others discussed below have attempted to contribute to the understanding of what (if anything) really occurred in the way of witchcraft and of how it may be explained. Anthropology (especially that of Evans-Prichard) has had an influence on how some historians have approached the topic.

The third project has been the study of the modern witchcraft religious movements in America, England, and other present-day Western societies. The study of modern witchcraft has involved anthropologists, sociologists, and other researchers who focus on new religions and religious movements.

TRADITIONAL WITCHCRAFT AND
SORCERY IN SMALL-SCALE SOCIETIES

Bird Flu and Witchcraft in Contemporary Cambodia

A recent newspaper account illustrates much conventional thinking about traditional witchcraft and sorcery and its context. On November 3, 2005, a story appeared on the front page of the *New York Times* under the headline "Poverty and Superstition Hinder Drive to Block Bird Flu at Source" (Bradsher 2005). The story told of a recent episode in a village in Cambodia involving a possible outbreak of bird flu. Half-starved chickens began to die, and then village children developed fevers as well. Some villagers took their sick children to a government clinic where they were diagnosed with human influenza, but other villagers believed the problem was "witchcraft." They blamed the only resident of the village not born there, a fifty-three-year-old woman who had married a local man and moved in eight years before. One day, after her husband had gone to the forest, the woman was brutally killed. A village man, who had been delegated to do so and later paid the equivalent of $30 donated by grateful neighbors, came to her house and, as she was cooking rice on the dirt floor, grabbed her hair, pulled her head back, and slit her throat with a machete, almost cutting her head off. The story had first been told in a local newspaper article about sorcery. The killer, who was surprised to have been reported to the police, was arrested and sentenced to fifteen to twenty years in prison. The neighbors who had paid the killer were not (after making further payments to the police) prosecuted. One villager (identified as not among those who had paid for the execution) said no one really knew the cause of the illness but that things had improved since the woman had been killed. The illness stopped and everyone became happy again. The story was accompanied by color photos of the village and several villagers.

The purpose of the story was to show how and why it would be difficult to control the spread of bird flu in places like Cambodia. But it is hard not to believe that what got the story on the front page was not in large part the villagers' attribution of supernatural evil to the woman and her slaying. After all, as far as bird flu is concerned, the episode turned out to be a false alarm. The chickens may have been sick, but they did not have the H5N1 virus. Indeed, without the sorcery or witchcraft and the killing, there would probably not have been a story at all. The story also fits with our assumption that witchcraft is exotic. The incident took place in a far-off Third World place that already had a well-known reputation for killing.

Several things in the story stand out. One is that the person blamed and executed was a woman, and another is that the woman was an outsider who had moved into the village after marrying a local man, and who therefore presumably lacked blood relatives who might have protected her. Less obviously, the story uses the terms "sorcery" and "witchcraft" interchangeably, as if these words mean the same thing. The story does not report the word in Khmer—the Cambodian language—that the villagers might have used to describe what they thought had occurred.

Anthropologists make a traditional (although not uniform) distinction between sorcery and witchcraft that goes as follows: sorcery is simply black magic—ritual activity aimed at harming, controlling, or influencing other persons in mystical ways. It can be done by anyone who has the means of doing it and the inclination to do so. It exists insofar as people attempt to practice or counteract it, although whether or not people actually practice sorcery, or simply believe that others do so, is again not easy to establish. Witchcraft, on the other hand, involves the belief that some persons are *inherently* evil in a way that can cause harm to others through psychic means, even without necessarily intending to do so. Witches may be believed to be evil as a result of being born so or as a result of having become so as, for example, with the European Christian notion of becoming a witch by making a pact with the devil. Witches may or may not be believed to engage in deliberate efforts to cause harm. While the notion of witchcraft implies deliberate activity (such as holding sabbats and making witch's brew), the harm done others can also be passive.

If this classic distinction is applied to the Cambodian woman who was killed, the implication of the story is that she was believed to be a witch. There is no mention in the account that anyone believed she performed rituals intended to make anyone's chickens or children sick or to cause any other sort of harm in the village. The story implies that the villagers believed that her mere presence was enough to cause trouble. Possibly the villagers believed that she engaged in black magic and this was left out of the newspaper story but, as it is, it would seem she was regarded as a witch in the passive sense. Although a clear distinction between witchcraft and sorcery of the sort noted above does not always hold up well in comparative terms, the notion that some persons have inherent malevolent spiritual qualities—or that they bring bad luck—is widespread.

The Azande and Other African Groups

In anthropology as in other fields, what scholars think about a topic or problem can be strongly influenced by particular studies. Such studies are frequently discussed and used as examples. They become paradigms for several possible reasons. One is that they were carried out at an early point in the development of the field; another is that the phenomenon in question tends to be particularly well developed or important in the particular society or region concerned; and a third is that the account produced by the ethnographer is written in particularly clear, convincing, and vivid terms with telling examples. Malinowski's study of magic among the Trobriand Islanders of Melanesia is one such prominent example. It has survived long after his more general functionalist theoretical approach declined. It has given us the generalization that magic is not a substitute for rational effort but rather something that is likely to be used as a supplement to it in situations where outcomes are both important and uncertain or beyond complete human control.

Regarding witchcraft in small-scale societies, the defining case is unquestionably Evans-Prichard's study of the Azande, a central African people of the present-day southern Sudan and northern Congo. Evans-Prichard lived and studied witchcraft and related beliefs and practices among the Azande in the late 1920s, and his account was first published in 1937 (an abridged edition is still in print). At the time of his fieldwork, although the execution of convicted witches was no longer permitted, witchcraft beliefs and practices were otherwise ongoing and very common. By the 1980s these Azande had converted to Christianity though they had not abandoned their belief in witchcraft or the practice of making accusations, holding trials, and using oracles to establish guilt or innocence.[2]

As believed and practiced at the time of Evans-Prichard's study, Azande witchcraft had a number of characteristics. It was recognized as a distinct realm of activity and referred to as *mangu*, a term that Evans-Prichard had no hesitation in translating as witchcraft. *Mangu* was frequently and publicly discussed and acted on, and therefore easy to study. Indeed, Evans-Prichard stressed that the topic could not be avoided by anyone living in a Zande village. Witchcraft was a common explanation for misfortune including illness, accidents, crop failure, losses, miscarriages, and death, although talking about it, attempting to diagnose it, combat or punish it was not the same thing as practicing it, which was a matter of secrecy. Both men and women were thought to be witches but witchcraft worked differently according to gender. While it was believed that either men or women could bewitch men, it was held that only women could bewitch women. This might suggest that men were more likely to be bewitched than women, but Evans-Prichard does not say that this is so, and it was countered to some extent by the belief that all death was supposed to be the result of witchcraft (or sorcery). While the Azande thought at that time that only individuals practiced witchcraft, they also believed that group-based rituals could sometimes take place. These included a group of witches sitting around a pot cooking and eating human flesh.

For the Azande, witchcraft was based on an inherent characteristic, specifically a physical substance in the body of the witch, located in the area of the stomach. The Azande also thought that the witchcraft substance was inherited—among men from the father and among women from the mother. It was also supposed to grow over the course of life, so it was small in children and very large in older persons. But while the Azande believed that witchcraft was based on an inherent characteristic in the witch, it was also thought to harm to other persons only by the deliberate action of the witch. They supposed such efforts were motivated by jealousy and hatred. At least this was the general Azande view; in actuality persons accused of witchcraft and found guilty through the use of an oracle, might claim that any harm done was inadvertent rather than deliberate. In any case, a witchcraft attack was also believed to have a physical dimension. It was a force that passed through space in the form of a spot of light that moved rapidly from the witch to the victim. This light could be seen at night.

The Azande at the time of Evans-Prichard's study believed witchcraft to be dangerous and sometimes deadly. They discussed it openly and tried to prevent or counteract it by the use of magic. If they believed someone might have been bewitched they would consult oracles (especially the poison oracle) to learn if it was the cause of whatever was wrong and, if so, who was to blame. People did this by seeking the help of a witch doctor, whose specialty was to diagnose and take appropriate measures. If the person who did the bewitching could be persuaded to nullify it by the ritual of blowing out water, the harm might be canceled. The person who had been accused could be brought before the village court. If someone was believed to have died of witchcraft, the goal was to learn who was responsible and exact revenge. Those who had been harmed, including the family members of someone killed by witchcraft, could take punitive measures or demand compensation. Although convicted witches could previously be executed, this required the agreement of the local prince or king. Such permission was usually given only in instances of repeated offenses. By the time of Evans-Prichard's fieldwork, only lesser forms of retaliation or compensation could be pursued. In any case, alleged witches were not punished simply for being witches but for specific attacks against other persons.

The Azande also believed in sorcery, which they clearly distinguished from witchcraft, except insofar as both were considered harmful. Witchcraft was thought to be a purely psychic act requiring neither a spell, the manipulation of objects, nor the use of substances (medicines). Sorcery, by contrast, was a form of magic. But it was bad magic or medicine and therefore clearly distinguished from good or neutral forms of magic. Sorcery was also thought to be deadly and in actuality was more feared than witchcraft because its effects were assumed to work more quickly and violently and to be more difficult to counter. Azande princes who did not worry about being attacked by witchcraft did fear sorcery. Also, unlike witchcraft, sorcery was not discussed openly, and people were generally unwilling to accuse others of practicing it. In addition to sorcery aimed at killing or physically injuring someone, there were also forms that could cause other types of harm, including keeping a hunter from finding or killing game.

As noted, by the time of Evans-Prichard's fieldwork the British colonial regime in the Sudan had banned the execution of witches. This was a common colonial practice throughout Africa, according to the Africanist anthropologist Lucy Mair (1969: 157). She concludes that it is not possible to know with any certainty how common it was to execute witches in the precolonial period but does not think that it was actually frequent, and that lesser forms of punishment (such as banishment and the payment of fines) were more common. Also, as among the Azande, the general African practice was to take action only against persons who were accused of harming others through witchcraft. Individuals might be considered to be witches and gossiped about as such, but being a witch was itself not a crime. At the same time, colonial governments in some areas of Africa, in addition to forbidding the killing of convicted witches, outlawed accusations of witchcraft or sorcery altogether and made the conviction of such accusations punishable by imprisonment, because they thought the accusations themselves could cause serious harm. Africans tended to think that witchcraft and sorcery increased after it became illegal to deal with persons believed to engage in witchcraft and sorcery in traditional ways (Mair 1969: 161).

Anthropological observers have also supposed that natives' concerns or fright about witchcraft and sorcery had probably increased as a result of changes brought about by colonialism. These changes included the destabilizing effects of the introduction of capitalism, wage labor, migration, urbanization, advancement based on education, and the undermining of the authority of chiefs and elders. Colonialism also brought the introduction of Christianity based on the efforts of European missionaries and the prestige of Western technology, wealth, and culture. Like secular colonial authority, European missionary Christianity was not sympathetic to African concerns about witchcraft and sorcery and traditional ways of dealing with them. The introduction of Christianity often led to the development of new syncretic religious movements. In contrast to orthodox mission Christianity, the new religious movements addressed fears and suspicions about witchcraft and sorcery. Some movements were led by persons who claimed to be adept at detecting witches and offered protection against mystical forms of attack (Mair 1969: 164).

In the most recent period, the afflictions that have devastated some regions of Africa have sometimes been explained along traditional lines as consequences of witchcraft. It is not surprising that infection by AIDS should be explained in mystical terms in the same way that older forms of affliction have been. It is also not surprising that the outcome of soccer matches should also often provoke suspicions or accusations of witchcraft or sorcery, especially insofar as notions of mystical causation in modern sports are widespread in the world.

The Navajo

Witchcraft and sorcery have often been reported among various New World peoples. For North America, Clyde Kluckhohn's (1962) study of witchcraft among the Navajo has been the classic case, although it has not had the defining significance of Evans-Prichard's study of the Azande. The Navajo live in the American Southwest and are a part of a larger culture area identified as Southwestern that also includes the Pueblo peoples, the Apache, and other groups. The region is marked by a history of contact, conflict, and colonial domination and influence that extends back to the early sixteenth century, first by the Spanish and then by the Americans who subdued and confined the Navajo to what became the largest reservation in the United States.

Kluckhohn studied Navajo witchcraft at about the same time as Evans-Prichard did fieldwork among the Azande, although he did so in a series of shorter lengths of field time over a longer period. While witchcraft was not the only thing that Kluckhohn studied and wrote about concerning the Navajo, he regarded it as one of the key dimensions of Navajo social organization and culture and pursued it deliberately and systematically. If he had not made such an effort he would not have found much out, for unlike witchcraft among the Azande, it was not visible at the surface of Navajo life. Unlike Evans-Prichard, who learned a great deal about Zande sorcery through participant observation in daily life (engaging in gossip, watching oracles being consulted, listening to public accusations and trials, seeing witch doctors in action), Kluckhohn relied on formal and informal interviews. This was because nearly everything involving Navajo witchcraft was done in secret or at least out of public view, including action against alleged witches that could involve torture to obtain a confession (this being considered necessary to save or cure the victim) and/or execution. Kluckhohn stressed that getting information about witchcraft from Navajo informants was not difficult, if an investigator knew how to go about it and had established relationships of trust or, better yet, real friendship, built up over a period of time. He ultimately accumulated a large body of information in terms of persons interviewed and instances of witchcraft and sorcery learned about. He does not always make a clear distinction between what was believed or practiced in the past and what was current at the time of his study.

The circumstances of Navajo witchcraft differ from those of the Azande in other ways as well. Except for the colonial government's ban of the execution of persons found to be witches, Evans-Prichard hardly mentions outside influences and describes Azande beliefs and practices as though they were traditional and unchanged. In contrast, Kluckhohn stresses non-Navajo influences on the culture of Navajo witchcraft. He suggests, for example, that one of the reasons the Navajo were secretive about witchcraft around whites and reluctant to admit to believing in witches was that they were aware that most whites thought that witchcraft beliefs and practices were backward superstition and looked down on the Navajo for such things.

The Navajo recognized distinct kinds of activity that Kluckhohn classes as types of witchcraft. They have separate terms for these various practices but lack a common term or phrase for all of them, although one form seems to Kluckhohn to be very similar to the European notion of witchcraft. Kluckhohn translates each of these terms or phrases and uses them as technical terms but does not try to justify putting them all in his common category of "witchcraft." Nor does he make an effort to distinguish witchcraft from sorcery or discuss whether the Navajo themselves make any such distinction, although it would seem that they do not.

Witchcraft among the Navajo and the neighboring Pueblo groups also raises the question of outside influence. The Southwesternist anthropologist Elsie Clews Parsons attempted to sort out Spanish and indigenous elements in the witchcraft beliefs and practices of the Zuni that presumably would also cover other Pueblo groups as well. She concluded that while Zuni witchcraft undoubtedly has roots in pre-Hispanic traditions of sorcery, its development into true witchcraft can be attributed to Spanish influences (Parsons 1927). As for the Navajo, there are similarities (such as the importance of confessions and the use of torture to obtain them) between their witchcraft notions and practices and those of late medieval and early modern Europe. Further, the Spanish presence in the Southwest substantially overlaps the later part of the period of the witchcraze in Europe, and the Spanish did prosecute and execute witches in the region. In the case of the Navajo, such influence would have been mainly or entirely indirect, that is, via the Pueblos, but probably can't be ruled out of the question. At the beginning of his account, Kluckhohn states that he has no information bearing on possible Spanish influence on Navajo witchcraft but returns to it at several points later on and also alludes to similarities to and possible influences of the Pueblos.

Witchcraft in Melanesia and Southeast Asia

Outside of Africa, Europe, and parts of the New World, witchcraft has been noted especially in Melanesia. The idea that witchcraft is associated with something physical in the body of the witch that has already been noted for the Azande also occurs in New Guinea. Here, however, the physical thing is intrusive. According to a recent account by Pamela Stewart and Andrew Strathern (2004: 114–15) of witchcraft beliefs among one group in the Mount Hagen area, this takes the form of little witch stones that jump out of streams and lodge in the throats of people who have come to drink water after greedily consuming too much pork at a pig feast. There had also been earlier beliefs in this area about people becoming cannibal witches by drinking water that had been infected by human flesh put into it by other witches. In another area of New Guinea the intrusive thing that was thought to cause people to become witches was a small snake-like creature that entered the body and lived in the abdomen, thereby enabling the person so invaded to mystically kill others. Such ideas seem similar to the classic Western notion of the incubus.

In contrast to Melanesia, relatively little note has been taken of "true" witchcraft among Asian peoples. In Southeast Asia, for example, where beliefs and practices of magic and sorcery are certainly well developed, true witchcraft seems to be of less significance (Ellen 1998), the recent instance of witchcraft and bird flu in Cambodia discussed above notwithstanding. The Island of Bali—the only remaining center of historical Hinduism in Southeast Asia—is one exception. Here witches or *leyak* are well-known figures in mythology and ritual drama (Covarubias 1937: 321–57, Bateson and Mead 1942: 28–34; 164–71). Such witches seem be often regarded by the Balinese mainly as spirits or demons instead of evil humans with supernatural powers. The Balinese also appear to believe that real humans can be and are witches, but much less seems to be known about these than about the distinctly mythical and theatrical versions. Witchcraft accusations involving executions have also been very recently reported for Java as well, though without reference to a possible difference between witchcraft and sorcery (Siegel 2006).

WITCHCRAFT IN LATE MEDIEVAL
AND EARLY MODERN EUROPE

While anthropologists have studied witchcraft mainly in small-scale societies of Africa and elsewhere, Westerners in general are likely to think of it in regard to the Europe of several centuries ago. It is to this place and time that the current popular symbols of witchcraft—the pointed black hats, kettles of witch's brew, and broomsticks of Halloween—all hearken back. The study of witchcraft in late medieval and early modern Europe involves a different sort of project from the one concerning non-Western societies. The study of the latter has been largely an anthropological endeavor, based on participant-observation fieldwork and interviews with persons with firsthand knowledge. The study of European witchcraft in the past has been a historical effort based on written sources and mainly limited to the records produced by the Inquisition and other efforts to find witches, and by the trials of alleged witches.

As noted earlier, one of the problems with the study of witchcraft and sorcery is learning what—if anything—really takes place, rather than what other people *think* takes place and what they do on the basis of such beliefs or suspicions. The problem of knowing what people really practice in the way of witchcraft or sorcery is especially difficult in the case of the

European witchcraze because what did or did not occur is several centuries or more in the past. It is not possible to conduct participant observation of the sort carried out by Evans-Prichard among the Azande or to interview informants in the way that Kluckhohn did among the Navajo. There are transcripts of trials, records of inquisitions, and other written information that show what people were accused or convicted of doing rather than what they really did. Most of the persons who confessed to witchcraft did so as a result of torture or other forms of coercion. And of those who gave accounts voluntarily, there are other reasons to question their reliability, at least as records of what actually took place. Insanity and/or hallucinations have long been suspected. Accusations by others and circumstantial evidence such as "devil marks" found on the bodies of suspected witches played an important role in trials and convictions, but such evidence cannot be reexamined today.

To oversimplify somewhat, two lines of interpretation have tended to dominate scholarly thought about European witchcraft. One is that little or nothing took place in the way of witchcraft or sorcery, making it necessary to sharply distinguish witchcraft from the witchcraze as two entirely different things. The other line of interpretation is that beliefs and accusations about witchcraft practices were not exactly baseless, but that what took place was really either (1) something other than witchcraft or (2) something that was "imagined" (or hallucinated) by confessed witches.

Organized Witchcraft Did Not Exist

Let us begin with the first line of thought, which is that witchcraft practices or activities (at least of the sort of which peoples were accused and frequently convicted and executed) had no basis in reality. This line of interpretation has been pursued by historians rather than anthropologists, but understanding it as background is useful; it has probably been the dominant scholarly view of the witchcraze since the Enlightenment. This view has been propounded in the recent period especially by the historians Hugh Trevor-Roper and Norman Cohn. What these scholars deny is not only the obviously supernatural activities attributed to witches (such as flying on broomsticks or copulating with the devil) but also the existence of organized activities of any sort, as opposed to possible individual efforts at magic or sorcery; they deny that groups of people ever met for collective activities involving devil worship, black masses, or other communal witchcraft practices. For such scholars, what is interesting and important is not witchcraft but rather the belief in witchcraft by the church and state and its prosecution on a large scale—the witchcraze. And one thing that is significant about the witchcraze is its timing. For Trevor-Roper it is one of those interesting lessons that show history does not move in a straight line of improvement. As he explains it, the witchcraze did not occur when European civilization had supposedly reached a low point (the so-called Dark Ages) but rather when things were rapidly improving. It coincided with the decline of feudalism, the occurrence of Renaissance, the development of modern science, the beginning of capitalism, the discovery of the New World and sea routes to India and China, and the creation of European overseas empires and the growth of world trade and urbanization. In other words, the historical context of the witchcraze was not one of traditional backwardness and stability, but of growth and—in many realms at least—of what we like to think of as progress and cultural florescence:

> [In] the Dark Ages there was at least no witch-craze. There were witch beliefs, of course—a scattered folk-lore of peasant superstition: the casting of spells, the making of storms, converse with spirits, sympathetic magic. Such beliefs are universal in time and place . . . I am concerned with the organized, systematic "demonology" which the medieval Church constructed out of those beliefs and which, in the sixteenth and seventeenth centuries, acquired a terrible momentum of its own . . . we have to admit that the Church of the Dark Age did its best to disperse these relics of paganism which the Church of the Middle Ages would afterwards exploit. (Trevor-Roper 1969: 91)

This explanation of European witch-hunting is probably the most familiar today. The witchcraze, with its many prosecutions and executions, is thought to be based on fantasy and political paranoia, and therefore the persons—mainly women—who were tortured, tried, condemned, and executed were innocent victims, at least of the supernatural practices of which they were accused. Such explanations link the witchcraze to various developments. They hold that it was a reaction to troubling change, the Reformation, and other external developments, including the plagues and the spread of a highly virulent form of syphilis (possibly from the New World), famines, and displacements of the time. Trevor-Roper further asserts that the witchcraze of the sixteenth and seventeenth centuries is analogous to the anti-Semitism of nineteenth- and twentieth-century Europe, and the anticommunist extremism of the early 1950s in the United States, as the popular political term "witch hunt" suggests. If he were writing today he would probably note certain parallels with present-day attitudes and practices regarding terrorism, as other scholars have begun to point out (Stewart and Strathern 2004: 195).

Witchcraft Was Actually Class Struggle

The other line of thought has been that European witchcraft at the time of the witchcraze was something very real, but also very different from what those who created and perpetuated the witchcraze thought or claimed it was. Here there have been three sorts of explanations. First, witchcraft was really incipient class struggle; second, witchcraft was really the perpetuation of pre-Christian European religion among the common folk; third, witchcraft accounts were the result of hallucinations or delusions produced by psychotropic substances.

The argument that organized witchcraft was really an expression of class conflict goes back to the nineteenth century. It was promulgated by the Frenchman Jules Michelet in a book titled *La sorcière* and published in 1862 (Cohn 1974: 30–31). Michelet argued that witchcraft was a justified but hopeless expression of the struggle by medieval serfs against the nobility, making witchcraft in France a sort of precursor to the French Revolution. He interpreted the witch's sabbat as an occasion at which peasants came together at night to perform both ancient dances and satirical farces directed against oppressive lords and priests. While such things were going on as early as the twelfth and thirteenth centuries, by the fourteenth, when both the Church and the nobility were losing credit, the witch cults hardened into a ritual defiance of the social order (as epitomized by the Christian God) and took the form of what Michelet called "the Black Mass."

Another notable feature of Michelet's theory is that he put at the center of the witchcraft cult not a male devil but a priestess—specifically a female serf in her thirties. This priestess induces the peasants to give food for the communal meal, thus drawing them into the conspiracy, and she sets up a giant wooden figure of the devil with horns and a great penis. This is Satan imagined as the great serf in revolt but also as a nature god who makes the plants grow. The priestess ritually mates with Satan at the sabbat, sitting on his lap and simulating copulation, thereby receiving his spirit. Later she turns herself into an altar at which a man disguised as a demon makes offerings to Satan to promote a good harvest. And finally the priestess shouts in defiance at the Christian God and a horde of demons rushes out and jumps over fires to encourage the peasants to get over their fear of hellfire. All of this is a fantasy, according to Cohn (1974: 30), that has no basis in contemporary accounts—all of these were instead a matter of collective imagination and forced confession.

Witchcraft Was Pre-Christian Religion

The most important and widely accepted theory of the alternate nature of European witchcraft is that it was a disguised version of pre-Christian religion. The modern scholarly version of this thesis was developed especially in two books published in the first part of the twentieth century by Margaret Murray, but the argument in one form or another is much older.

According to Cohn (1974: 28–29), the argument can be traced to German scholars, one of whom included it in his comments about the records of a seventeenth-century witch trial. The specific assertion was that witchcraft was above all a nature religion that had once been the religion of all pre-Christian Germans. After the conversion to Christianity this nature religion survived among the common people but was condemned by the church as devil worship and therefore was practiced in secret. As Christianity spread among the common people, so did the notion that the old religion was devil worship but, because it was believed to be vital as a means of influencing nature, it was nonetheless retained. However, it also came to be assumed that anyone practicing devil worship would also use the rituals of witchcraft to harm others.

Margaret Murray's twentieth-century version of the argument was propounded in her books *The Witch-Cult of Western Europe* (1921) and *The God of the Witches* (1931). Murray was a respected Egyptologist and held a faculty position the University of London. Like many intellectuals and scholars of the time, she had been strongly influenced by James Frazer's *The Golden Bough*, which "launched a cult of fertility cults." Frazer's general idea, as elaborated at length in twelve volumes, was that many different kinds of later rituals were derivative of magic once performed to enhance the reproduction of plants and animals. Murray's argument became widely known and generally accepted by the public in the middle decades of the twentieth century, as a result of her books and other publications that included the main entry for witchcraft in successive editions of the *Encyclopedia Britannica* over a forty-year period.

Murray's interpretation of European witchcraft goes as follows. Down to the seventeenth century a pre-Christian religion persisted throughout Europe and included followers from all levels of society, from royalty to peasantry. The core belief involved a two-faced horned deity. First shown in Upper Paleolithic cave art, this god later became the Roman god Dianus (or Janus). In Europe he was the god of fertility, crops, and the seasons, and therefore thought of as periodically dying and being reborn. At the village level the god took the form of the horned being who presided over the witches' assemblies. With the Reformation and the Inquisition, the village incarnation of the horned god came to be viewed by local opponents and hostile religious authorities as the devil, so that witchcraft appeared to be a form of Satan worship. The witch's sabbat was a real weekly meeting held for practical ritual purposes, including the promotion of fertility in crops, animals, and humans, the curing of the sick, and the harming of enemies through black magic. People did not fly through the air on broomsticks but walked to the meetings. The devil's marks referred in the witch trials were in actuality tattoos of the sort commonly applied by pre-Christian European peoples (Murray 1970: 100).

Figure 8.1. A drawing of a cave image from Les Trois Frères cave in the French Pyrenees, offered as evidence by Margaret Murray in *The God of the Witches* that the devil of medieval Christian witchcraft belief was really a pre-Christian horned deity that can be traced to the Paleolithic.

In sum, according to Murray, all of the various beliefs and practices attributed to witches and the practice of witchcraft in medieval and early-modern Europe can be explained in one way or another as the survival of an ancient pre-Christian religion. This ancient religion, moreover, was like that of the Greeks and Romans and many other peoples. While not evil in nature, it was not associated with a moral code concerned with relationships among humans. This was the true folk religion of Europe. At least until the Reformation, Christianity was only a veneer, especially where the rural masses were concerned.

Murray's thesis also encompasses the broader ethnological history of
Europe. Here she argues that the perpetuation of the cult of the horned
god of fertility was the effort of an aboriginal race of small people who
had been driven into marginal areas by successive invasions from the
east. These little people lived in remote areas of Great Britain, Ireland, and
continental Europe, practiced animal pastoralism, and dwelt in small
round houses. They are the reality behind the fairies, goblins, elves, and
dwarfs of European folklore and folk religion. Because of what has happened to fairies in recent European folklore and Western popular culture
in general, we are inclined to overlook their earlier link with witchcraft.
(During the witchcraze witches were thought to be closely associated
with fairies; indeed, involvement with fairies was a crucial diagnostic feature of witchcraft, enough to have a person condemned and executed.) It
was the shy and elusive original inhabitants of Europe who passed on
their religion to the later arrivals who became the witches of medieval and
later periods (Murray 1970: 46–56).

While long enjoying some academic respect and a lot of popular appeal,
Murray's explanation of the nature of European witchcraft was eventually
attacked as highly improbable. No one denied that many pre-Christian
European religious traditions (e.g., those surrounding Christmas and
Easter) survived to become Christian ones. Folklorists, anthropologists,
and historians have been pointing out such syncretism for a long period
and it is still accepted. But the possibility or likelihood that a whole religion based on pagan European gods that were worshiped down to the
time of the Reformation was a different matter. How, it was asked, could
Christian authorities have overlooked the widespread existence of such a
popular cult for more than a thousand years before attempting to expose
it, label it as heresy and devil worship, and destroy it?

Lucy Mair, an anthropologist and a specialist on African witchcraft,
concludes that Murray's thesis does not fit at all with what anthropologists have learned about witchcraft and religion. Murray argues that European witchcraft was not really witchcraft at all but was only labeled and
opposed as such by the Church. Mair counters this with the assertion that
the beliefs evidently held by ordinary Europeans during the period of the
witchcraze as well as the sorts of accusations made by such persons at the
time are similar to those widely documented for African societies. In both
Europe and Africa, witchcraft, in addition to being a way of dealing with
evil in the world, reflected the tensions and conflicts of social life in the often difficult circumstances of village society.

But if so, why did the church and civil authorities not get involved with
prosecuting alleged witches until a late phase of Christian European history? Her answer is similar to the explanation offered by historians like
Trevor-Roper—that the historical circumstances of the late medieval and

early modern period (plagues, the Reformation, and so forth) caused the witchcraze. Mair suggests that the church (both Catholic and Protestant versions) became convinced of the reality and danger of witchcraft as a result of the increased religious complexity and turmoil of Europe. In situations of religious complexity, in which organized religions compete for power and the loyalty of followers, heresy becomes a matter of great importance and the tendency is to demonize the competing or minority religion. Such tendencies to demonize competing religions involve the universal fantasy attributes of the witch, such as the ritual murder of children and the use of their body parts for cannibal feasts and sorcery. In the early history of Christianity, when Christians were a minority within Judaism, they were accused by traditional Jews of such practices, while in a later phase, in which Jews became a minority in European society, the accusation was turned around (Mair 1969: 226–32).

Witchcraft Beliefs, Experiences, and Hallucinations

If organized witchcraft did not really exist, and if some of the things that witches confessed to doing were impossible, then these were matters of fantasy and imagination. If this were the case, how did such bizarre beliefs and accounts originate? One possibility is that they were hallucinations brought on by the effects of psychotropic (mind-altering) substances that were incorporated into the human body in one way or another. The ingestion of such substances could have been deliberate or accidental, and if deliberate it could have been either because the visions were desired or because the materials involved were taken as medicine for pain relief or some other healing purpose.

The historian Norman Cohn (1974:38) treats the hallucinogenic explanation of witchcraft in the same way he does other recent interpretations— as tendencies to look at the past through the lens of the present. In this instance, the 1960s hallucinogenic experiences, including both those involving traditional plants, especially peyote, and the newly created chemical ones, namely, LSD, came into vogue among hippies, artists, folk musicians, political dissidents, and antiwar activists and students. The popular cultural interests and practices involving hallucinogens also had a counterpart in science and scholarship. This included an interest in the role of vision-producing substances in religious practices and experiences, specifically the possibility that witchcraft was also related to the use of hallucinogens. By suggesting that scholars were projecting the present into the past, Cohn implies that such views were mainly a matter of imagination. In any case, he does not otherwise take such explanations seriously.

While the 1960s (and later) popular and scientific interest in hallucinogenic substances and experiences undoubtedly nourished interest in their possible role in European witchcraft, the idea had been around a long time. E. B. Tylor (1889: 2:418) suggested that medieval witch ointments brought visionary beings into the presence of the patients, transported them to the witch's sabbat, and enabled them to turn into beasts. Tylor did not suggest which specific ingredients might have been involved. However, in the twentieth century observations along this line became common. In a work published in 1924 the pharmacologist Lewis Levin noted it was the ointments used by "fanatics" that produced their visions of intercourse with evil spirits, and cited datura as one such ingredient (Harner 1973: 129).[3]

The awareness of the possible role of mind-altering substances in witchcraft beliefs and experiences appears to be much older than the nineteenth century. Harner notes that some scientists had suggested as early as the sixteenth century that witches were delusional and that the delusions were produced by the application of unguents or ointments containing potent plant substances, including ones (mandrake, henbane, nightshade) now known to be hallucinogenic. The general ingredient in these various members of the potato family is atropine and other closely related tropane alkaloids, all having hallucinogenic effects about which humans have long been aware. These plants, which are mentioned as ingredients in witches' preparations, have two other relevant characteristics. The first is that the hallucinogenic effects of atropine can work by absorption through intact skin as well as by ingestion in other ways. The other is that these and other plant-based hallucinogenic substances can be extremely dangerous in their other mental and physical effects. Their toxicity can result in death. It is perhaps significant that the effects of the substances can to some extent be controlled by their mode of incorporation into the body—through the skin, in the form of unguents or ointments as opposed to eating or drinking them, for example (Harner 1973: 128). Harner therefore concludes that crucial ingredients in witch's brew were hallucinogenic plant ingredients, which were applied as ointments rather than drunk as potions.

Like Margaret Murray, Harner thus believes there were real witches in late medieval and early modern Europe. At least, there were persons using potent psychotropic plant substances, having hallucinations of night flying and sabbats, orgies, devil worship, and so on, and of sometimes confessing these to the authorities. Some scholars have added to this the possibility that accidental or nondeliberate exposure to plant-based hallucinogens might have contributed to incidents of hysteria and hallucination. This might have involved the side effects of plant drugs used for other purposes—such as medicines provided by midwives (who were often accused of witchcraft) to relieve pain or otherwise aid in childbirth. It might have also involved the effects of consuming grain contaminated by hallucinogen-containing fungi or rotten food or polluted water. The evidence for any of these possibilities would seem to be circumstantial, but some connection with witchcraft experiences seems likely. However, the possible influence of hallucinogenic substances does not address the issue of whether or not group activities were involved as opposed to individual ones.

MODERN WITCHCRAFT OR NEO-PAGANISM

According to Christine Larner (1982: 50–51), a historian of preindustrial European witchcraft, two types of contemporary Western groups identify themselves as practitioners of witchcraft. The first type expressly embraces "evil" and is centered around Satanism and sex. She suggests such groups have a long if irregular history extending back to the eighteenth-century Hell Fire Club and include various twentieth-century successors. The main ritual is usually some version of the black mass (in which Christian symbolism is inverted), but such groups are very eclectic.[4] The commonness of such groups is not addressed. The second type of contemporary witchcraft involves practitioners who consider themselves witches but not Satanists. These persons see themselves rather as inheritors of pre-Christian European religion. Larner (1982: 51) writes:

> [These] groups tend to be connected with each other. Occasionally members write to me to explain that they are the true surviving witches. They have the characteristics of a sect, though there is little proselytizing. The basic belief is that they are a fertility religion, which had to go underground during the period of Christian dominance. They meet to perform 'ancient rites', which consist essentially of forms of dance. None of these groups date from earlier than the 1920s, which is when the idea of witches as innocent exponents of an underground rival religion was first invented and popularized by Dr. Margaret Murray. The key document for these groups is the article by Murray in the 14th (1929) edition of the *Encyclopaedia Britannica*, which was replaced only in the 1968 reprinting by one by Clyde Kluckhohn, and subsequently in the 15th (1974) edition by one by Max Marwick.

Other scholars trace the roots of such groups to the late nineteenth century, as we shall see below. It is these modern, non-Satanist groups that have been studied by anthropologists and sociologists.

In the English-speaking world, organized modern witchcraft emerged first in England and then spread to the United States and elsewhere. Such groups became well-known in the 1960s and widespread in the 1980s. The American versions are not entirely the same as the British or United Kingdom ones, but both are to a considerable extent based on broader cultural developments common to both countries and Western societies in general. In both places also adherents and those who have studied them use a number of different terms more or less interchangeably to refer to adherents and to their beliefs and practices. In a way, the terms "witch" and "witchcraft" are the most important and significant for adherents, linking them to the persecuted witches of earlier centuries and, through them, to the religious traditions of pre-Christian Europe. These terms are also the most potent in distancing practitioners from Christianity. By the same token, these terms are also the most controversial.

According to Sabina Magliocco (2004: 72), an anthropologist who has studied witchcraft in the United States, some American adherents consider these words to have negative and stigmatizing implications and feel they should be avoided. "Pagan" or "neo-pagan" (Magliocco uses pagan and neo-pagan interchangeably) are widely used by both adherents and scholars. These terms are somewhat more neutral than witch and witchcraft, and also perhaps intended to include a broader range of groups. Judging from Tanya Luhrmann's account of English witchcraft practitioners in the 1980s, the most commonly used term in England for modern witchcraft is "magic." While this includes magical practices in the narrower sense of manipulation of the supernatural, it also means all of the other things involved in modern witchcraft, including worship of the Goddess. If there is a single "official" inside term for modern witchcraft as a religion, it is Wicca. This term, though taken from much older English usage, is generally assumed to be modern. It is less well-known than "witch" or "witchcraft" and avoids the satanic associations of these terms. Finally, witchcraft has been shortened to "the Craft" to create an inside term.

As the diversity of terms suggests, modern witchcraft does not involve a single set of beliefs, ritual practices, or a single organization. According to all of the scholars who have studied the present-day witchcraft or neo-pagan groups, diversity prevails. However, modern practitioners do belong to groups and have well-known leaders.

Modern English Witchcraft

The fullest anthropological account of modern witchcraft in England is based on a study done by Tanya Luhrmann (1989) in the 1980s. Although Luhrmann is an American, her study takes little note of either the United States or continental European developments or variations. Her research was undertaken while she was a graduate student in anthropology at Cambridge University and, as might be expected, is theoretically oriented. Though her study was not set in any particular village or neighborhood, she did classic participant observation of modern witchcraft as it was practiced in and around London and Cambridge. This involved finding and developing informants, witnessing and participating in rituals, learning to read tarot cards, being accepted by other practitioners and initiated into a coven. Her informants included businesspeople, computer programmers (who, according to Luhrmann, have a particular affinity for magic), government civil servants, and scientists, among all of whom ritual seems to take precedence over belief.

Luhrmann concludes that modern witchcraft is basically an urban development. Urban areas have bookstores and shops dealing in occult materials and the largest concentrations of the sorts of persons likely to be interested in magic and witchcraft. This means that in England modern witchcraft was, at the time at least, concentrated in London, although the sacred sites and important ritual locations are commonly in the surrounding countryside. Most adherents are middle-middle class rather than lower- or upper-middle class. However, some of the individual practitioners she discusses or refers to are upper middle class in terms of education and career—including an occasionally highly placed civil servant, university lecturer, or research scientist.

In regard to the question of origins and continuity, Luhrmann explains that neo-paganism in England was created in the 1940s by Gerald Gardner. Gardner was civil servant with an interest in ethnology and folklore. He was inspired especially by Margaret Murray's previously discussed argument that European witchcraft was organized pre-Christian fertility religion. He published several fictitious ethnographies in the early 1950s of supposedly contemporary witchcraft groups that had been practicing in secret since the time of the persecution. He also claimed to have been initiated into one such group in 1939, although Luhrmann does not seem to have been convinced that he was.

Beyond Gardner and the influence of Murray, modern English witchcraft can be traced to the Victorian Era, most specifically to a late-nineteenth-century fraternal order known as the Temple of the Golden Dawn. Claiming to have discovered an ancient Rosicrucian document that revealed an old secret society of rituals and spiritual powers, dissident Freemasons founded this organization in 1887. This was the height of a period of turmoil over science and religion, and interest in psychic research, spiritualism, literary romanticism, English folklore and heraldry, and theosophy, which claimed to be both scientific and based on Tibetan Buddhism. The Temple of the Golden Dawn attracted upper- and middle-class members, and especially members of the literary world, including W. B. Yeats, who at one point was head of the London Temple. The Temple of the Golden Dawn did not claim to be involved in witchcraft and may not have been cognizant of a possible claimed link between European witchcraft and pre-Christian religion. However, several people now regarded as lineal ancestors of modern English witchcraft groups were members. These included most importantly Aleister Crowley, who is viewed by adherents as a founder of one of the main divisions. The temple broke up and was reassembled in the early decades of the twentieth century into several groups that moved back toward Christianity but held on to occult beliefs and practices. The new groups included other founders of modern witch-craft divisions (Luhrmann 1989: 38–39).

Modern American Witchcraft

The American versions of modern witchcraft or neo-paganism derive from the British ones but there are differences. To begin with, there are dif-ferences in the environment or landscape and its implications. The ancient architectural landscape of England, Wales, Scotland, and Ireland, and its meaning, helps to give neo-pagan religious practices an identity and a na-tionalist legitimacy that does not exist in the United States or Canada. To be a present-day neo-pagan, witch, magician, or adherent of the Craft in England involves an identity with the indigenous cultural and religious past of the country, of which there are abundant and often spectacular re-minders. Here the landscape has many vestiges of ancient pre-Christian religious traditions in the form of stone circles, dolmens, and other mon-uments, of which Stonehenge is the best known. Such ancient ruins are of-ten the sites of modern pagan rituals.

The ethnic context is also different. Neo-pagans in the United States, like those in England, regard modern witchcraft as a revival of indigenous pre-Christian religious traditions. But even Americans of northern Euro-pean ancestry are often several or more generations removed from Eu-rope and of mixed ancestry. In her account of American neo-paganism and witchcraft, Loretta Orion (1995: 142) writes that when modern British witchcraft was imported into the United States it was transformed in var-ious ways. The Americans developed a more informal ritual style, and they incorporated more shamanism—part of the Native American influ-ence. American neo-pagans have also developed an emphasis on the earth as a "living, conscious divine being" (this also presumably drawn from Native American sources as well as an alignment with the environmen-talist movement). And finally, American devotees have added a tradition of psychotherapy and naturalistic medicine that was largely lacking in modern British witchcraft.

The religious and cultural context of modern witchcraft is also differ-ent in other ways on the two sides of the Atlantic. Based on the accounts of both Orion and Magliocco, it would seem that American adherents are less likely to be open about what they believe and practice than their English counterparts. Luhrmann (1989: 339) points out that part of the explanation of modern witchcraft in England is that people live in an in-creasingly tolerant world, at least where some things are concerned. (Or, to bring this up to date, the preferences and activities of middle-class

English people who claim to be practicing indigenous pre-Christian traditions must seem entirely harmless in light of ongoing tensions involving immigrant Muslim peoples in Great Britain.) The possibilities for religious diversity are more limited in the United States. Religious tolerance and freedom are probably no longer what they were in the 1980s in either the United States or Great Britain, but aside from that, they are not and probably were never quite the same.

There is also greater regional diversity in the popularity and the tolerance or acceptance of neo-paganism in the United States than in the United Kingdom. Witchcraft or neo-pagan groups are concentrated in the most liberal areas of the United States: the upper Atlantic region, followed by the upper Midwest and the Pacific Coast. Conversely, they are lacking or rarer in the traditional Bible Belt, the South, and the intermountain West. Beyond such regional differences, they flourish in and around urban areas with concentrations of universities and colleges, such as Boston and New York, on the one hand, and the Bay Area of the West Coast, on the other.

As individuals, American adherents of modern witchcraft described by Orion and Magliocco seem at least roughly similar to the English ones discussed by Luhrmann. Orion (1995: 62–66) offers succinct, numerical descriptions of American neo-pagans that, while based on her own limited surveys, are probably generally applicable to those around the country:

> Thirty-eight percent of the respondents to my questionnaire are male; 58 percent are female; 4 percent identified themselves as androgynous. The data support my field observations; by rough count I consistently found twice as many women as men.
>
> . . . In response to the question regarding sexual preference, I discovered a high percentage of non-heterosexual Neopagans. Sixty-one percent declared themselves heterosexual, and 11 percent declared themselves gay, 28 percent bisexual. A total of 38 percent, then, declared a sexual preference other than heterosexuality.
>
> . . . The Neopagans are well educated, and in their academic studies and occupations they reveal a pervasive interest in the arts and healing. Seventy percent have four or more years of education beyond high school, compared to only nineteen percent of the [overall] population. Thirty-six point five percent of those who attended college . . . and responded to my question regarding their major area of study revealed an interest in the arts and humanities. Only 9 percent of college freshmen in the general population selected the arts and humanities . . . only two [of 139] selected business.
>
> . . . The largest category of employment for Neopagans (22 percent) is "helping and healing." The next largest category of employment is "arts and entertainment." With writers included in that category, the total rises to 20 percent. Following that the next most significant category of occupation is "computer related." [Luhrmann found many computer programmers among practitioners of magic in England.]

In terms of ideological values, adherents of modern witchcraft appear from all accounts to be strongly oriented to the causes of feminism or gender rights, environmentalism, and to artistry, creativity, self-fulfillment, and personal development. Christianity and other traditional organized religions are regarded as patriarchal in various ways. In contrast, pagan or pre-Christian religion is deemed to involve feminine fertility and goddess worship. Environmental values are thought to be manifest in various ways in neo-paganism, including its association with Mother Earth, fertility, pantheism (the belief that God exists in all things), nature worship, and outdoor rituals and celebrations. Artistry, creativity, and self-fulfillment are emphasized in that individuals and groups are free to innovate and to develop or alter ritual practices in accord with their own needs, values, or interests, so long as these do no harm.

Probably to a greater extent than in England, American adherents of present-day witchcraft, Wicca, or paganism appear to regard their beliefs, practices, and groups as religion and therefore as deserving of the same respect and protection as any other religions. Christian fundamentalists and evangelicals, on the other hand, tend to regard witchcraft as Satanism or devil worship, and therefore as grounds for denying it the status of a religion. As this was being written, a controversy was in progress in Nevada over whether the Wicca symbol (a five-sided star, or pentagram, enclosed in a circle) might be incorporated into a grave marker of a soldier killed in the Iraq War. The government authority denied the request on the grounds that the Wicca emblem was not on the official list of religious icons (though the pentagram was subsequently accepted as a result of court rulings).

NOTES

1. Modern witches or neo-pagans have been described by anthropologists in at least five scholarly books (Greenwood 2000; Luhrmann 1989; Magliocco 2004; Orion 1995; Pike 2004).

2. See the documentary film *Witchcraft among the Azende* (Singer 1981).

3. *Datura* (a New as well as an Old World plant) was also identified by Clyde Kluckhohn (1962:48; 175–76) as a common ingredient in medicines created by the Navajo for various purposes, including witchcraft.

4. Depictions of such groups have attracted much attention in the popular entertainment industry and are more likely to be mainly familiar to the public through Hollywood movies rather than scholarly studies or serious journalism. Two recent examples are the Roman Polanski film *The Ninth Gate* (1999), starring Johnny Depp, and the Stanley Kubrick film *Eyes Wide Shut* (1999), starring Tom Cruise and Nicole Kidman.

REFERENCES AND FURTHER READING

Adler, Margot. 1979. *Drawing Down the Moon: Witches, Druids, Goddess-Worshippers, and Other Pagans in America Today.* New York: Viking.

Bateson, Gregory, and Margaret Mead. 1942. *Balinese Character: A Photographic Analysis.* New York Academy of Sciences, Special Publications 2.

Bradsher, Keith. 2005. "Poverty and Superstition Hinder Drive to Block Bird Flu at Source." *New York Times,* November 3.

Cohn, Norman. 1974. "Was There Ever a Society of Witches?" *Encounter* 43(6): 26–41.

Covarrubias, Miguel. 1937. *Island of Bali.* New York: Knopf.

Dundes, Alan. 1981. "Wet and Dry, the Evil Eye." In *The Evil Eye: A Casebook,* edited by Alan Dundes, pp. 257–312. New York: Garland.

Ellen, Roy. 1998. Introduction to *Understanding Witchcraft and Sorcery in Southeast Asia,* edited by C. W. Watson and Roy Ellen, pp. 1–25. Honolulu: University of Hawaii Press.

Evans-Prichard, E. E. 1937. *Witchcraft, Oracles, and Magic among the Azande.* Oxford: Oxford University Press.

Favret-Saada, Jeanne. 1981. *Deadly Words: Witchcraft in the Bocage.* Cambridge: Cambridge University Press.

Fortune, R. F. [1932] 1963. *Sorcerers of Dobu: The Social Anthropology of the Dobu Islanders of the Western Pacific.* New York: Dutton.

Golden, Richard, ed. 2006. *Encyclopedia of Witchcraft: The Western Tradition.* Santa Barbara, Calif.: ABC-CLIO.

Greenwood, Susan. 2000. *Magic, Witchcraft, and the Otherworld: An Anthropology.* Oxford: Berg.

Harner, Michael J. 1973. "The Role of Hallucinogens in European Witchcraft." In *Hallucinogens and Shamanism,* edited by Michael Harner, pp. 125–50. New York: Oxford University Press.

Kluckhohn, Clyde. [1944] 1962. *Navaho Witchcraft.* Boston: Beacon.

Larner, Christine. [1974] 1982. "Is All Witchcraft Really Witchcraft?" In *Witchcraft and Sorcery,* edited by Max Marwick, pp. 48–53. London: Penguin.

Luhrmann, T. M. 1989. *Persuasions of the Witch's Craft.* Cambridge: Harvard University Press.

Macfarlane, Alan. 1970. *Witchcraft in Tudor and Stuart England: A Regional and Comparative Study.* London: Routledge & Keegan Paul.

Magliocco, Sabina. 2004. *Witching Culture: Folklore and Neo-Paganism in America.* Philadelphia: University of Pennsylvania Press.

Mair, Lucy. 1969. *Witchcraft.* New York: McGraw-Hill.

Marwick, Max, ed. [1970] 1982. *Witchcraft and Sorcery: Selected Readings.* 2nd ed. London: Penguin.

Murray, Margaret Alice. 1921. *The Witch Cult in Western Europe.* Oxford: Oxford University Press.

———. [1931] 1970. *The God of the Witches.* Oxford: Oxford University Press.

Orion, Loretta. 1995. *Never Again the Burning Times: Paganism Revived.* Prospect Heights, Ill.: Waveland.

Parsons, Elsie Clews. 1927. "Witchcraft among the Pueblos: Indian or Spanish?" *Man* 27: 106–12, 125–28.

Pike, Sarah M. 2004. *New Age and Neopagan Religions in America*. New York: Columbia University Press.

Siegel, James. 2006. *Naming the Witch*. Stanford: Stanford University Press.

Singer, André. 1981. *Witchcraft among the Azande. Disappearing World*, Granada Television.

Stewart, Pamela, and Andrew Strathern. 2004. *Witchcraft, Sorcery, Rumors, and Gossip*. Cambridge: Cambridge University Press.

Thomas, Keith. 1971. *Religion and the Decline of Magic*. New York: Scribner.

Trevor-Roper, H. R. [1956] 1969. *The European Witch-Craze of the Sixteenth and Seventeenth Centuries and Other Essays*. New York: Harper & Row.

Tylor, Edward B. [1871] 1889. *Primitive Culture: Researches into the Development of Mythology, Philosophy, Religion, Language, Art, and Custom*. 2 vols. 3rd American ed. New York: Holt.

Walker, Deward, ed. 1970. *Systems of North American Witchcraft and Sorcery*. Anthropological Monographs of the University of Idaho.

Watson, C. W., and Roy Ellen. 1993. *Understanding Witchcraft and Sorcery in Southeast Asia*. Honolulu: University of Hawaii Press.

9

✑

Spirit Possession, Spirit Mediumship, and Shamanism

All over people believe that human beings are animated by souls that can exist outside of the body in one way or another. Edward B. Tylor concluded that such notions were the beginning of religion, which developed further as people supposed that other things in the natural world were also animated by souls and began to act accordingly. He argued that people originally came by the belief in souls as a result of experiences with dreams, trance states, illness, and death. In dreams, the soul was believed to leave the body, move about, and have experiences. Sickness resulted when the soul was absent from the body for longer periods, and death took place when it left permanently. For people who continue to believe that physical or mental illness can be caused by the loss of a soul from the body, curing will consist in part at least of finding and retuning it to the body. Tylor (1889: 1:103) noted the widespread belief that a sneeze indicated that the soul was passing out of the body or that a spirit was entering it, hence the present-day Western practice of saying "bless you" when a person sneezes, although the reason for doing this is no longer generally known.

The assumption that human bodies or personalities are spiritually permeable, both to the exodus of their own souls and to the intrusion of spirits from without, is the basis for several widespread traditions of religious belief and practice with which we shall be concerned in this chapter—spirit possession, spirit mediumship, and shamanism. Of these, spirit possession and spirit mediumship are matters of relative agreement among anthropologists and other scholars who work on religion. Shamanism is more complicated and is the subject of acrimonious disagreement among cultural anthropologists and more recently among archaeologists as well, and it requires lengthier consideration.

SPIRIT POSSESSION AND SPIRIT MEDIUMSHIP

The term "spirit possession" (or often simply "possession") is generally used for what occurs when someone's personality has been taken over, supposedly by an alien spirit. Exactly what is believed to happen varies. In some instances possession is thought to entail the actual penetration of a person's body and mind by an alien spirit. This is typically what is assumed to occur in East Asian forms of possession. In other instances possession is believed to be a matter of a spirit holding a person in its grasp. For example, in some African and Afro-New World cultural traditions of possession, the spirit is thought to ride the possessed person like a horse. Sometimes spirit possession can have a marital or sexual dimension and can lead to pregnancy and childbirth.

Anthropologists generally recognize two basic forms of spirit possession, each involving its own ritual procedure. In one type, those concerned suppose that possession is involuntary and takes place without conscious awareness of the person affected, and in the other is voluntary or deliberate. With involuntary possession, a person is overcome and speaks with the voice of the invading or controlling spirit. It is commonly assumed by those who accept possession as reality that the person possessed is unconscious, or at least powerless to resist, and therefore cannot be held responsible for whatever she or he may do. However, the term "involuntary" can be misleading. Spirit possession cults refer to ritual activities in which participants expect and welcome possession by external spirits or gods. They often use dancing and music to aid in the onset of the trance experiences that are associated with possession. Voodoo and other Afro-Caribbean and Afro-Brazilian religions are well-known examples in which such forms of possession are expected and sought by participants. In such cases the notion of "involuntary" no longer describes what takes place.

Those who experience involuntary possession can regard what occurs in either positive or negative terms. An example of positive involuntary possession would be speaking in tongues (glossolalia) or other activities taken to be possession by the Holy Ghost (the power of God) in some forms of Christianity. Possession by external spirits is also widely viewed as a dangerous affliction. The symptoms of a person attacked may be either mental or physical (or both), but in either case it is assumed the person possessed is in need of help or curing; that is, the invading or possessing spirit must be persuaded or forced to leave the afflicted person.

The process by which such a spirit is driven out or persuaded to depart is exorcism. As with positively regarded forms of possession, incidents of spirit affliction are often dealt with by groups formed for this purpose. The spirits thought to possess people are of various types. They may be ghosts—spirits of dead persons, especially (in Asia at least) those who have died bad deaths and as a result have not made it to the land of the dead. Such spirits lurk around the places where they died or were buried and may possess people who come to such places. They may be nature spirits associated with certain trees, rivers, or swamps and attack and possess persons who have disturbed them. A further, and in some places very common, possibility is that possessing spirits have been sent by another person, in which case spirit possession is a form of sorcery.

Spirit Mediumship or Voluntary Possession

If a person is believed to deliberately summon or invoke external spirit beings into his or her personality and thereby gives them a voice, the activity is generally known as spirit mediumship (or, less often, voluntary possession). It is generally assumed that the ability to do this is learned and is normally a practice that a person undertakes at the request of others, often

Figure 9.1.   Chinese spirit mediums in Kelantan, Malaysia, engage in a ritual of exorcism. They are preparing a spirit boat in an annual ceremony used to rid the village of harmful spirits and evil influences.

Figure 9.2.   When ready, the spirit boat is carried down to the riverside and burned.

for a fee. The specific purposes for which spirits are summoned and given voice vary, but several are especially common. One is to consult them about why a person is ill or otherwise afflicted, or about what may occur in the future; a second is to seek their help in curing or some other activity; and a third is to enable the living to communicate with the dead, which also may be done for many of the same reasons that living persons communicate with one another. In societies with cultural traditions of ancestor worship, (efforts at) communication through a spirit medium with deceased relatives is very common and important.

Whether for curing or some other purpose, the ritual event at which spirit mediumship takes place is commonly referred to as a séance. Our popular image of such an event comes mainly from Hollywood movies. People sit around a table in a darkened room while a medium, sometimes dressed in costume, goes into a trance and pretends to contact those "on the other side," while playing tricks to convince everyone that ghostly things are really happening. It is an image that also lends itself well to melodrama and farce. However, Hollywood séances are very different from those often described by anthropologists. In East and Southeast Asia, for example, séances usually involve music (especially powerful drumming) and dancing and often have the character of a play or performance in which mediums—wearing costumes—act out the characters of the different spirits who possess them. As with spirit possession cults,

Figure 9.3. A Malay spirit medium (often referred to in the literature as a shaman) attempting to cure a woman in a séance performance of *main peteri* in 1967, when such practices still flourished in rural Kelantan, west Malaysia.

spirit mediumship is generally associated with trance or "alternative states of consciousness."[1]

Involuntary Spirit Possession as Psychopathology and Spirit Mediumship as Psychotherapy

Two sorts of explanations are commonly offered for involuntary spirit possession and spirit mediumship. This first is psychological and functional. What is experienced and interpreted as possession is assumed to be emotional trauma. The person who manifests symptoms of involuntary possession is experiencing internal conflict, depression, anxiety, or other negative emotional states and is expressing them in a traditional way that is readily understood by everyone and is likely to gain help. A person who is suffering from some organic physical ailment will also experience fear or anxiety, especially if it involves severe pain or does not respond to organic medical treatment or proceed through an expected cycle of improvement. Having an exorcist séance for a person experiencing psychological or physical illness will do several things that are likely to help if not necessarily cure. It will demonstrate that others are concerned and provide an explanation for suffering and a means of dealing with it. Further, such an explanation can be a bridge between modern and traditional views of illness and other afflictions. Rather than regarding beliefs and practices connected with spirit possession as backward superstition to be put aside in favor of modern biomedical diagnosis and treatment, such a psychological interpretation offers respect for customary interpretations and procedures without requiring that anyone accept the literal truth of spirit possession, mediumship, and exorcism.

This is the explanation that Melford Spiro gives of spirit possession and spirit mediumship among the Burmese in his book *Burmese Supernaturalism*:

> Within the Burmese framework, the exorcist is a religious practitioner, expelling harmful supernaturals from the bodies of their victims through the assistance of benevolent supernaturals. If, following the exorcism, the victim returns to his normal behavior, it is assumed that the ceremony has been a success, i.e., the harmful supernaturals have been expelled.
>
> . . . From the naturalistic point of view . . . the alleged victim of supernatural possession is mentally ill, suffering from psychological dissociation; the exorcist is a psychotherapist; and the exorcistic séance is a form of psychotherapy. Although modern therapists may be offended by this designation of Burmese exorcism, the exorcistic séance described in this chapter certainly satisfies the minimum definition of "psychotherapy" proposed by some psychiatrists. (Spiro 1967: 194–95)

Involuntary Spirit Possession as Protest and Empowerment

The other sort of explanation, which is by no means incompatible with the first, is sociological. It can be called protest possession. Anthropologists who have studied involuntary spirit possession have often found a pattern. According to the British anthropologist Ioan Lewis (1989), who has made a broad study of this pattern and has developed the fullest explanation of it, those who are attacked and become possessed (and often those who attempt to cure them) tend to represent the poorer or more marginal members of a society. In many instances this means women, especially in societies in which women are placed in a position of inferiority, dependence, and economic deprivation as a result of religion or custom. The general assumption is that women and others in such positions are likely to experience emotional distress and that the only (or at least the most effective) way of expressing this, the way that would most likely be taken seriously and that might lead to an improvement would be through the "idiom of possession." In societies in which this is the case, women and others who become possessed are not blamed for their troubles and those around them recognize the need to obtain help. In such places, where people accept the reality of malevolent spirits and their capability of entering into and taking over the personalities of humans, possession is treated seriously. This does not mean, however, that some people are not skeptical of incidents of possession and of the motives of those involved.

Lewis (1989: 64–71) attempts to explain the circumstances and process of protest possession as follows: To begin with, it is found in situations of religious complexity (which will be discussed further in the final chapter). Protest possession does not seem to be found, or at least to work very well, in societies in which there is a simple or single religious tradition that includes spirit possession as a part of the mainstream of belief and practice. This is apt to be the case with indigenous religions. In such societies, while the religious activities of men and women may be clearly differentiated, the differences are usually not a matter of marked superiority and inferiority. Here also anyone is liable to be possessed, and if this is so possession does not serve as a means of protesting or criticizing anything.

The situation is quite different in societies that have more complex or multiple religious traditions, specifically ones in which there is both what Lewis calls a "central morality cult" and one or more "peripheral cults." This occurs when a world religion is present, in which case the central morality cult is associated with the official doctrines or mythology, institutions, and moral requirements of the society, be they those of Christianity, Islam, or Buddhism. Although there is great variation within all of these world religions, their traditional forms tend to both differentiate between the participation of men and women and to assign women an inferior and often marginal position. Women participate in the main morality religion and are subject to its requirements and strictures but their participation is often limited and they have little or no opportunity to achieve influence or authority in it. Here also spirit possession and spirit mediumship constitute peripheral cults—peripheral in terms of their status and respectability. Both are associated with women as well as to some extent with certain types of men.

Lewis's main concern is with spirit possession traditions within Islam. His particular research concerned patterns of spirit possession in Somalia, a mainly tribal Muslim society marked by strong gender inequality. This inequality is based on both the formal legal strictures of Islamic law (which are interpreted by male tribal elders) and the customary practices of patrilineal descent and patriarchal authority, which tend to undermine the property rights that women are accorded by Islam. Women suffer insecurity in association with polygyny because their husbands can divorce them easily. Spirit possession is a consequence of the stresses to which women are subject, but spirit mediumship offers one of the few means by which women can exert influence and exercise authority. Other women care for women who are thought to be possessed. Possession by spirits, known as *sar* or *jinn*, is believed to cause a variety of mental and physical maladies. In some regions of Africa, the beliefs and practices involving spirit possession, mediumship, and exorcism are referred to as *zar* cults, after the name of the type of possessing spirits involved.

Lewis notes several specific situations that are apt to produce the symptoms that are interpreted as possession. One can involve a younger, unmarried woman who becomes severely disturbed after a man withdraws from a promise of marriage. If the engagement has not yet been formally agreed to by the families of both the man and the woman and the man changes his mind or his family is unwilling to accept the woman, neither she nor anyone else can do anything about it in terms of law or custom. The symptoms in such a case are likely to be depression and lassitude. Other situations involve married women. One is the possibility of divorce, another is a husband taking a new wife, and a third is a husband favoring one wife over another or withdrawing attention from an older wife.

If, for these or any other reasons, a woman shows signs of being possessed by a *sar* spirit, other women will advise a séance at which a spirit medium will seek to learn what is wrong and how to make it right. This will generally be expensive entertainment and new clothing and jewelry for the woman who has been possessed as the price for the spirit to leave. Men have an ambivalent view of what takes place. They are likely to be skeptical and cynical but, at the same time, not entirely so because the existence of evil *jinn* is sanctioned by the Qur'an, which cannot be doubted. They are therefore likely to accept the expense of exorcism in order to restore harmony. Lewis stresses that both men and women in Somali society have an explicit "sex war" view of marriage and relations between the sexes and that women feel considerable solidarity because of this.

Spirit Possession among Malay Schoolgirls and Factory Workers in Malaysia

Incidents of spirit possession that fit at least broadly with Lewis's general arguments are well-known from Malaysia. By now the traditional interpretations may have been largely replaced by modern Western psychiatric ones that label what takes place as "hysteria." In the 1970s and 1980s, however, the afflictions to be described here were considered in both ways, depending in part on the type of people engaged in the interpretation. In this period episodes of spirit possession hysteria were common in some areas. In the more traditional and rural part of Malaysia with which I am familiar, spirit possession hysteria was common among adolescent schoolgirls. This should not be taken to mean that the context was traditional. Mass schooling in Malaysia was at that time relatively recent, especially for women. Moreover, one way to interpret what took place is to see the incidents as reflecting psychological and social stresses that derive from putting young women in a situation that they have not been in before: in close and sustained proximity to, and in competition (for very limited opportunities to continue on to higher levels of schooling) with large numbers of young men.

The episodes that occurred differed from those described by Lewis in several ways, the most important being that more than one person was affected at a time. At some point during the school day and for no apparent (to anyone involved) reason a girl would begin to scream, laugh, or cry and not respond to efforts to help or inquiries about what was wrong. Soon others would begin to act in a similar way. The school might then be closed and the girls sent home. When the girls regained normal consciousness they would sometimes report seeing or feeling spirits. If the school was located near a place where Japanese soldiers had died during World War II, the disturbance was attributed to their ghosts. Another cause that was considered probable was that a boy had used love magic on the girl and it had a more powerful affect than anticipated.

Whatever the assumed cause, the incidents often continued or recurred over time. School authorities might interpret the incidents as "hysteria" rather than as spirit possession and try to deal with them accordingly. However, it was discovered that the best way to end the incidents was to proceed as though they were episodes of possession, by bringing in a Muslim religious specialist or a traditional curer who engaged in rituals of exorcism and cleansing.

It turned out that spirit possession in the 1970s and 1980s was not limited to the relatively traditional areas of the country such as Kelantan. Episodes were also taking place in the most modern areas of the country in and around the rapidly developing urban centers of the west coast. Those affected were young Malay female factory workers employed in the plants set up by Western corporations to produce calculators, computer parts, and other gear associated with the rapidly growing field of consumer electronics. These incidents were studied, described, and analyzed by the anthropologist Aihwa Ong. She interprets the episodes in various ways but, basically, her analysis is very much in line with Lewis's theory of spirit possession, although the specific situation was different.

Ong (1987: 141) notes the seeming paradox of traditional spirit possession occurring in the ultramodern context of a multinational, west coast (the modern, developed geographic region of peninsular Malaysia), high-tech factory. But, as in the adolescent female school pattern, the context was actually a mixture of traditional and modern elements. The women were from traditional backgrounds and subject to traditional social controls and stereotypes, even if they were less traditional than those on the east coast. Traditional attitudes toward women depend on their status. Virgin daughters and married women are highly regarded, but divorced and widowed women are a problem in traditional rural society. Men are attracted to them but also fear them. Such women are sexually experienced and are thought to be inclined to trap men with love magic. The women are raised to believe in many kinds of malevolent spirits and are familiar with spirit possession.

Ong argues that spirit possession episodes represented a form of protest against exploitation (low wages, low status, long hours, and generally unpleasant working conditions) in a situation in which more positive means of objection (such as unionizing or seeking more favorable government regulation) were precluded, although she also notes other contributing strains. She does not say that the women were consciously using spirit possession as a strategy of resistance or protest, any more than Lewis did so regarding Somali or other African women, or in general terms. But neither does she say that such a possibility was totally absent from their understanding or motives.

Episodes of possession could be highly disruptive. Forty women were involved in one incident and 120 in another. One American manager asked how he was going to explain the loss of 8,000 hours of production to a ghost sighting (Ong 1987: 204). But again spirit possession did not necessarily lead to real improvements. Village elders blamed the spirits. Factory managers tended to blame the women who become possessed, seeing them as hysterical, as victims of their own superstitions and poor eating habits, rather than acknowledging the strains and difficulties of factory work, let alone the conflicts the women faced because of their situation (as sexually mature but not under the control of a husband or family, looked down on as pleasure-seeking and perhaps promiscuous). Management went through the process of engaging a traditional Malay *bomoh* (curer, exorcist) and sponsoring rituals of cleansing and exorcism, but also adopted the policy of firing women who were possessed on more than one occasion.

SHAMANISM

The first references to what later came to be identified as shamanism go back at least to the ancient Greeks. According to the historian Gloria Flaherty (1992: 3),

> Such practitioners and their followers have aroused the curiosity of intellectuals at least since the fifth century B.C., when Herodotus recounted the death-defying feats of Scythian soothsaying poets Aristeas and Abaris. Herodotus also reported on the delight the Scythians took in sweat baths

and in the long, deep inhalation of burning hemp. Classical scholars throughout the ages have not only continued to study Herodotus, but they have also pointed out numerous other 'shamanic" practices of antiquity. Some scholars have attributed the late Hellenistic novel to the trances of shamans, while others have seen in those trances the origins of theater and fairy tales. Still others have believed shamans responsible for the very creation of Greek mythology.

Though its etymology is disputed, the word "shaman" is generally assumed to come from the Evenk or Tungus of eastern Siberia. Other derivations, including Sanskrit, Pali, and Chinese have also been claimed, and the practice was unquestionably widespread over a large area, usually said to include central and northern Asia. Just how and when the term "shaman" came to be taken from the Evenk and incorporated into European languages is not known with certainty, although various claims have been made, all going back several centuries or more. According to Flaherty, different terms for shamanism were in use throughout Europe until the eighteenth century, by the end of which, however, "shaman" had come to predominate. She thinks that German or German-educated explorers were responsible, while others have claimed that Russian explorers and missionaries were crucial.

"Shaman" and "shamanism" as general terms of reference for various practices came into widespread use in the eighteenth century. Though variously conceived, shamanism became widely important for intellectuals, musicians and artists, and medical doctors. The apparent similarity of shamanistic practices among American Indians to those of Siberian and central Asian peoples was taken as a link that connected the two peoples. On the assumption that shamanism in the New World was brought along with many other cultural practices from northern Asia, it was supposed that shamanism in the Old World was at least old enough to predate the settling of the Americas.

As anthropology developed in the late nineteenth and twentieth centuries in Europe and America, the importance attributed to shamanism as a topic and as a concept varied. In continental Europe and especially in Russia and Scandinavia, shamanism remained an important focus of research and analysis for local folklorists and anthropologists. However, it did not, at least until recent decades, gain much attention among British anthropologists (Lewis 1986: 78–79). Here scholars and researchers concentrated instead on witchcraft and sorcery, spirit possession, and spirit mediumship as topics or categories of religion—perhaps because these fit better with the regions (especially Africa and parts of the Pacific) where their research interests were concentrated. Found widely as it was also among Native Americans, shamanism became a well-established interest in American anthropology at an early point. Clifford Geertz (1973) dismissed shamanism in 1965 in his seminal article on religion ("Religion as a Cultural System") as an insipid topic of no interest. But by then it was already on its way to renewed and then greatly increased interest for researchers and scholars—and this time for British anthropologists as well (e.g., Lewis's comparative study *Ecstatic Religion: A Study of Shamanism and Spirit Possession*, first published in 1971).

The increased interest in the 1960s and thereafter has been widely attributed to the popular and intellectual interest in altered states of consciousness, especially those of a hallucinogenic nature, one of the hallmarks of 1960s popular culture. The first of Carlos Castaneda's bestselling if controversial accounts of the Yaqui Indian shaman Don Juan (discussed below) and his own hallucinogenic adventures with mescaline was published in 1968. Scholarly conferences and volumes on hallucinogens and their uses in shamanism and other religious practices soon took place. The expansion of ethnographic research by American, British, and other anthropologists in the Amazon that followed especially the trail blazed by Lévi-Strauss contributed further to the ethnological picture.

The Work and Influence of Mircea Eliade

The modern scholarly study of shamanism derives especially from the work of Mircea Eliade. A Romanian-born, French-educated scholar of comparative religion, Eliade spent his career mainly in the history of religions program at the University of Chicago. His crucial work was *Shamanism: Archaic Techniques of Ecstasy*. First published in French in 1951 and then in a revised English version in 1964, it was six hundred pages in length, a literal magnum opus on which Eliade worked for five years. Neither the valuable firsthand accounts by ethnographers nor the theoretical and comparative studies by anthropologists and other scholars have surpassed Eliade's book as an encyclopedic overview of shamanism by a single scholar.

Eliade begins his book by trying to establish what shamanism is and is not. It is above all a technique of ecstasy, a means by which the shaman experiences trance during which his soul leaves his body and ascends to the sky or descends to the underworld. Although shamanism is a religious phenomenon, it is not in itself a religion. By this he means that it is a not a complete religion, that people who follow shamanism also have other, quite separate religious beliefs and practices, and that shamanism can be found in association with a range of different religions in various places.

Defining Shamanism Broadly or Narrowly

At the same time, Eliade's work has also been prominent in the controversies that have developed over shamanism in the past several decades. The controversies begin with definitions. As is true of many things concerning religion, shamanism can be defined broadly or narrowly, and the more broadly it is defined the more widely it will be seen to occur. At the popular level shamanism can include almost anything in the way of healing or ritual specialization of a non-Western sort. Anthropologists are apt to be somewhat more careful but do not necessarily distinguish, for example, between shamans and spirit mediums. Lewis (1986), for example, takes a broad approach to shamanism to show that involuntary spirit possession, deliberate spirit possession (or spirit mediumship), and the control of spirits (or shamanism) are closely related and can be seen as phases in the shaman's "career."

Those who advocate a narrower approach to shamanism do so for several reasons. One is the view that the term has been used in so many ways that it has little value as a means of identifying or explaining anything in particular. But if the term is to mean something more specific, how is it to be decided what exactly this should be? One obvious answer is to use the term to mean what it meant in its "original" Siberian or Central Asian setting. Indeed, this has often seemed to be a good reason for taking a narrow approach. The scholars who take this view have tended to focus on the core shamanist cultures or closely connected cultures, for example, the New World arctic.

But here there are two problems. One is if geographical or ethnological lines are to be drawn around shamanism where specifically are they to be drawn? No one seems to suppose that the concept should be restricted to the practices of the Tungus or other neighboring peoples who have the term in its original form. Most scholars who are experts on Siberian, Central Asian, or Eurasian arctic shamanism seem to think that more or less exactly the same tradition also occurs among the New World arctic peoples as well. But if shamanism is extended to the New World arctic, from Alaska to Greenland, what about the subarctic peoples to the south and so on, to the southern tip of South America? The other and related problem is, geographical or ethnological proximity aside, just what is it that sets Central Asian and arctic shamanist practices apart from nonshamanist ones?

The Basic Features of Shamanism

Eliade provides a bridge between the broad and the narrow approaches to shamanism. He takes the position that, strictly speaking, shamanism is a tradition of belief and practice of Central Asia and Siberia, and therefore the features found in this region should be regarded as defining its essential nature. Nonetheless, he also concluded that shamanism, conceived in terms of its classic Siberian features, extends far beyond this core area in various directions. As we have seen, Eliade's minimal definition is that shamanism is above all a technique of ecstasy, a means by which the shaman experiences trance during which his soul leaves his body and ascends to the sky or descends to the underworld. A more satisfactory approach might be to note a number of core features from his analysis that form the "full" or "classic" pattern and use them as criteria for wider comparisons, as follows:

1. The belief in a cosmos with many spiritual beings that can help or harm human beings, some of whom can be controlled or influenced by shamans—humans who have been chosen, initiated, and trained (Eliade 1964: 5–6).
2. The belief that the cosmos consists of distinct levels that include, broadly, an upper world, a middle world that is experienced through the natural senses, and an underworld that is the realm of the dead (Eliade 1964: 259–66).
3. The belief that not only do humans have souls that leave the body during illness and dreams and permanently at death, but that they can sometimes be overtaken and returned by the shaman with the assistance of spirit helpers (Eliade 1964: 215–24 passim).
4. A tradition of recruitment whereby shamans do not seek their vocation and often resist it. While shamanism may be hereditary, it is typically assumed that shamans are called by the spirits who wish to form a relationship with them, one that is sometimes thought to be sexual or marital in nature. The call may involve either dreams or bouts of physical or mental illness that recur and resist efforts to cure, and is interpreted by trained shamans as a summons that must be accepted, refusal meaning death or permanent insanity. Often there is a traditional schema of suffering, symbolic death, and resurrection (Eliade 1964: 33–35; 67–88).
5. The practice of initiation whereby shaman candidates undergo training by other shamans and ceremonies through which they gain control over their familiar spirits (Eliade 1964: 110–44).
6. The belief that the shaman goes on spiritual journeys to the upper world and the underworld in order to recover lost souls and thereby to heal or to guide souls of the dead to the realm of the dead (Eliade 1964: 215–58).
7. The shaman acquires various paraphernalia that are used in ritual activities, usually items of dress or adornment and other objects. By

far the most important and widespread item in the material culture of shamanism is the drum. Quartz or other rock crystals are noted from different areas of the world (Eliade 1964: 52; 168–76).

Not each and every one of these features alone would serve to differentiate shamans from other sorts of ritual specialists, but two in particular can be stressed: the belief that the shaman (1) is chosen or "called" by the spirits and that once initiated (2) has the ability to travel to other worlds. Such basic features presuppose some of the other, less distinctly shamanistic ones, including the belief in spirits and in spiritual worlds. There are also mixed or marginal cases in which one of these features is present but not the other.

Figure 9.4. A Bidayuh Dayak shaman in a trance telling of his of his journey in search of the soul of the man he is attempting to cure, in Lundu in northwestern Borneo, east Malaysia.

The Occurrence of Shamanism

According to Eliade's survey, the occurrence of shamanism across the world can be summarized as follows:

1. The "classic" form is found in the societies of Siberia and central Asia (and beyond that across the Eurasian arctic), although the present-day version has undergone some alteration from an earlier and truer form.
2. There are further extensions that have all or most of the main features of classic shamanism, including

   a. The indigenous traditions of many peoples of the Americas, from the arctic (Alaska to Greenland) to the southern tip of South America, which are a consequence of the original migration into the region by shamanism-practicing peoples, supplemented in the arctic and subarctic areas by more recent influences from northern Asia.
   b. The practices of various indigenous peoples throughout mainland Southeast Asia and Indonesia (insular Southeast Asia).
   c. Those also of various peoples (especially indigenous or tribal groups) in South Asia.

3. In addition, there are indigenous or tribal peoples whose religious practices have elements of shamanism but who lack what could be called real shamanism: Melanesia, Australia, and the other Pacific islands.
4. Extinct or ancient Old World religious traditions that may have elements of shamanism, including those of various Indo-European peoples.
5. Asian religious traditions that have ancient elements of shamanism that have been absorbed and transformed and that have in turn influenced the classic shamanist traditions of central and northern Asia. Such Asian religions include Lamaism in Tibet and Taoism in China.
6. Several East Asian religious subtraditions that are commonly identified as shamanism but that have only some of the features of classic shamanism. These include most notably the Korean (discussed in chapter 11) and Japanese versions.
7. Other areas of the world remain outside of Eliade's discussion, notably Africa, to which Eliade makes few references.

Shamanism, Modes of Adaptation, and Levels of Social, Political, and Religious Organization and Gender

Over time, anthropologists studying shamanism have attempted to explain its occurrence or development in terms of its association with other social and cultural traditions. Patterns of adaptation have been the main focus of such efforts, and hunting has been generally singled out as having a particular link with shamanism; this link is assumed to have a prehistoric origin. Whatever the merits of the argument that shamanism is among the oldest or original sorts of religious activity (discussed below), efforts to associate it with hunting (or hunting and gathering) adaptations in present-day ethnographic terms have not been very convincing.[2] Yet core or classic shamanism, as defined in terms of the features noted above, does seem to be associated with certain kinds of societies rather than others. This is not always apparent, however, because the term "shamanism" is sometimes applied when it is not really present In Southeast Asia, classic shamanism flourishes among the traditionally small-scale or tribal peoples of the interior and upland or mountainous regions of both the insular region and the mainland; that is, among people who follow what are otherwise indigenous practices, traditionally live by shifting cultivation, and until recently existed beyond or on the margins of state control. Conversely, the full pattern does not seem to occur among the larger-scale lowland, wet-rice cultivating peoples who adhere to one of the world religions and who have long been organized into states.[3]

But why does classic shamanism exist in one type of society and not another? One possibility is that the interior and highland tribal societies have "always" or "for long" had shamanism as a part of their overall culture or way of life. If, as many scholars claim, shamanism is an ancient complex of belief and practice, then the relevant question may be not why some types of societies have it, but why other types do not. One part of the answer to such a question may be that classic shamanism does not survive well as the world or universal religions become dominant.

This can be seen in what seems to have taken place in China, Korea, and Japan as well as in Southeast Asia; as world religions, literacy, and urbanization have developed, shamanism has been absorbed or altered and marginalized. While spirit possession and spirit mediumship (along with beliefs in sorcery and various kinds of magic) have continued to flourish throughout the region, the worldview or cosmology of classic shamanism, perhaps, was incompatible with the doctrines of the world religions. Or perhaps classic shamans were considered to be too powerful or threatening and competitive to be accepted by the elites and authorities of these religions.

The anthropologist Joan Townsend, who has studied shamanism in Nepal as well as among Native Americans, argues that what tends to happen is partly a matter of gender.

> Shamans can be either male or female—although in a particular society, one or the other sex may be in the majority or hold the position exclusively. There seems to be a tendency for males to predominate as shamans in small societies, such as foraging, while in somewhat larger cultivating societies,

both men and women are well represented. In large, stratified societies such as Korea and Japan, women mainly fulfill the role, although in Nepal male shamans outnumber female shamans. The tendency for women more than men to be shamans in some large societies may be a reflection, in part, of the relegation of shamanism to the periphery when large universalistic religions are present. Men then tend to gravitate to the greater power and prestige positions of the dominant religion, leaving women to conserve the "folk" shamanic traditions as well as spiritual healing, mediumistic and mystical practices. (Townsend 1997: 439)

Shamanism as a Paleolithic Religion

Although the archaeology and prehistory of shamanism are sharply contested, many scholars believe that it can be traced to the Paleolithic. This assumption rests on several kinds of evidence. One is the wide distribution of shamanism in the world—especially the occurrence of many or most of the same basic features noted above in both the Old World and the Americas. The general assumption here is that the more widespread some tradition is in the world (especially one that does not have an obvious technological or other adaptive advantage), the older it probably is. The commonalities in shamanism in northern Eurasia and the New World arctic can perhaps be in part attributed to contact and diffusion over the past thousand years or so, but this is much less likely in the case of shamanism in South America. The possibility that the various basic features of shamanism were independently invented seems less likely than that they were part of the Paleolithic culture brought by migration over the Bering land bridge, and from there eventually to the tip of South America. If shamanism was brought by migration from northern Asia and if such migration took place 10,000 or more years ago, then some form of shamanism was already in place in northeastern Asia by that time.

The antiquity of shamanism has also been linked to a hunting adaptation and therefore to a special relationship with animals, since the Paleolithic peoples were all hunters. If so, shamanism might have developed anywhere in Paleolithic Eurasia and spread over the region and eventually to the Americas, then declining in areas where other forms of subsistence developed instead (or as other possible changes took place). According to this line of reasoning, classic shamanism remained in this region because of its remoteness from currents of change and its continuing dependence on hunting (and later animal pastoralism).

Shamania: The Controversy over Prehistoric Art and Shamanism

Those who argue that shamanism can be traced to the Paleolithic also base their interpretation on Ice Age art, specifically the cave paintings of southwestern Europe that have for many decades been taken to be an indication of the presence of shamanism long ago. The famous Dancing Sorcerer of Les Trois Frères (figure 3.2) in particular has been taken to be a drawing of a shaman. This image combines human and animal characteristics—in this case the head and antlers and body and tail of a deer (or a wolf) and the arms and hands and legs and feet of a human. However, the figure can be interpreted in more than one way. It has been seen to be the image of a shaman wearing a deer mask (La Barre 1990: 267), but it could just as well be a depiction of a supernatural creature (see below).

While scholars interested in shamanism have looked to cave art for evidence of its origins or antiquity, those interested in cave and rock art have looked to shamanism as an explanation of its meaning and purpose. Of all the issues surrounding shamanism this one has been the most forcefully and bitterly contested. Prehistoric rock and cave art have always been difficult to account for and remain so. In most instances there is little or no continuity between the art and existing peoples, meaning there is no ethnographic context. Therefore, there is the problem of inferring the motives, purpose, and cultural meaning that lie behind the art. In the case of art found in underground caverns in conditions totally lacking natural light (at the time the drawings were made) it seems reasonable to infer that the images were created in association with rituals, if only because other motives are hard to imagine; however, discerning what sort of rituals may have been involved is a different matter. In the case of images created in aboveground cave entrances, under rock shelters and on open rock faces the range of possible purposes seems much greater, and includes territorial marking, signaling, and even humorous expression.

In the first part of the twentieth century, the favored explanation for those inclined to see prehistoric art in ritual terms was that of hunting magic. Animals shown being pierced with arrows or spears are the main and most obvious evidence for the hunting magic hypothesis, though such scenes are not common or even present in many instances (Bahn 1998: 234–35). Depictions of pregnant or copulating game animals suggesting efforts to promote fertility also fit with the hunting magic argument—although, again it has been claimed that such images are not common. In recent decades the hunting magic interpretation of prehistoric rock and cave art has gone out of fashion and been replaced with shamanism, at least among scholars who wish to go beyond "literal" interpretations (ones that profess mixed motives, stress variation, and stress uncertainty). The shamanist argument is that rock and cave art was produced in association with shamanist rituals, presumably by shamans under the influence of hallucinogenic substances or in states of altered consciousness produced in other ways. Assertions of this sort have been around a long while in regard to specific groups or areas. In North America rock art has often been ascribed to shamanism in earlier as well as later periods (i.e., the first half of the twentieth century as well as the second).

While shamanist interpretations of rock and cave art have been around for many decades, those offered since the late twentieth century are much more extensive, complex, and controversial than the earlier ones. They have been applied to a wider range of places and presented a much fuller interpretation of what supposedly occurs in terms of shamanist beliefs, rituals, and altered states of consciousness. For cave art the leading collaborative proponents of such interpretations are Jean Clottes (a French specialist in European Ice Age cave art) and David Lewis-Williams (a South African prehistorian who began his work with Bushman rock art). Their interpretation is complex and involves several sorts of arguments.

The basic idea is that the cave art was produced by shamans or in association with shamanic activities. The animals so frequently created are really the spirit helpers of shamans, rather than simply animals to be hunted or shown for their importance for other cultural reasons or for their impressive beauty. Rather, the motifs are the result of trance states, which proceed through three stages (Clottes and Lewis-Williams 1998: 92). There are first geometric patterns or designs. These are zigzags, wavy lines, dots and grids and spirals that reflect the optical or non-hallucinogenic images experienced during the initial stage of trance. Next there are those of the second stage of trance, in which real hallucination begins and the geometric designs are replaced by more familiar or discernable images of animals (or less commonly of humans), scenes, or activities. Finally, there are the images produced during the third stage. These are marked by several kinds of distortion including ones involving the relative size and placement of the things shown (for example, very large animals depicted above or below small ones). Most notably, such third-stage forms include the combining of human and animal parts as in the "sorcerer" images of Les Trois Frères (figures 3.2 and 8.1).

The final part of Clottes and Lewis-Williams interpretation seeks to explain why shamanic cave art was produced in caves. Caves were entrances to the underworld of the shamanic cosmos. The descent into the cave was the shaman's spiritual journey to the lower world. The walls of the cave were not simply the surface on which the art was created but the membrane of the lower world through which contact was made. Here the crucial image is the common stencil of the human hand. In creating such images what people were really doing was "sealing their own or others' hands into the walls" (Clottes and Lewis-Williams 1998: 95).

Shamanist interpretations of prehistoric art have attracted considerable criticism, some of it strident. The main point of such criticism is that there is no evidence to link Ice Age art to shamanism beyond assumption (Bahn 1998: 237). The leading critic has been the prehistorian and specialist in prehistoric art Paul Bahn (1998: 249). In the *Cambridge History of Prehistoric Art*, Bahn refers to such explanations as "shamania" and discusses them elsewhere in articles with titles that include "Membrane and Numb Brain" and "Save the Last Trance for Me." The latter article is in a recent volume produced by the International Society for Shamanistic Research titled "The Concept of Shamanism: Uses and Abuses" (Francfort and Hamayon 2001), the main thrust of which could be summarized by saying the "uses" part of the title might as well have been left out.

The critics of the shamanist interpretation of rock and cave art do not dismiss the possibility that shamanism could ever have been involved. Rather, they regard it as generally unproved. One problem noted is that the evidence for shamanism in rock and cave art is generally limited to the images themselves. This is entirely so for the ancient instances, such as the Upper Paleolithic cave art of Eurasia, and largely so of the more recent rock art that has some association with ethnographically known peoples. Moreover, in the case of those instances with ethnographic connections, the connections are either more limited than claimed or distorted, or both. A further point of criticism is that while ritual may have been involved it was not necessarily shamanic, and even if it was there is the question of whether the images produced were created by shamans in trances themselves or by others, or created during the séance or later from memory.

The critics of the shamanist interpretations of rock and cave art have also drawn on or merged their objections with the criticisms made of ethnological interpretations of shamanism (e.g., cultural anthropologist Alice Kehoe's [2000] argument for limiting the notion of shamanism to Central Asia). This overlooks the considerable difference between interpretations of shamanism in rock and cave art and in ethnological interpretations based on firsthand accounts. The fundamental problem with the former is a lack of evidence that, to critics, makes such interpretation or explanation hypothetical if not far-fetched. The problem with the ethnology of shamanism is the opposite one of too much evidence; that is, more than most theorists of shamanism or critics of theories of shamanism such as Kehoe and Bahn seem willing to synthesize and evaluate.

Some archaeologists and prehistorians of rock art feel that criticisms of the shamanistic interpretations of cave and rock are wrong or go too far and therefore discourage likely or possibly productive new lines of inquiry and understanding. For example, this is the position taken in a recent book by James Pearson (2002) who reviews the general approach and work done on prehistoric Native American rock art in particular. The sometimes negative attitudes toward both the ethnological study of shamanism and the shamanic interpretation of rock and cave art have probably been influenced by the popularization of shamanism and by its association with New Age ideas. Let us now consider shamanism from this perspective.

NEO-SHAMANISM:
CARLOS CASTANEDA AND MICHAEL HARNER

While Eliade's book greatly increased scholarly awareness of shamanism and its various forms around the world, what is referred to as neo-shamanism is largely the creation of two individuals: Carlos Castaneda and Michael Harner. Both began as anthropologists but left orthodox anthropology for other efforts.

Carlos Castaneda and Don Juan

Castaneda initiated the popularization of shamanism with a series of books that began in 1968 with the publication of *The Teachings of Don Juan* and that went on to included ten volumes in all. Castaneda was at the time an anthropology graduate student at UCLA and, by his account, Don Juan was a Yaqui Indian from Sonora, Mexico. Castaneda recounts that he first met Don Juan in 1960 in Arizona while seeking information on native plants. He subsequently became an apprentice to Don Juan, who introduced him to three hallucinogenic plants then in use by Indians in the region including peyote (*Lophophora williamsii*), Jimson weed (*Datura inoxia*), and a mushroom (possibly *Psilocybe mexicana*). Castaneda's experiences with these drugs are vividly described in *The Teachings of Don Juan* and *A Separate Reality*, both best-sellers, and in his other books. Along with the Harvard psychologist Timothy Leary and a few other researchers and scholars who wrote popular accounts of their experiences with synthetic or natural hallucinogenic substances, Castaneda's books became a part of the popular drug culture that began in the 1960s. Perhaps because he told of his experiences and of the knowledge he obtained in relation to his relationship with a Yaqui Indian, his writings also contributed to the creation of the New Age movement.

Although *The Teachings of Don Juan* was first published by the University of California Press (as was a thirtieth anniversary edition in 1998) and although Castaneda was awarded a Ph.D. in anthropology by UCLA in 1973, his writings were controversial in academic and intellectual circles, and they now appear to be rapidly fading in interest.[4] Nor is it clear from Castaneda that Don Juan was, initially at least, supposed to be a shaman. In a preface to the 1998 edition of *The Teachings of Don Juan*, Castaneda repeatedly refers to Don Juan as a shaman, but he does not do so in the original or in the other early books. Instead he calls him a "sorcerer" or other such names. The first application of the term "shaman" to Don Juan in the published literature seems to have been by reviewers or commentators. The identification of Don Juan as a shaman seems to have been made because he was familiar with hallucinogenic plants and because he traveled between different worlds. Otherwise, little else about Don Juan's shamanistic practices or, for that matter, about other dimensions of his life is provided.

Michael Harner and the Foundation for Shamanic Studies

Michael Harner, who built on what Castaneda had begun, clearly associates Castaneda and Don Juan with shamanism. Harner himself had first studied shamanism in the 1950s among the Jivaro and other Indians of the Peruvian Amazon. His initial publications were scholarly studies, including the edited collection *Hallucinogens and Shamanism*. In 1980 he moved into popular literature with *The Way of the Shaman*. More than a popular account, however, this book was intended to be a manual that would teach Western readers how to find and use shamanic knowledge and how to become shamans themselves. Harner believes that shamanic knowledge is real and can be discovered and developed through training into a method of healing and spiritual development. Adopting a broad view of shamanism as an ancient form of healing that has been kept alive by so-called primitive peoples who lack advanced technology, he sets out a series of steps by which anyone can move from what he calls (following Castaneda) an ordinary state of consciousness (OSC) to a shamanic state of consciousness (SSC).

As with Castaneda, hallucinogens played an important role in Harner's initial venture into shamanism. He had been told by the Conibo Indians, among whom he was staying in the early 1960s, that if he wished to learn about their religion he would have to take the shaman's sacred drink made from *ayahuasca*, the "soul vine." He was also "told that the experience would be very frightening." He took the drink and experienced striking auditory and visual hallucinations:

> Overhead the faint lines became brighter, and gradually interlaced to form a canopy resembling a geometric mosaic of stained glass. The bright violet hues formed an ever-expanding roof above me. Within this celestial cavern, I heard the sound of water grow louder and I could see dim figures engaged in shadowy movements. As my eyes seemed to adjust to the gloom, the moving scene resolved itself into something resembling a huge fun house, a supernatural carnival of demons. In the center, presiding over the activities, and looking directly at me, was a gigantic, grinning crocodilian head, from whose cavernous jaws gushed a torrential flood of water. Slowly the waters rose, and so did the canopy above them, until the scene metamorphosed into a single duality of blue sky above and sea below. All creatures had vanished. (Harner 1980: 3)

This was only the beginning. Harner subsequently returned to live with the Jivaro to study shamanism and have further plant-induced hallucinogenic experiences.

Following these narrative accounts and a brief overview of shamanism based on Eliade's book and a review of native North American practices, Harner offers the first lesson on how to make a journey down through the tunnel to the lower world. For this exercise the aspiring shaman needs either the proper drum or a cassette recording of shamanic drumming, as well as someone to assist by beating the drum, at least if a real drum is used. He then supplies detailed instructions about what to do and what the experience should be like, as well as a series of accounts of what those who have completed the journey have experienced.

It is notable that the instructions for this journey include the avoidance of any narcotic or alcoholic substances for the preceding twenty-four hours. More generally, while having reported that his own shamanistic experiences with Amazon Indians involved the use of hallucinogens, Harner states that "in some cultures shamans take mind-altering substances, but in many others they do not. In fact, some psychoactive materials can interfere with the concentration shamanic work demands" (Harner 1980: 44).

So the book continues, interspersing descriptions of various facets of shamanism (mainly focusing on Native American versions), with instructions about how to do it. There is a chapter on power animals, which are the guardian spirits of North American native shamans. Everyone has one or more such power animals. It is only a matter of knowing how to get in touch with them.

In addition to his own research among Amazon Indians and other traditional practitioners of shamanism, Harner's book was based on his experiences in instructing Westerners and conducting workshops. The purpose of these efforts was not only to teach individuals to explore their own consciousness and inner potential in new ways but also enable them to use their power to heal others. In order to develop and promote the benefits of shamanism among Westerners, Harner has been teaching shamanism since the early 1970s.

Along with the promotion of shamanism among contemporary Westerners as a method of personal development, healing, and counseling, Harner and his associates have sought to perpetuate or revive traditional forms of shamanism among indigenous peoples. Shamanism among Native Americans, the tribal peoples of Central Asia and the arctic and elsewhere has been under assault as the world religions spread and governments promote religious and cultural modernization. As a result, shamanism had come to be regarded as religiously incorrect and backward, and consequently its ancient wisdom and benefits are widely threatened with extinction.

The Foundation for Shamanic Studies in Mill Valley, California, was created in 1987 by Harner to study shamanism, provide training in the theory and techniques of "core shamanism," and support indigenous shamanic practitioners. According to its website (www.shamanism.org), the foundation currently offers more than 200 courses to over 5,000 persons each year. The general philosophy is to offer shamanism as a supplement to scientific medicine or standard mainstream psychotherapy rather than as a replacement. As a means of perpetuating and reviving traditional shamanism, the foundation attempts to provide support and recognition for shaman masters everywhere as living treasures. The website also offers online sales of books, cassettes, and shamanic paraphernalia including drums and rattles.

How similar are the neo-shamanist beliefs and practices promulgated by the Foundation for Shamanic Studies and those of traditional indigenous forms of shamanism? As we have seen, the latter vary substantially across cultures. Harner's neo-shamanism appears to have drawn more from Native American forms (e.g., the notion of power animals) than from Asian ones. At the same time, in dropping the use of hallucinogens, neo-shamanism moves away from Native American (or at least Latin American) forms and toward the Asiatic ones, in which the use of mind-altering plant substances plays a less significant role or is totally absent.

NOTES

1. In one form of Malay spirit mediumship known as *main peteri*, mediums prepare themselves for possession first by dancing faster and faster to drums and gongs and then by rapidly rotating the upper body. The process of entering a trance state and becoming possessed in this way is referred to as *lupa*, the literal meaning of which is "to forget."

2. For example, in Southeast Asia, where shamanism of the true or classic sort flourishes among some groups, it has no particular association with a hunting and gathering adaptation.

3. The term "shaman" has been sometimes been applied to ritual specialists in these societies. For example, Melford Spiro (1967) does so regarding some Burmese ritual practitioners and Carol Laderman (1991) does so regarding Malay ones.

4. Two volumes of critical discussion of Castaneda were edited and published by Richard De Mille (1976, 1980). Castaneda's books have been translated into twenty-seven languages. He died in 1998.

REFERENCES AND FURTHER READING

Atkinson, Jane Monnig. 1989. *The Art and Politics of Wana Shamanism.* Berkeley: University of California Press.

———. 1992. "Shamanisms Today." *Annual Review of Anthropology* 2: 307–30.

Bahn, Paul. 1997. "Membrane and Numb Brain: A Close Look at a Recent Claim for Shamanism in Paleolithic Art." *Rock Art Research* 14(1): 62–68.

———. 1998. *The Cambridge Illustrated History of Prehistoric Art*. Cambridge: Cambridge University Press.

———. 2001. "Save the Last Trance for Me: An Assessment of the Misuse of Shamanism in Rock Art Studies." In *The Concept of Shamanism: Uses and Abuses*, edited by Henri Francfort and Robert N. Hamayon, pp. 51–93. Budapest: Akadémiai Kladó.

Bernstein, Jay H. 1997. *Spirits Captured in Stone: Shamanism and Traditional Medicine among the Taman of Borneo*. Boulder: Lynn Rienner.

Blacker, Carmen. 1975. *The Catalpa Bow: A Study of Shamanistic Practices in Japan*. London: Allen & Unwin.

Bourguignon, Erika. 1991. *Possession*. Prospect Heights, Ill.: Waveland.

Castaneda, Carlos. [1968] 1998. *The Teachings of Don Juan: A Yaqui Way of Knowledge*. Berkeley: University of California Press.

Clottes, Jean, and David Lewis-Williams. 1998. *Shamans of Prehistory: Trance and Magic in the Painted Caves*. New York: Harry N. Abrams.

DeBernardi, Jean. 2006. *Chinese Popular Religion and Spirit Mediums in Penang, Malaysia*. Stanford, Calif. Stanford University Press.

De Mille, Richard, ed. 1976. *Castaneda's Journey: The Power and the Allegory*. Santa Barbara, Calif.: Capra.

———. 1980. *The Don Juan Papers: Further Castaneda Controversies*. Santa Barbara, Calif.: Ross Erikson.

Eliade, Mircea. [1951] 1964. *Shamanism: Archaic Techniques of Ecstasy*. New York: Pantheon.

Flaherty, Gloria. 1992. *Shamanism and the Eighteenth Century*. Princeton: Princeton University Press.

Francfort, Henri-Paul, and Robert N. Hamayon, eds. 2001. *The Concept of Shamanism: Uses and Abuses*. Budapest: Akadémiai Kladó.

Furst, Peter T. 2003. *Visions of a Huichol Shaman*. Philadelphia: University of Pennsylvania Museum of Archaeology and Anthropology.

Geertz, Clifford. 1973. *The Interpretation of Cultures*. New York: Basic Books.

Guenther, Mathias. 1999. "From Totemism to Shamanism: Hunter-Gatherer Contributions to World Mythology and Spirituality." *Cambridge Encyclopedia of Hunters and Gatherers*, edited by Richard Lee and Richard Daly, pp. 426–33.

Harner, Michael. 1973. *Hallucinogens and Shamanism*. New York: Oxford University Press.

———. 1980. *The Way of the Shaman: A Guide to Power and Healing*. San Francisco: Harper & Row.

Hultkrantz, Åke. 1992. *Shamanic Healing and Ritual Drama*. New York: Crossroad.

Jakobsen, Merete Demant. 1999. *Shamanism: Traditional and Contemporary Approaches to the Mastery of Spirits and Healing*. New York: Berghahn.

Kehoe, Alice Beck. 2000. *Shamans and Religion: An Anthropological Exploration in Critical Thinking*. Prospect Heights, Ill.: Waveland.

Kendall, Laurel. 1985. *Shamans, Housewives, and Other Restless Spirits*. Honolulu: University of Hawaii Press.

———. 1988. *The Life and Hard Times of a Korean Shaman: Of Tales and the Telling of Tales*. Honolulu: University of Hawaii Press.

La Barre, Weston. 1984. *Muelos: A Stone Age Superstition about Sexuality*. New York: Columbia University Press.

———. [1972] 1990. "Hallucinogens and the Shamanic Origins of Religion." In *Flesh of the Gods: The Ritual Uses of Hallucinogens*, edited by Peter T Furst, pp. 269–78. Prospect Heights, Ill.: Waveland.

Laderman, Carol. 1991. *Taming the Wind of Desire: Psychology, Medicine, and Aesthetics in Malay Shamanistic Performance*. Berkeley: University of California Press.

Lewis, I. M. 1986. *Religion in Context: Cults and Charisma*. Cambridge: Cambridge University Press.

———. [1971] 1989. *Ecstatic Religion: A Study of Shamanism and Spirit Possession*. London: Routledge.

Olmos, Margarite Fernandez, and Lizabeth Paravisini-Gebert. 2003. *Creole Religions of the Caribbean: An Introduction from Vodon and Santería to Obeah and Espiritismo*. New York: New York University Press.

Ong, Aihwa. 1987. *Spirits of Resistance and Capitalist Discipline: Factory Women in Malaysia*. Albany: State University of New York Press.

Park, Willard Z. 1938. *Shamanism in Western North America: A Study in Cultural Relationships*. Evanston, Ill.: Northwestern University Press.

Pearson, James L. 2002. *Shamanism and the Ancient Mind: A Cognitive Approach to Archaeology*. Walnut Creek, Calif.: AltaMira.

Sather, Clifford. 2001. *Seeds of Play, Words of Power: An Ethnographic Study of Iban Shamanic Chants*. Kuala Lumpur: Tun Jugah Foundation.

Schiller, Anne. 1997. *Small Sacrifices: Religious Change and Cultural Identity among the Ngaju of Indonesia*. New York: Oxford University Press.

Siikala, Anna-Leena, and Mihály Hoppál, eds. 1998. *Studies on Shamanism*. Helsinki: Finnish Anthropological Society; Budapest: Akadémiai Kladó.

Spiro, Melford E. 1967. *Burmese Supernaturalism: A Study in the Explanation and Reduction of Suffering*. Englewood Cliffs, N.J.: Prentice-Hall.

Thien Do. 2003. *Vietnamese Supernaturalism: Views from the Southern Region*. London: RoutledgeCurzon.

Thomas, Nicholas, and Caroline Humphry, eds. 1994. *Shamanism, History, and the State*. Ann Arbor: University of Michigan Press.

Townsend, Joan. 1997. "Shamanism." In *Anthropology of Religion: A Handbook*, edited by Stephen Glazier, pp. 429–69. Westport, Conn.: Greenwood.

Tylor, Edward B. [1871] 1889. *Primitive Culture: Researches into the Development of Mythology, Philosophy, Religion, Language, Art, and Custom*. 2 vols. 3rd American ed. New York: Holt.

Walter, Mariko Namba, and Eva Jane Neumann Fridman, eds. 2004. *Shamanism: An Encyclopedia of World Beliefs, Practices, and Culture*. Santa Barbara, Calif. ABC-CLIO.

Winkelman, Michael. 1997. "Altered States of Consciousness and Religious Behavior." In *Anthropology of Religion: A Handbook*, edited by Stephen Glazier, pp. 393–428. Westport, Conn.: Greenwood.

———. 2000. *Shamanism: The Neural Ecology of Consciousness and Healing*. Westport, Conn.: Bergin & Garvey.

Winzeler, Robert L. 1993. *The Seen and the Unseen: Shamanism, Spirit Mediumship, and Possession in Borneo*. Borneo Research Council Monograph Series 2.

———. 2004. "Southeast Asian Shamanism." In *Shamanism: An Encyclopedia of World Beliefs, Practices, and Culture*, edited by Mariko Namba Walter and Eva Jane Neumann Fridman, pp. 834–42. Santa Barbara, Calif. ABC-CLIO.

10

⸜⸝

Religious Movements and the Origins of Religion

Religious movements among indigenous peoples have long been a major item in the stock-in-trade stock in the anthropology of religion. Defined in the simplest terms, a religious movement can be any general and rapid change in religious beliefs and practices that is adopted by some group. Religious movements as we know them have several other characteristics as well. One is that the changes, and the people who have adapted them, have a known and named identity, both to themselves and to outsiders, although the specific terms used by insiders and outsiders may not be the same. Another characteristic is that such movements tend to occur within a broader context of contact, change, and conflict, although just how much and how rapid cannot be specified; nor do all situations of contact, change, and conflict necessarily produce religious movements. A final characteristic is that movements as such have a limited duration. Several of the world religions (not to mention a large number of developments within them) are often assumed to have begun as movements, but none is today referred to as such. Although no one can give a particular number of years or decades, sooner or later one of several things happens: the movement dies out or disappears from view, some of its innovations perhaps absorbed into existing belief and practice, or else it becomes an established, named religion or a version or sect of one.

In addition to these general characteristics, religious movements often have two other features as well. One is a known leader or originator, usually a visionary (in the literal sense of this term) often referred to as a prophet; the other is that, if there is a known founder, it is the name of this person that may become the name of the movement. Religions or religious movements named after known or assumed founders are so well-known that it is the exceptions that are worth mentioning. These exceptions include some of the movements, which have occurred among indigenous peoples in colonial situations in which anthropologists have often taken a particular interest, such as some of the best-known Native American movements.

Religious movements have occurred throughout history and have been labeled by anthropologists and others in different ways according to one or another of their central characteristics or doctrines. Those that emphasize the abandonment of foreign ways and a return to indigenous ones are called *nativistic* (Linton 1943); those that involve a messiah are known as *messianic*, and those proclaim an end or a transformation of the world are referred to as *millennial* or *millenarian*. In some instances, more than one such feature may be present; the Ghost Dance was both millenarian and nativistic (but not messianic). For the past several decades, however, anthropologists have often referred to all types as *revitalization* movements, a notion deriving from an effort by the American anthropologist Anthony Wallace to characterize their common features and analyze the general nature and sequence of development.

Whatever they are called and whatever exact forms they take, religious movements occur widely in the world, as they have throughout history. Anthropological attention has focused on those in Africa and especially Melanesia and North America. There are several possible reasons for this, including their commonness or frequency in the latter two areas (at least in some periods), their often spectacular character, and their political nature. In what follows I will first summarize and discuss several movements, including ones from North America, Melanesia, and Southeast Asia that exemplify some of the main differences as well commonalities. After that we will look at the theory of revitalization and its current status.

THREE NATIVE AMERICAN MOVEMENTS

The Delaware Prophet

In 1762, following the defeat of the French and their Indian allies by the English, a prophet named Neolin appeared among the Delaware people, who were then living in the Ohio territory in the present-day United States.[1] The movement he created was both political and nativistic, for the prophet preached the union of tribes and a return to the old Indian way of life. It was also unquestionably religious in that a spirit, whose title was translated as the Master of Life, had commanded Neolin to do these things in a vision. The vision was recounted as occurring in the following way: Neolin ("the Enlightened") was eager to meet the Master of Life and one day decided to travel to the spirit world. In order to know the way, he performed a ritual and fell into a deep sleep and dreamed that he was simply to begin to walk and by doing so would eventually reach his destination. He started off the next morning and traveled for eight days. Then at sunset, while he prepared to camp for the night by a small stream in an opening in the forest, he noticed three wide paths leading in different directions. After preparing his camp and making a fire, he saw that even as it grew darker the paths into the forest had become more visible. Frightened by the strangeness of what was before him, he decided to leave and make camp elsewhere, but then he remembered his dream and the purpose of his journey and remained where he was. The next morning he chose the widest path and followed it until noon, when a fire rose from the earth in front of him. He went closer but the fire grew before him until he was frightened and turned back.

After returning to his camping place, Neolin took the next widest path but was turned back in the same way. After returning again he took the last path, on which he continued all day until he suddenly saw before him a shining mountain. The mountain was steep and he could see no way up. He was about to give up when he saw a bright, beautiful woman clad in snow-white garments seated a short way up the mountain. She spoke to him in his own language, saying that the Master of Life lived on the summit of the mountain and that Neolin should ascend and meet him. But before he could go up, he was to leave his clothes and gear behind and bathe in the nearby river. Neolin did as he was told and then asked how he could ascend the mountain, which was steep and as slippery as glass. The woman replied that he could do so by using only his left hand and foot. Though this seemed impossible, Neolin began to climb in this way and with difficulty reached the top (Mooney 1973: 662–64).

At this point the woman vanished and Neolin saw a plain on which there were three villages composed of well-made houses arranged in an orderly manner. He began to approach the main village but remembered that he was naked. He was about to turn back when he heard a voice tell him that it was all right to continue. Neolin advanced to the gate of the village where he was met by a handsome man who also wore white garments. The man offered to lead him to meet the Master of Life. Admiring everything around him, he was led to the Master of Life who took him by the hand and told him to sit on a hat with a gold rim. Afraid of spoiling the hat, Neolin was reluctant to sit down until told again to do so. After he was seated, the Master of Life addressed him and said, "I am the Master of Life. Listen to what I shall tell you for yourself and for all the Indians." The Master of Life then spoke of the situation in which the Indian people found themselves: "The land on which you are, I have made for you, not for others. Wherefore do you suffer the Whites to dwell upon your lands? Can you not do without them?" (Mooney 1973: 664–65)

After explaining how the Indians had gotten themselves into their sad circumstances, the Master of Life went on to state what they should do regarding the whites, and this was very different in the case of the French and the English (which before the revolution included the American colonists):

> I do not, however, forbid suffering among you your Father's children [the French]. I love them; they know me; they pray to me. I supply their own wants, and give them that which they bring you. Not so with those who are come to trouble your possessions [the English]. Drive them away; wage war against them; I love them not; they know me not; they are my enemies; they are your brother's enemies. Send them back to the lands I have made for them. Let them remain there. (Mooney 1973: 665)

The Delaware prophet was then given a prayer carved in Indian "hieroglyphics" on a wooden stick that he was told to deliver to his chief after returning to earth:

> Learn it by heart, and teach it to all the Indians and children. It must be repeated morning and evening. Do all that I have told thee, and announce it to all the Indians as coming from the Master of Life. Let them drink but one drought [of alcohol], or two at most, in one day. Let them have but one wife, and discontinue running after others people's wives and daughters. Let them not fight one another. Let them not sing the medicine song, for in singing the medicine song they speak to the evil spirit. Drive from your lands those dogs in red clothing [the British]; they are only an injury to you. When you want anything, apply to me, as your brothers do, and I will give to you both. Do not sell to your brothers that which I have placed on the earth as food. In short, become good, and you shall want nothing. When you meet one another, bow and give one another the (left) hand of your heart. Above all, I command thee to repeat morning and evening the prayer which I have given thee. (Mooney 1973: 665)

Neolin was then led back down the mountain, where he dressed and returned to his village. There his friends were surprised to see him for they had thought he had been lost. They asked him where he had been, but he only pointed to the sky and proceeded to the house of the chief, to whom he delivered the prayer and the message from the Master of Life.

The message brought by the Delaware prophet spread rapidly from group to group and produced widespread ferment. It led to the creation of a confederacy of northwestern tribes under the leadership of the famous chief Pontiac, aimed at preventing the further progress of the English.

While the confederacy had some initial success, it was eventually over-whelmed and defeated. When the American Revolutionary War began, the Indian groups aligned themselves with the English as the lesser of two evils, again choosing the losing side. (Mooney 1973: 668–69: Wallace 1972)

The religious fervor that spread among the Indian groups along the American frontier in the latter part of the eighteenth century was neither the first nor the last. Religious hope and enthusiasm associated with vi-sions and prophecy moved in a wave among Native Americans from the eastern part of what became the Unified States to the west. In addition, in the Southwest, along the Rio Grande River, the Pueblo revolt of 1680 was also linked to visions, this time of the Tewa prophet Popé, who had been given magical powers by the ancestral spirits and commanded to make an effort to rid the country of the Spaniards.

James Mooney and the Ghost Dance

James Mooney discussed these (and many other) instances of prophetic inspiration, widespread fervor and resistance in *The Ghost Dance Religion and the Sioux Outbreak of 1890*. The title of Mooney's book referred to the climactic and best-known religious reaction to the conquest and subjuga-tion of the indigenous peoples of North America. Ghost Dance was a translation of the various Native American terms used for the movement as it developed on the Great Plains.

Mooney was an early ethnologist who worked for the Smithsonian In-stitution (Moses 1984). When news of the Ghost Dance began to spread in 1890, he was doing research among the Cherokee, most of whom, like other surviving remnants of the Indians that had occupied the lands of the United States to the east of the Mississippi, had been forced to resettle in Oklahoma. Mooney sought and received permission to investigate and went directly west to learn what was occurring among the southern Cheyenne and Arapaho. What he found was more widespread and im-portant than had been supposed. The study Mooney had expected to last weeks continued over much of the next three years. It involved firsthand research among the Kiowa, Comanche, Apache, Caddo, and Wichita as well as the Cheyenne and Arapaho, all of whom had been moved at var-ious times to Indian Territory or present-day Oklahoma. It also included travel to other regions and research among the Sioux at Pine Ridge, South Dakota, the Paiute of Mason Valley Nevada, and the northern Arapaho and Shoshoni of Wyoming. On a subsequent trip he also visited the Navajo, Hopi, and other Southwestern groups among whom apostles of the Ghost Dance had been proselytizing. All told, Mooney spent twenty-two months in travel and field research. It was not exactly modern an-thropological fieldwork in the style of Malinowski, but Mooney believed in gaining the trust of those he interviewed as the basis of accurate information, participated in dances and ceremonies, regarded Indian people as his friends, and was sympathetic to them and the movement.

Mooney was well aware of the cultural differences among seemingly similar Native American groups. He stressed variations in receptivity to the Ghost Dance movement and the importance of local and regional developments. Information about the ritual procedures of the Ghost Dance was transmitted orally, by individual contact and instruction. It was reinterpreted according to the cultural background and historical context of the various tribes. It was one thing for the Paiute of Nevada, among whom it had originated with the visions and prophecy of Wovoka, and quite another among the Lakota and other groups east of the Rocky Mountains, among whom it had the greatest impact. But Mooney also argued that there were strong continuities between the earliest Indian religious movements in eastern colonial North America, including that of the prophet Neolin, and the Ghost Dance of the west at the end of the nineteenth century. The Ghost Dance religion had strong Indian and shamanic elements, including the importance of dancing as the crucial ritual activity, visions and dreams, and ritual paraphernalia, especially the ghost shirts. It also had Christian biblical elements, especially the prophetic, messianic, and apocalyptic notions spread by missionaries.

Mooney's book was written at a time when the conquest and settlement of a large part of the North American continent by white Americans was generally viewed as a great triumph, national destiny, or at least inevitability. Mooney stressed that Indian religious revivals and the seemingly futile armed resistance they sometimes engendered were born of desperation. Moreover, the movements were common human reactions to defeat and demoralization that could be seen widely throughout human history and across culture, including Western and white American history and religion. He listed as parallels (and then described in more detail in his last chapter) the visions and prophecies of the biblical period, Mohammedanism, Joan of Arc, the Dance of St. John, the Flagellants, the Ranters, Quakers, French prophets, Jumpers, Shakers, Methodists, and the Kentucky revival. He did not say so, but he hinted that religions in general often began with dreams, trance states and visions, prophecy, dancing, and emotional release and that these tended to recur in the context of civilized religions as well as tribal ones (Mooney 1973: 928–52).

Mooney reported that as a religious movement the Ghost Dance had an unspectacular beginning in the Nevada desert. Wovoka, the prophet of the 1890 Ghost Dance, was not the first Paiute to have such visions. A man named Wodziwob had similar visions in 1870 and had communicated them locally with limited effect.[2] The Paiute of western Nevada were an odd case, Mooney thought, in comparison to many other Indian groups at the time. They did not seem to have suffered to the same extent as the eastern, Midwestern Prairie, and Plains groups. They had not undergone the military defeat, dislocation, loss of freedom, starvation, and nearly total destruction of their way of life that had befallen many groups, often in a short period of time, especially on the Plains. The local Paiute had fought only once with whites, the battle of Pyramid Lake in 1860. At the time of his visit, the Paiute had seemed to adjust comparatively well to the arrival of the whites, who were living mostly in scattered mining settlements and on isolated ranches. The Paiute had developed a distinctive semiacculturated way of life. They spent part of the year working for ranchers, who regarded them as good workers in a region where labor was in short supply. They also spent part of the year engaged in traditional hunting and gathering activities. Their material culture reflected this partial and selective adaptation to white ways and technology. They had accepted white clothing, guns, and many other things they purchased with the money they earned by selling their labor, but they had retained their own type of house.

Given Mooney's (1973: 764–72) rather positive evaluation of what had and had not happened to the Paiute and other desert-dwelling groups of the western Great Basin, it seemed somewhat strange that the Ghost Dance had begun here, especially given his own inclination to explain Indian religious revivalism in terms of disruption, defeat, and despair. Mooney attempted to explain this seeming contradiction by stressing the difference between the movement as initiated among the Paiutes by Wovoka and what it became to the east of the Rockies. He thought that what had happened to Wovoka himself was more a personal crisis than a reaction to social and cultural decline and despair.

Mooney (1973: 771–73) acquired three different versions of Wovoka's visions, including one from the prophet himself.[3] According to Wovoka, his visions had occurred some six years before the interview. The occasion was an eclipse of the sun. Wovoka fell asleep in the daytime and was taken up to the other world. Here he saw God and all the people who had died long ago engaged in their old-time sports and occupations, and all were happy and forever young. The other world was a good place and full of game. After showing him all this, God told Wovoka that he must return and instruct his people to be good and love one another, to not quarrel, and to live in peace with the whites. God said also that people must work, not steal or lie, and put away all of the old practices that savored of war. He said that if the people did these things, they would be reunited with their friends in the other world, where there would be no more sickness, death, or old age. God then told Wovoka that all of this could be hastened by a ritual dance that he revealed. The dance should be performed for five days. Finally, God gave Wovoka powers to control the weather, to make it rain or snow, and appointed him to be his deputy on earth in the west.

The second version, which was given by a Paiute informant, was somewhat different from and more dramatic than Wovoka's. In this account, Wovoka had gone into the mountains with his family to cut wood for a man named Dave Wilson. One day he heard a great noise above him and, after moving toward it, he fell down dead and was taken by God to heaven.

Both of the Paiute versions of what happened to Wovoka have a strong shamanist dimension—they hold that Wovoka ascended to heaven. This also happened to the Delaware prophet, except he got there by climbing to the top of a magic mountain. The third version—the one Mooney favored—leaves out the shamanic journey (or at least Mooney left it out of his account). This was a version provided by a neighboring white rancher for whom Wovoka sometimes worked. The gist of this account was that Wovoka's visions resulted from a severe fever, when the rancher had cared for him. During the fever, a solar eclipse happened to occur. This was an event interpreted by the Paiute as caused by a monster devouring the sun, and therefore the occasion of great fear and excitement. Wovoka's vision resulted from the combination of his fever and the excitement caused by the eclipse (Mooney 1973: 773).

Following his vision Wovoka began to preach, perform miracles with the weather, and teach the dance to the Paiutes. Wovoka gained a local following but the real impact of the Ghost Dance religion came with its spread to other Native American groups, especially among those dwelling far to the east. In Mooney's words, the "great underlying principle of the Ghost Dance doctrine is that the time will come when the whole Indian race, living and dead, will be reunited upon a regenerated earth, to live a life of aboriginal happiness, forever free from death, disease and misery" (Mooney 1973: 777). The white race being new to the Indian world had no place in this transformation and would cease to exist after it occurred. The apocalypse would eventually come without human action but might be anticipated in dreams through the dance. According to Wovoka, the time was near but after several predictions failed to materialize he left the exact date open.

As news of Wovoka and his vision and prophecies spread, Indians from throughout western North America traveled to see him and carried his prophecies and instructions back with them. The movement spread rapidly in 1889 and 1890, though different groups took it up to varying extents, and Christian converts did not become involved. Different groups then proceeded to create different versions on the basis of their own mythology and situation.

Mooney observed that the dance took on a more militant and antiwhite character when it crossed the Rockies and moved onto the Plains. It was here in the latter part of the nineteenth century that resistance to white encroachment had been greatest and where defeat had been most rapid and traumatic. Mooney stressed that it was only among the Sioux (Lakota) that the Ghost Dance was linked to violent resistance to whites. He noted that Wovoka, in addition to emphasizing that Indians were to live in peace, disclaimed any responsibility for the ghost shirts. These shirts, the most emblematic of all objects associated with the Ghost Dance, were believed to confer invulnerability on their wearers.

The Ghost Dance did not last long as religious movements go. Some Indian groups had been doubters and skeptics all along and others who had initially been devotees became so after the expected transformation of the world did not occur. While Wovoka had not by the time of Mooney's visit given up on his vision, he was said to have become tired of being visited by Indians from distant places and wanted to be left alone. The spread of

Figure 10.1.   An Arapaho Ghost Dance shirt published in James Mooney's *The Ghost-Dance Religion and the Sioux Outbreak of 1890.*

the news among Indians of the disaster at Wounded Knee did not bring an end to the Ghost Dance. For a while it continued to travel, as new groups took it up. By the time Mooney wrote his report in 1893, however, he claimed that the Ghost Dance was essentially over as a pan-Indian revival. Among most of the tribes it was already extinct. The Shoshoni and some other groups had lost faith after the failure of the first predictions. The Paiute had been dancing a year before (in 1892) and the Kiowa, having previously abandoned it, were again dancing as of 1893. In Oklahoma, especially among the Cheyenne, Arapaho, Caddo, Pawnee, Wichita, and Ohio, the Ghost Dance was frequently performed as a regular part of tribal ceremonies, but it had lost the feverish expectation of previous years. Here it had instead become something closer to the Christian hope of eventual reunion with departed friends in a happier world at some unknown future time (Mooney 1973: 927).

The general term that Mooney used for the Ghost Dance and other such movements was "revival," which was widely used at the time for Christian efforts at reawakening and fundamentalism. Although Mooney sometimes referred to Wovoka as a messiah, Wovoka regarded himself, as did his followers, as a messenger of divine revelation rather than a savior, though he was believed to have certain mystical powers, including an ability to control the weather.

Peyotism and the Native American Church

Religious movements among Native Americans did not end with the Ghost Dance. By the time the fervor had subsided, another new pattern of ritual practice had already begun. What became labeled by scholars as peyotism or the Peyote Cult and by adherents as the Peyote Way, began in Oklahoma and spread throughout the west and beyond.[4] This development lacked messianic and apocalyptic themes or any expectations that the whites would disappear, the ancestors would come to life, and buffalo would return. It emphasized acceptance of the world as it is, participation in communal rituals, and visions achieved through the use of peyote. While not devoid of elements of resistance and separatism, peyotism proved to be more enduring as an alternative to Christian conversion than the Ghost Dance.

"Peyotism" and related names reflect that the ritual practices include the eating of the dried tops (or buds) of the peyote cactus (*Lophophora williamsii*), containing mescaline, a potent hallucinogen. The use of peyote (the word is from the Aztec *peyotl*) to produce visions has a long history in Mexico and the American Southwest, although in the latter region the plant has a limited range along both sides of the Rio Grande River. Scholars including J. S. Slotkin (1956) distinguish between the long-standing ritual use of peyote by individuals as a vision-producing medicine and what became the organized peyote religion. Slotkin (1956: 34) concludes that the peyote religion began around 1885 among the Kiowa or Comanche then living on a reservation in Oklahoma and spread to other areas (especially the plains) over the next several decades. An early and enduring interpretation was that the movement gained momentum after 1891 as a consequence of the failure of the Ghost Dance, although the exactness of the relationship between the two developments has been questioned.

Although beliefs and practices vary from one place and tradition to another, peyotism developed as a syncretic tradition. It combined the older and widespread Southwestern ritual use of peyote as a vision-inducing medicine with Christian doctrine and practice, as reinterpreted along Indian lines. The consumption of peyote came to be defined as a sacrament reminiscent of Communion. The early rituals were primarily intended for curing but eventually developed into a general service held from Saturday night through Sunday.

Peyotism had no prophet or single founder. However, two individuals, both of mixed Indian and white descent, were crucial in developing and spreading the movement or, more accurately, two distinct versions of it. The first was Quanah Parker, a Comanche leader and the son of a white mother and a Comanche father who favored Indian cooperation with whites. Parker or Quanah, as he is often known, was the founder of the Half Moon tradition or the Tipi Way (because the services are held in a tipi). John Wilson, founder of the other tradition, known as the Big Moon or Cross Fire tradition, was a Caddo Indian of Caddo, Delaware, and French descent. A Catholic, Wilson's version of the Peyote Way contains more explicit Christian symbols and practices than does Quanah Parker's more Indian one. Both traditions succeeded and spread because the peyotists were willing and able to confront conservative white opposition and use the courts and other institutions and work with white allies. While peyotism initially spread like the Ghost Dance through traditional contact and word of mouth, it also came to be widely known through new institutions that brought together Indians from distant tribes, including the Carlisle Indian School in Pennsylvania, a rather ironic development given that the purpose of such institutions was to advance the acculturation and assimilation of Indians to white ways. Peyotism eventually spread as far north as Canada and to more than fifty tribes.

From early on peyotism aroused controversy, among both Indians and whites who had dealings with them. Among Indians, traditional shamans and Christians, as well as adherents of modernization and acculturation, opposed it. Not surprisingly, much of the opposition concerned the use of peyote. Partly as a defensive strategy and using Christian church organization as a model, peyotists began to organize themselves as the Native

American Church (then as the Native American Church of North America, to include Canadian adherents as well), first in 1918 in Oklahoma (where James Mooney—who was also among the first non-Indians to have witnessed and noted the peyote ceremony while researching the Ghost Dance in 1891—was involved as an organizer and supporter) and then in eleven more states by 1960. The church presently claims about 1,800 chapters and 250,000 members. It eventually came to be strongly associated with pan-Indian nationalism. Gaining status as an officially recognized religion enabled adherents to claim the right to use peyote under the guarantees of religious freedom provided by the First Amendment of the U.S. Constitution. Such a right as far as peyote was concerned had long been challenged and continued to be. In 1978, Congress passed the Native American Religious Freedom Act, which exempted the use of peyote for religious purposes by members of recognized Indian tribes. In 1990, the U.S. Supreme Court decided against the religious right to use peyote in a termination of employment case. In 1993, Congress passed the Religious Freedom Restoration Act, but this was struck down on the same grounds as those of the 1990 decision—that the right to religious freedom does not trump otherwise valid laws. However, antipeyote laws are not enforceable on Indian reservations, and most law enforcement organizations have not attempted to halt peyote-related activities.

CARGO MOVEMENTS IN MELANESIA

At the time of the Ghost Dance in North America, religious movements were occurring among indigenous peoples in other parts of the world. Those that took place in the southwestern Pacific have received particular attention in anthropology.

The Tuka Movement in Fiji

Fiji provides an early example known as the Tuka movement (the name Tuka is believed to derive from two Fijian words that together meant "something that stands forever"), which was founded in the early 1880s (Worsley 1968: 20 n.) by a Fijian man named Ndugumoi, who had a series of visions. Like Wovoka, Ndugumoi had a father who had experienced visions many years before. A further parallel was that Ndugumoi had also worked for whites in Tonga at one point. Unlike Wovoka, however, Ndugumoi, a hereditary priest in traditional Fijian religion, got in trouble with the British colonial authorities and was exiled to the remote Lau Islands for sedition.

His mission began after he was freed and returned in 1882. In addition to announcing his visions, Ndugumoi also claimed that he had escaped from the whites who believed him to be in Tonga. In fact, he said, he had left his body in Tonga while his spirit had returned by ship, escaping when the vessel was passing a sacred mountain. He had gotten away in spite of attempts by whites to kill him by tying an anchor around his neck and throwing him overboard. He had escaped by swimming unharmed and unnoticed to shore, and was therefore invulnerable to efforts to kill or harm him.

After Ndugumoi's miraculous return, he took the title of Navosavakandua, which was applied to the chief justice of Fiji, which meant literally "he who speaks once" in reference to his life and death powers over those brought before him. He also began to reveal his visions. In many respects they were similar to those of Wovoka and other Native American Indian prophets that told of apocalyptic change. He prophesied that ancestors would soon return to Fiji, and when they did a great transformation would take place—the faithful would enter the Glorious Paradise, the lands of Fiji would become independent again, and whites, including traders, government officials, and missionaries, would be driven into the sea.

There were also themes that link the Tuka cult to the broader tradition of Melanesian movements. For those who believed in the new world, the shops would be filled with canned salmon, calico cloth, and other goods brought by ship. In addition the prophecy drew from the Fijian creation myth in which twin brothers were defeated and forced to sail away into exile. According to Ndugumoi, these divine twins were about to return. The Europeans were aware of this and, while pretending to be surveying the reef, were actually watching the horizon for the ships bringing the divine twins and the ancestors.

Like many religious movements that developed following the introduction of Christianity into a region, Tuka doctrine combined indigenous and biblical themes. This included a version of creation featuring two gods, Jehovah and Ndengei, the Fijian snake deity. When the latter lost a contest to the former, it was driven away, leaving Jehovah to create the peoples of the world. An antiwhite theme included the claim that Jehovah was a Fijian deity rather than the one claimed by missionaries. Whites had deliberately deceived the Fijians when they wrote the Bible by substituting the names Jehovah and Jesus Christ for those of the divine twins.

Religious movements gain importance to the extent that they spread and develop in organizational terms and, from the white or government perspective, to the extent that they bring unrest or threaten resistance, especially violence or rebellion. Navosavakandua preached widely and set

up an elaborate organization. The rituals that were created featured
dances that also combined indigenous and imported forms, the latter involving the colonial constabulary drill, including salutes, marching, and
words of command. The antiwhite doctrinal themes, organization efforts
and success, and the militaristic ritual practices worried the colonial authorities. They reacted when the prophet set a date for the millennium
and began to issue threats to the government. Navosavakandua was arrested and sentenced to a year in prison, as new rumors spread about government efforts to kill him being foiled by his invulnerability. He was later
banished for ten years to Rotuma Island ten miles to the north and died
on his way home after release. His followers refused to believe the news
of his death due to his reputation for invulnerability. The Tuka movement
continued to reappear in different places or guises for many years. Religiously oriented unrest and resistance continued well into the twentieth
century, with lesser revivals taking place in relation to both World War I
and World War II (Worsley 1968: 17–29).

The Notion of Cargo

The Tuka movement in Fiji is an early example cf a cargo cult, although
the explicitly cargo themes (the expectation that in the transformed world
there would be shops filled with calico cloth, canned salmon, and other
goods) appear minor. Why did cargo become a defining element in
Melanesian religious fervor?

In standard usage, the term "cargo" refers to the contents carried by a
ship or a plane—the goods transported from one place to another. However, in the pidgin languages that developed in the islands of the southwestern Pacific, cargo came to mean all of the material things (including
tools, weapons, cloth and clothing, canned food and other foodstuffs, and
much else) or wealth of the white man that arrived in ships and later in
planes. There were several things about cargo that made it particularly
important in the eyes of the native peoples of Melanesia. To begin with,
compared to their own, the material culture of the whites was striking.
Further, prestige property in the form of pigs, certain kinds of shells,
feathers, dog teeth, and other things was highly important in Melanesia,
where political power was closely associated with the possession, display,
and exchange of valued material objects. Finally, the origins of the white
man's cargo were basically a mystery. None of it was made locally; all of
it came by ships that arrived and departed randomly.

The use of the term "cargo cult" to label the religious movements of
Melanesia implies that they were simply motivated by materialistic desires. A cargo movement was one that had as its goal the acquisition,
partly by ritual means (as well as in some instances the use of ordinary

physical force), of the cargo possessed by whites. Cargo movements, however, varied from one place and time to another, and anthropologists and other scholars who have studied them do not necessarily agree on their meanings or causes. But the general understanding is that the desire to acquire white cargo was based in part at least on the belief that cargo was necessary for gaining power over whites or driving them away.

The anthropologist Peter Worsley (1968), who has provided the best general account of the Melanesian movements, argues that they are basically religious forms of resistance to exploitation and appropriation, the loss of power, and the creation of class and ethnic hierarchies in a colonial situation. The distinctive religious aspects of the movements are a matter of Melanesian culture, but the social, political, and economic causes or context are similar to many religious movements over the world and throughout history. In general terms, such an interpretation is not very different from Mooney's explanation of the Ghost Dance.

As Worsley and other scholars have shown, colonial subjugation and exploitation were particularly harsh in the areas of Melanesia where cargo movements developed. This was so in part because of the generally limited nature of indigenous political integration. Unlike many of the Polynesian societies of the Pacific, the Melanesians, with few exceptions, lacked highly developed chiefdoms. Such chiefdoms were respected as forms of authority and tradition by Europeans (especially the British), and that probably helped deter some of the abuses and exploitation that took place in much of Melanesia. Among the worst of these activities was "blackbirding," whereby labor recruiters captured men and sent them to work on plantations in distant places, including Australia, a practice not far removed from the slaving activities of an earlier period.

The Logic of Cargo Movements

To summarize, the Melanesian movements have generally been explained along the following lines:

1. Indigenous Melanesian society was very competitive, and status was generally achieved rather than inherited. Accumulating and giving away property was a major way of competing for status. Religious activity had a strongly practical focus.
2. Europeans arrived with types and quantities of goods, or cargo, never before seen or known. The goods simply appeared with no indication of how they are made or where they came from.
3. Indigenous society was destabilized and then transformed. There may or may not (depending on the area) have been conflict initially, but eventually a colonial state was created, native land in some

areas was appropriated, natives were often captured and pressed to work on European plantations. A rigid hierarchical class system was created.

4. European missionaries also arrived and urged conversion to Christianity as a means to salvation and a better life. The Christian doctrines that were preached had limited relationship to indigenous ones, despite some parallels in mythology. Many individuals converted under the assumption that life would improve but it did not. Conversion often led to disillusionment.

5. Here or there a convert familiar with Christian doctrines of salvation and the millennium had a vision that synthesized indigenous and imported ideas. A part of the belief is that the Europeans acquired the cargo that was intended for the natives, or that the European missionaries held back the important ritual secrets necessary to obtain the cargo and the way of life and power that went with it.

6. Various developments followed. People accepted the new doctrine and practiced the rituals advocated by the prophets of cargo. Some destroyed their old property and gardens in anticipation of the expected transformation. In some instances efforts were made to attack, destroy, and drive out the Europeans. Other movements were peaceful and focused on the millennium and the arrival of the cargo.

7. Violent or otherwise disruptive movements were suppressed by the European colonial regime, leaders were arrested, imprisoned, or exiled or, if killings occurred, perhaps executed.

8. The failure of the transformation to occur and the cargo to arrive along with, in some instances, the suppression of the movement often led to its end in one area, to be followed, however, by the same or a similar one elsewhere.

Later Cargo Cults and Nationalist Movements

Following the initial wave of cargo movements in the late nineteenth and early twentieth centuries, there was a new surge after World War II. This war and its aftermath in Melanesia were severe and destabilizing. The Melanesian Islands were a major theater of the Pacific war. The Japanese drove out the British and Australians early on and occupied the islands. A few years later, in some of the largest land and sea battles of the entire war, Allied forces drove out the Japanese and reoccupied the islands. The developments during and after World War II were quite different in some ways from those of earlier periods. But the cargo associated with the war and its aftermath of military bases (and again brought by ship and planes from distant places) was far more awesome than that associated with earlier developments. The problem in this case was not so much the sort of subjugation and exploitation experienced by the natives in earlier phases of colonial rule. It was rather the influx of vast technology, new organizations, cultural influences, and economic opportunities followed by their rapid disappearance after the war with the closing of bases and the departure of troops, practically overnight. The years after the close of the war brought the return of colonial rule and, while change and development were promised, little occurred.

The later movements were in some ways similar to previous ones. Rumors of ghostly ships and planes arriving with new cargo spread, and in some instances airstrips were cleared and model planes were built. Prophets had visions and preached about what the people should do to become modern and developed and obtain the wealth now in the hands of others. However, unlike the earlier cargo movements the later ones were in some instances precursors to modern nationalism, as movement leaders in some instances became politicians (Worsley 1968: 182–94).

THE BUNGAN MOVEMENT IN THE INTERIOR OF BORNEO

The Bungan movement of the interior of northern central Borneo is worth a look because it shows needs, motives, and developments that have not yet been considered. It illustrates a desire catalyzed (if not created) by outside agents of change that led indigenous peoples to alter but not abandon their old set of religious practices. Bungan was not based on the kind or degree of trauma and dislocation involved in the Native American or Melanesian cargo movements discussed above. Nor did it involve any of the militant anticolonial and nativistic efforts associated with some of these movements.[5]

The Bungan movement was created in the late 1940s in Indonesian Borneo by a Dayak man named man named Jok Apoi, whose precise ethnic identity is in doubt (he was either Kayan or Kenyah, but probably the latter because Bungan was a Kenyah divinity), as is his religious affiliation; he may or may not have been a Christian before his revelation. The anthropologist Peter Metcalf, who took an interest in the Bungan movement because it spread to the Berawan, the small Orang Ulu ethnic group he studied in the 1970s, describes what occurred in the following way:

> In the most frequently told version, Jok Apoi was a poor man who year after year failed to produce enough rice to feed his family. Then, he had a dream in which he was confronted by Bungan, a gentle female deity often portrayed as the wife of the supreme deity Bali Penyalong. She told Jok Apoi that his crops had failed because he observed all the traditional taboos, rather than tending to his farm. This is the same pragmatic message that missionaries

were urging on interior folk at the time, as an inducement to become Christian. Bungan instructed Jok Apoi to disregard the bad omens that previously kept him at home, and to disregard also the expensive or inconvenient taboos, such as those surrounding trophies of the headhunt. Jok Apoi did as he was told, and his farm prospered. Despite the ridicule of the noble elite, others increasingly followed his example. (Metcalf 1989: 215)

As is sometimes the case with religious movements, Bungan had its greatest influence not where it had originated in the Indonesian Apo Kayan plateau, but across the mountains among the Orang Ulu (or Up-river) groups in Sarawak. One possible reason Bungan did not really take hold where it originated was that Christianity was already more firmly established than it was among the Orang Ulu of Sarawak. To many of the Orang Ulu, Bungan seemed to offer the best of both the old religion and Christianity. It was nativistic but it eliminated the practices that supposedly perpetuated backwardness.

In 1956, a party of Bungan missionaries traveled down the Baram, preaching as they went. They converted many among both the old religionists and those who had recently gone Christian. Yet they were more successful among the former than the latter. At its zenith of influence in the late 1950s and early 1960s, Bungan could probably claim as many adherents in the Baram river watershed as Christianity. The traditional religion had meanwhile all but disappeared. (Metcalf 1989: 215)

In the case of the Berawan in particular, Bungan made no headway until a local prophet had a vision and urged conversion. The prophet in this case was a young man named Sadi Pejong who as a teenager had been involved in opening an already full mausoleum so that another body could be added, an experience that disgusted him and led him to believe that the decline of the Berawan was due to their two-stage mortuary practices. Probably already aware of the Bungan movement among the neighboring Kenyah, Sadi Pejong had a series of strange dreams in the mid-1950s. The dreams combined elements of Berawan cosmology with things he had seen during World War II:

In one dream a mystical airplane landed on the river outside of the long-house and took him on a heavenly tour. After a particularly intense vision in which he received instruction from Bungan herself, he made his inspiration public and announced a new order. (Metcalf 1989: 216)

The result was that some Berawan adapted the Bungan innovations while others did not. Eventually Bungan lost ground, but this was to Christianity rather than the old religion. It would have been difficult or impossible to return to the old religion because many of the ceremonial

Figure 10.2. Orang Ulu Christian symbolism in a Kayan longhouse wall mural in central Borneo (Sarawak, east Malaysia): Veneration of the Cross including dragons offering flowers. Photo by Lim Yu Seng, reproduced with the permission of the Sarawak Museum, Kuching, Sarawak, Malaysia.

activities of which it consisted were communal or village-wide in nature. Today Christianity has become the religion of nearly all of the Orang Ulu peoples, including the Berawan. The Bungan, however, has not yet disappeared entirely. In addition to existing to some small extent among the longhouse dwellers it was taken up later by the hunting and gathering Penan, most of whom have given up their nomadic ways and settled into fixed villages.

REVITALIZATION

In an article first published in 1956, Anthony Wallace attempted to show that all religious movements can be analyzed as efforts at what he called *revitalization*. In the half century since the article appeared, "revitalization" has become a common way that anthropologists refer to religious

Figure 10.3. A Kenyah Orang Ulu interpretation of the crucifix in the old Roman Catholic church at Long San, Upper Baram, Sarawak, east Malaysia. Photo by Lim Yu Seng, reproduced with the permission of the Sarawak Museum, Kuching, Sarawak, Malaysia.

movements, although it is not clear that what Wallace meant by revitalization applies in all instances.

Wallace (1956) defined revitalization as a "deliberate, organized, conscious effort by members of a society to construct a more satisfying culture." The revitalization process involves five stages:

1. *Steady state.* This is the normal state of society and culture. The basic needs (physical and psychological) of the vast majority of the population are being met. Chronic stress may exist but it is within tolerable limits.
2. *The period of increased individual stress.* The specific causes of stress can include various things but the overall context is frequently one of contact, subjugation, and acculturation. While individuals can tolerate a certain amount of stress, such processes of deterioration can

lead to what Wallace calls "mazeway disintegration," by which he means the cultural or cognitive maps by which people live begin to lose their validity. People lose confidence in their culture.

3. *The period of cultural distortion.* At this stage different types of people respond in different ways. Rigid or conservative persons prefer high levels of chronic stress to making adaptive changes. Those who are more flexible try limited changes. Yet other individuals adopt "regressive innovations," which include alcoholism, indolence, extreme dependency on others, disregard of sexual norms, family and kin obligations, depression, and self-reproach. Some such innovations may themselves become cultural patterns.

4. *The period of revitalization.* Such processes of cultural and social deterioration can lead to the death of the society in one or another way. However, a revitalization movement frequently forestalls such dire consequences. A revitalization movement will need to accomplish at least six things.

   a. *Mazeway reformulation.* This means someone has to imagine a solution or a new way of life. That someone is usually a prophet, or less often a messiah, who has undergone dreams, hallucinatory or mystical experiences in which a supernatural being appears. This being explains the prophet's own and his society's troubles as existing partly or entirely as a result of the breaking of certain rules and promises salvation if various injunctions are followed and rituals performed, or personal and social disaster if they are not. The dreamer or visionary is rejuvenated, gives up old destructive habits like alcoholism, and begins a new life of energy and purpose.

   b. *Communication.* Revitalization will only occur if the doctrine is spread and accepted by others. The message contains two kinds of appeals for the target population. One is the proposition that followers or converts will come under the care and protection of supernatural beings and the other is that adherents will benefit materially from the implementation of the new cultural program. If successful, the prophet acquires apostles or disciples who help spread the revelations.

   c. *Organization.* A successful movement will have an organizational structure in the form of a hierarchy, with the prophet at the top, close associates (or special disciples) next below, and then general followers. At this point the movement becomes a campaign organization that is pervaded by a sense of charisma (an aura of mystical or magical power) that comes as a result of the prophet having entered into a special relationship with a supernatural being as a result of his or her revelations. The followers think of the charisma of the prophet as a form of mystical power.

d. *Adaptation.* This follows organization and includes all of the changes that are made in order to cope with resistance to what is in effect a revolutionary organization. Such changes may include alterations in doctrine to make the movement acceptable to a greater range of people or to counter the hostility of nonbelievers, or a combination of both.

e. *Cultural transformation.* This occurs if the movement is successful. However, it may not occur for various reasons. Movements are more or less "realistic," more or less adaptive, and occur in contexts that are more or less conducive to their success. Success takes the form of a reduction in the personal pathological behavior of adherents and in the creation of viable programs of positive adaptive cultural transformation or reform for the group.

f. *Routinization or normalization.* At this stage the movement is no longer revolutionary, though this does not mean that it becomes static. At this point also the movement relaxes control over many aspects of life except in the realm of doctrine and ritual. The movement has now become a "church."

5. *The new steady state.* Once this set of changes has taken place and if the results endure, a new steady state may be said to exist.

A Reevaluation of the Theory of Revitalization

One of Wallace's central claims about the importance of his theory of revitalization movements was that it covered and explained all the types of religious movements that had previously been referred to by a variety of terms. But is revitalization, which implies a positive pattern of change, always (or even often) an appropriate term? Revitalization movements do not really involve revitalization, he suggests, until they actually get to stage 4 (the period of revitalization). This seems to be not entirely logical or satisfactory. It would seem better to have a more general term for movements that lead to revitalization as well as ones that do not. Of course, the right such term would be simply "religious movement," which is any social effort that has a significant mystical or supernatural dimension. Some religious movements from the beginning do not seem to have much potential for successful revitalization.

This leads to a second problem. Although he did not say so, Wallace seemed to envision religious revitalization in terms of movements that encompass entire societies or large segments of them. This is not surprising in that Wallace was writing at a time when anthropologists traditionally studied small-scale societies in a holistic manner. Religious movements among such groups often involve whole societies or at least regions or tribes or villages or large parts of them. This is less likely to be the case with religious movements in larger, complex societies. They may involve only scattered individuals or families, neighborhoods, or regions, but it is harder to see how they will revitalize or change the larger society unless they continue to grow and become very large—which does not happen most of the time. And even if religious movements grow, they do not necessarily revitalize anything except perhaps the lives of some individual members who give up alcoholism or drug addiction or some other pathology. And this is not what Wallace meant by revitalization as a process leading to the creation of a whole new steady state.

Recently Wallace's original theory of revitalization has been reevaluated by a number of scholars involved in studying situations to which the theory might apply, specifically ones concerning Native Americans and Pacific Islanders (Harkin 2004). These reevaluations, which have been published as chapters in a book (*Reassessing Revitalization Movements: Perspectives from North America and the Pacific Islands*), make it clear that the theory of revitalization as originally formulated by Wallace is no longer accepted. In a short foreword to the volume, Wallace himself makes this point. He explains that he originally formulated the theory of revitalization as an outgrowth of his research on the early-nineteenth-century Seneca prophet Handsome Lake that was eventually published as *The Death and Rebirth of the Seneca*, but much later (in 1970) than his original article on revitalization. The Handsome Lake movement fits closely with Wallace's formulation of the revitalization cycle, but Wallace thought the same process could be seen in other religious movements as well.

NOTES

1. The summary of the Delaware movement given here is taken primarily from James Mooney's (1973) account of 1896. Wallace (1972: 117–21) includes an account and discussion of the movement in his *Death and Rebirth of the Seneca*.

2. Mooney incorrectly reported that Wovoka was the son of Wodziwob.

3. See Michael Hittman's *Wovoka and the Ghost Dance* for a recent and thorough discussion of Wovoka and the literature about him.

4. Unless otherwise noted, the summary presented here comes from the Religious Movements Homepage Project at the University of Virginia under "Native American Church," which appears to provide the most up-to-date information. There are several books by anthropologists about peyotism and the Native American Church (La Barre 1962; Slotkin 1956; Stewart 1987). David Aberle (1982) has written at length about peyotism among the Navajo in particular.

5. The Bungan movement has been described by several anthropologists (Metcalf 1989: 214–17; Rousseau 1998: 21–37) who studied one or another of the groups involved, although firsthand reports are meager.

REFERENCES AND FURTHER READING

Aberle, David. 1982. *The Peyote Religion among the Navajo.* 2nd ed. Norman: University of Oklahoma Press.

Billings, Dorothy K. 2002. *Cargo Cult as Theater: Political Performance in the Pacific.* Lanham, Md.: Lexington.

Harkin, Michael E. 2004. "Introduction: Revitalization as History and Theory." In *Reassessing Revitalization Movements: Perspectives from North America and the Pacific Islands,* edited by Michael E. Harkin, pp. xv–xxxvi. Lincoln: University of Nebraska Press.

———. 2004. *Reassessing Revitalization Movements: Perspectives from North America and the Pacific Islands.* Lincoln: University of Nebraska Press.

Hittman, Michael. 1997. *Wovoka and the Ghost Dance.* Lincoln: University of Nebraska Press.

Jebens, Holger, ed. 2004. *Cargo: Cult and Culture Critique.* Honolulu: University of Hawaii Press.

Jorgensen, Joseph G. 1986. "Ghost Dance, Bear Dance, and Sun Dance." In *Handbook of North American Indians.* Vol. 11, *Great Basin,* edited by Warren D'Azevedo, pp. 660–72. Washington, D.C.: Smithsonian Institution.

Kehoe, Alice B. 1989. *The Ghost Dance: Ethnohistory and Revitalization.* New York: Holt Rinehart & Winston.

La Barre, Weston. 1962. *They Shall Take Up Serpents.* Minneapolis: University of Minnesota Press.

———. 1975. *The Peyote Cult.* Hamden, Conn.: Archon.

Lawrence, Peter. 1989. *Road Belong Cargo: A Study of the Cargo Movements in the Southern Madang District, New Guinea.* Prospect Heights, Ill.: Waveland.

Linton, Ralph. 1943. "Nativistic Movements." *American Anthropologist* 45: 230–40.

Mair, Lucy. 1958. "Independent Religious Movements in Three Continents." *Comparative Studies in Society and History* 1: 113–36.

Metcalf, Peter. 1989. *Where Are You, Spirits: Style and Theme in Berawan Prayer.* Washington, D.C.: Smithsonian Institution Press.

Mooney, James. [1896] 1973. *The Ghost-Dance Religion and the Sioux Outbreak of 1890.* Fourteenth Annual Report of the Bureau of American Ethnology. Glorieta, N.M.: Rio Grande.

Moses, L. G. 1984. *The Indian Man: A Biography of James Mooney.* Urbana: University of Illinois Press.

Rousseau, Jérôme. 1998. *Kayan Religion: Ritual Life and Religious Reform in Central Borneo.* Leiden: KITLV Press.

Slotkin, J. S. 1956. *The Peyote Religion: A Study in Indian-White Relations.* Glencoe, Ill.: Free Press.

Stewart, Omar C. 1987. *Peyote Religion: A History.* Norman: University of Oklahoma Press.

Thornton, Russell. 1986. *We Shall Live Again: The 1870 and 1890 Ghost Dances as Demographic Revitalization*. Cambridge: Cambridge University Press.

Wallace, Anthony F. C. 1956. "Revitalization Movements: Some Theoretical Considerations for Their Comparative Study." *American Anthropologist* 58: 264–81.

———. 1972. *Death and Rebirth of the Seneca*. New York: Vintage.

———. 2004. Forward to *Reassessing Revitalization Movements: Perspectives from North America and the Pacific Islands*, edited by Michael E. Harkin, pp. vii–xi. Lincoln: University of Nebraska Press.

Worsley, Peter. 1968. *The Trumpet Shall Sound: A Study of "Cargo" Cults in Melanesia*. New York: Schocken.

11

⌘

Anthropology and Religion in a Global Context: The World Religions, Conversion, and Complexity

Until after World War II, anthropological studies of religion focused mainly on the indigenous beliefs and practices of small-scale societies lacking written traditions. The theoretical discussions and arguments about magic, religion, ritual, witchcraft, movements, and other matters were largely concerned with religion in these types of societies. Such religious beliefs and practices were first described by missionaries, colonial officials, and travelers and later by anthropologists, including Bronislaw Malinowski, E. E. Evans-Prichard, James Mooney, Clyde Kluckhohn, Elsie Clews Parsons, Victor Turner, and many others. Postmodernist criticism notwithstanding, the richness and enduring value of this tradition of research and analysis can hardly be overstated.

The indigenous religious traditions of small-scale societies have continued to be important. Recent and present-day theoretical discussions about religion by anthropologists and other scholars continue to make special reference to the beliefs and practices of such groups. At the same time, over the past half century anthropological studies of religion have broadened to include those of a wider range of societies and religious traditions. To some extent this shift has occurred because many of the adherents of indigenous religious traditions have converted to one or another of the larger, externally based religions of the world. Also, however, it has occurred simply as a part of a broader move in anthropology to include the study of large-scale societies.

Various terms have been used for the named religious traditions that, among other things, span wide geographical areas, including "major" and "great." Scholars now commonly refer to them as I have done throughout this book—as world religions. Although not everyone's list will be exactly the same, those usually included are Judaism, Christianity, and Islam (sometimes referred to as the religions of Abraham or the Semitic religions), on the one hand, and Hinduism and Buddhism (sometimes referred to as the Indic or Asian religions), on the other.

Widely used in the field of religious studies and the topic of thick books and popular survey courses, the notion of world (or major) religions is less well accepted in anthropology. Some anthropologists regard any such conceptual category as simplistic and as perpetuating negative and hierarchical views of other religious traditions and as naively positivistic. It lumps together too much religious and cultural diversity under a few headings and it fits some of the so-called world religions better than others. Yet for all of its problems, the concept of world religion, or something like it, seems inevitable in any comparatively oriented discussion of religion.

In this chapter we begin with a consideration of the world religions and then examine how anthropologists have studied world religions and what they have contributed in the way of specific examples of complex traditions. Next we will look at patterns of conversion in several places in the developing world. And finally we will consider why, and with what consequences, the adherents of indigenous religious traditions have joined one or another of the world religions.

THE WORLD RELIGIONS FROM AN ANTHROPOLOGICAL PERSPECTIVE

As noted in chapter 2, for Americans and probably for Westerners generally, the world religions form the clearest model of what religions are: a matter of belief or faith, a separate realm of life, something you can have only one of at a time, mainly spiritual rather than practical, associated with dedicated buildings, and the basis of morality. Let us look more closely at some of the main characteristics of the world religions and at the extent that various ones actually exemplify them.

Named Identity

It is worth reiterating that the world religions have named identities that are recognized by their adherents and usually everyone else in the regions in which they are present. Today at least, the named identity of particular religions is linked to the view of religion as something distinct that people believe, practice, or follow. Adherents of the various world religions are Jews, Christians, Muslims, Buddhists, or Hindus, although they may also be something more specific (Protestant or Catholic, Sunni or Shiite, and so on).

Religious identity is often linked to ethnic identity but it is not the same thing. In local communities, being identified with a particular ethnic group often means being identified with a particular religion. To be an Arab in most places means to also be identified as a Muslim (though some Arabs are Christian and others are Druze), and to be a Thai means also to be identified as a Buddhist. The equation, however, does not usually work when turned around. Most Buddhists, Muslims, and Christians are aware (and generally emphasize) that their religion is known and practiced by many different peoples in many different places. When I first went to Malaysia in the 1960s, one of the first things that Malays (who are all Muslims) wanted to know was whether there were Muslims and mosques in the United States and, if so, how many. Subsequently the conversion of Muhammad Ali was a popular topic, including the question of what it meant that he was a black man—and what about the so-called Black Muslims, why were they not just Muslims? What did Islam have to do with color? (Nothing, in their view.) And later still, had I heard that the British pop singer (and a white man) Cat Stevens had entered Islam?

The characteristic of having a named religious identity tends to sharply distinguish the followers of the world religions from the believers and practitioners of indigenous religious traditions. And this distinction is usually to the disadvantage of the latter. That is, those who are identified as being nonfollowers of one or another world religion are often vulnerable to being accused of "not having a religion," and sometimes this is a matter of government policy, as in Indonesia.

Sacred Texts, Written Languages, and Restricted Literacy

The world religions are sometimes also referred to as "religions of the book" because they are each based on a body of written texts that in most instances have been in existence for a long period of time. The belief commonly held by the adherents of the various world religions that they are superior is based in part on their status as written rather than oral traditions.

The main books on which the various world religions are based are not all of the same nature. The Qur'an of Islam is the simplest of the central written texts of all of the world religions. Relatively brief, it is believed to be the literal word of God as conveyed in Arabic to the Prophet Mohammed by the angel Gabriel. Complete and unchanged, it is considered to be the absolute bedrock of Muslim doctrine and practice, law and morality. The Christian Bible, on the other hand, is at the opposite extreme in terms of complexity. It consists of many books written at different times in different languages and circumstances. Its principal divisions are the Old Testament (the texts of Judaism) and the New Testament (the life and teachings of Christ). However, it is also believed by most Christians to be a single book and in some sense the word of God.

However simple or complex, the core written texts of the world religions are important in many ways. Adherents regard them as providing an authoritative guide to essential belief, practice, and wisdom and ethics, which among other things provides a basis for later fundamentalist movements. In addition, the book itself may serve as a major physical symbol of the religious beliefs and values. Consider the things that are done with the Bible in addition to studying it, including swearing on it in a court of law or in taking an oath of office (in early 2007 in the United States a minor uproar erupted over the first congressman sworn in with a Qur'an, even one owned by Thomas Jefferson), carrying it around, or waving it about in a political speech or sermon.

The great importance of written texts in the world religions does not mean, however, that all of the adherents of these religions can read them. Often in the world many people are not able to read at all and, of those who can, many may not comprehend the language or script in which the sacred texts are written, although they may be able to correctly recite it. Situations in which only a portion—often a small portion—of a religious community is capable of reading the sacred texts are referred to as ones of *restricted literacy*, a widespread and important pattern that has been explored by anthropologist Jack Goody (1968) and others. Situations of restricted or partial literacy have prevailed in most places throughout most of the history of the various world religions and have had several consequences. One is that those who can read and write the sacred language will have a particular status, a reputation for wisdom, special knowledge, and often mystical power. Because of this, written inscriptions of words or phrases from the sacred texts are prepared and used as charms or for other magical purposes. Traditionally worn or carried as amulets for protection, sacred inscriptions are often placed in automobiles and other motorized vehicles to prevent accident and injury. Today in both Buddhist and Muslim Southeast Asia those who can read and write the sacred language (especially those with reputations for mystical power) are sought out to prepare charms and amulets.

Universality and Localization

The world religions are more or less by definition universalistic—not limited to particular local ethnic groups, or even states or countries. They have spread far beyond their points of origin over large areas of the world. This does not mean that indigenous religious beliefs and practices do not extend beyond particular groups of people. Certain indigenous religious traditions may occur over very wide areas. As we have seen, shamanistic beliefs and practices have been identified and described in many places in the world. However, even if the similarities are sufficient to say the many instances that have been identified by observers as shamanism are "the same," shamanism is not a world religion or even a regional one. It has no common named identity among its various practitioners in different places. There are no "shamanists" (except perhaps the modern neo-shamanists) in the sense that there are Buddhists, Muslims, Christians, Jews, and Hindus.

Some world religions are more universalistic than others. The world religions are historical entities that arose and developed within and among the states and empires of the Old World. Just before the beginning of the European conquest and settlement of the Americas, Christianity, Islam, Hinduism, and Buddhism were each largely concentrated in distinct zones: Christianity in Europe, Hinduism in South Asia, Buddhism in Central and East Asia, and in parts of South and Southeast Asia; Islam (probably the most widely distributed of all at that time) was established in parts of Central Asia, South Asia, throughout the Middle East and across northern Africa. The conquest and settlement of the New World by the Spanish and Portuguese, and then other European peoples, drastically enlarged the domain of Christianity—both through the massive transatlantic migration of European Christian peoples and through the eventual conversion of most of the surviving native inhabitants, along with that of blacks brought as slaves from Africa. In the Old World, the main change in the territories of Buddhism, Islam, and Christianity in the same period included the expansion of Islam and, to a lesser extent, Christianity into Southeast Asia, and of both of these into Africa below the Sahara. As a result of these developments, the many and varied forms of Christianity (but above all Roman Catholicism) now occupy the widest region of the world.

Christianity, Islam, and Buddhism are the most universalistic of the world religions in several ways. In terms of identity, the adherents of these religions have the clearest and most emphatic view that their beliefs and practices can (or should) be for all peoples. However, even as these religions have spread they have not remained the same. They have also become localized; that is, as they have spread they have also adapted to local circumstances and incorporated local religious beliefs and practices. In some instances an extensive blending or *synchronization* takes place. Local new, or hybrid, versions of the various world religions develop (and sometimes spread). Such processes of localization have sometimes been attributed to distance or a decline of contact where religions have been carried and established over great distances. This is part of the explanation given for the particular ways in which Islam developed in Southeast Asia.

Judaism and Hinduism are somewhat more restricted as world religions, though in different ways. Judaism has remained very small in terms of numbers of adherents as the world religions go. Unlike the other world religions, Judaism has not been and perhaps could not have been throughout most of its history, a proselytizing religion. It has been geographically fragmented into enclaves in widely dispersed areas of the world, mainly among much larger Christian and Muslim populations, until the formation of the modern state of Israel. Many Jews tend to look at themselves (as others also view them) in ethnic as well as religious terms, although there is no single Jewish ethnic tradition or language. The two main divisions of Jews (Ashkenazi and Sephardic) are primarily linguistic and geographical rather than doctrinal or religious in nature.[1]

The situation of Hinduism is complicated in a number of ways. The beliefs, practices, and institutions of Hinduism are ancient, but the term itself dates only to the nineteenth century. The pan-Hindu identity of modern times is also recent. Further, although the numbers of adherents of what today is called Hinduism are vast (many hundreds of millions) they are concentrated in the Indian subcontinent (India and Nepal) and the adjacent island nation of Sri Lanka. Hinduism is also closely linked to a pan-Indic civilization in a way that Buddhism is not; or, to put it differently,

Figure 11.1.   The south causeway and gate of the city of Angkor Thom in Cambodia.

Figure 11.2.   The overgrown Angkor temple of Ta Prohm.

Buddhism broke away from India in a way that Hinduism has not. In particular, the multiplicity of beliefs and practices found throughout the vast region of greater India are bound up with the extraordinarily complex and pervasive patterns of hierarchical class and status ranking known as caste or the caste system.

At the same time, dimensions of Hindu religion and civilization (especially art, architecture, and notions of kingship) clearly did at times in the past extend far beyond its present boundaries in South Asia. In this regard Hinduism, although not known as such, was more of a world religion a thousand years ago than it is at the present time. By that time it had spread far beyond the Indian subcontinent into and throughout much of Southeast Asia. Here it was not only a religion but also a political system that centered on god kings who were worshiped as incarnations of Shiva and Vishnu. Along with Buddhism, which was present at that time and probably not well separated from it, Hinduism was associated with some of the most extensive and finest monumental religious architecture ever created. Today long-established Hinduism (in striking contrast to Buddhism) remains in Southeast Asia but in a more limited way. While it is an element or subtradition in the complex religion of the Thais, Burmese, Javanese, Cambodians, and others it is a complete or primary (or named) religion only in one small area centering on the island of Bali.

Colonialism, Diaspora, and the World Religions

Over the past hundred years or so, Hinduism has entered a new phase as a world religion, one established especially by the globalizing effects of British colonialism. Today Hinduism has been spread widely in association with the appeal of some of its beliefs and practices (meditation, yoga, philosophy, and healing) to Westerners and others, some of whom have become disciples of various Indian spiritual leaders, although such devo-

Figure 11.3. A south Indian devotee with limes hung with hooks from his chest, a small steel trident through his cheeks, and carrying a *kavadi*, arrives at the Murugan Hindu temple in Kuching, east Malaysia, during Thaipusan in 1999.

tees would probably not regard themselves as Hindus. Hinduism is also practiced by immigrant or overseas Indian communities in various places in the world. These communities, (consisting largely of southern Indian ethnic groups) are the legacy of the British colonial empire as it developed in the second half of the nineteenth century and the first half of the twentieth. They were established in various British colonies in the Caribbean, the Pacific Islands, and Hong Kong, although the main center of the Indian Hindu diaspora has been in Southeast Asia, especially the zone of plantation rubber cultivation in the western region of the Malay Peninsula. In the 1980s, countless small Hindu temples could still be seen on plantations or former plantations throughout this region. Large numbers of Indians have by now also migrated from plantations to cities including Kuala Lumpur and Singapore. The most vibrant expressions of contemporary overseas Hindu religious practice are found in these urban places, in the public celebrations of festivals, especially that of Thaipusan. The latter is devoted to Murugan, a major south Indian divinity, the main part of which involves a procession to a major temple by devotees carrying offerings or bearing burdens of sacrifice involving the piercing of the flesh of the cheeks, back, and chest. In the pluralistic settings in which they take place, such public processions are ethnic and political as well as religious in the narrow sense.

Like the Indians of the British colonial and postcolonial diaspora, the Chinese who settled abroad (again, above all in Southeast Asia) also brought their religious beliefs, practices, and institutions with them. Books on world religions may include "Chinese religion." So conceived, Chinese religion is usually said to consist of Buddhism, Taoism, and Confucianism, all of which are based on the literary and philosophical beliefs and practices of elite. The Chinese who moved to Southeast Asia and other overseas locations during the colonial era brought with them their village or folk religious beliefs, practices, and institutions rather than elite Chinese philosophical traditions. Today many of the Chinese settled abroad have converted to Christianity while others practice Buddhism. In the case of the latter this is not usually the traditional Mahayana forms of East Asia, but rather the Theravada ones of the Thais, Cambodians, and other lowland Southeast Asian peoples. In addition, Chinese folk religion (with which locally derived traditions have often been mixed) involving household ancestor worship, spirit mediumship, and local temples housing various gods and festivals continues to thrive throughout Southeast Asia. The folk religions traditions practiced widely outside of China by ethnic Chinese are world religions in a sense, but they are hardly universalistic. And, as in the case of the Indian communities, the public celebrations of Chinese religion are also demonstrations of ethnic, political, and cultural vitality.

Figure 11.4. At a rural Chinese folk religious festival in Kelantan, west Malaysia, women and girls make offerings to the village gods (*tokong*).

Evangelism

With the additions or exceptions note above, the world religions are widespread because they have been more or less deliberately spread by their adherents, either as a consequence of conquest or expansion or as simple missionization. The followers of the universalistic religions suppose that their beliefs and practices are available to all peoples (or at least all peoples capable of understanding and practicing them). They generally assume that everyone would be better off if those outside of the religion were within it. In some instances there is an obligation to promote the spread of the religion and to gain converts. Such religions are said to be proselytizing or evangelical. In Max Weber's phrase, they are religions of "ethical prophecy."

Christianity is such a religion, although some denominations are more avidly evangelistic than others. Americans and probably many other Westerners are generally aware that if someone knocks on their front door with a religious message or leaves a pamphlet it will probably be someone from one or another of a limited number of Christian denominations. The Church of Jesus Christ of Latter Day Saints (Mormons) is a prominent example of a version of Christianity that has grown enormously since its founding, in part through well organized and vigorous missionary efforts, both at home in the United States and abroad. The Seventh-Day Adventists are another example.[2]

Suffering and Salvation

In keeping with the tendency of Westerners to conceive of religion primarily as a matter of belief or faith, discussions of similarities and differences among the world religions often focus on matters of doctrine or what anthropologists call worldview. Max Weber and others who have followed his lead have noted that the world religions have in common certain ideas about suffering and the world into which people are born. While they have different goals and while there are major differences within their subtraditions, the world religions have generally been world rejecting in their basic philosophy and have emphasized salvation (Bellah 1965). This is especially true of Islam, Christianity, and Buddhism, though it has also been so at some periods more than others. The view of the world religions as based primarily on a doctrine of suffering and salvation tends to obscure their practical side.

THE ANTHROPOLOGICAL STUDY OF THE WORLD RELIGIONS

How have anthropologists studied the world religions and what have they been able to contribute to their understanding? By and large they used the same techniques they apply to indigenous religions—fieldwork and participant observation in particular places involving ordinary people. The results have been studies of Islam in Indonesian, Moroccan, or Turkish towns and villages; Hinduism in rural India or Sri Lanka; Christianity in Irish, Mexican, and Italian communities; Buddhism in the Burmese or Thai countryside. In some respects, the religious beliefs and behavior found in such places have not been much different from that encountered in the tribal villages with indigenous religions. Nonetheless, perhaps the main contribution anthropologists have made by studying the world religions in relatively small local communities has been to show that religion in such places has been more complex and differentiated than would be supposed. Such complexity has, however, been interpreted in various ways.

Theoretical Developments

The complexity and diversity that anthropologists encountered when they began to study the world religions required new theoretical tools. Some of these were borrowed from the sociology of Max Weber, the leading analyst and interpreter of world religions until that time. Weber is known above all for his study of the relationship of Protestantism and modern capitalism (specifically his effort to link Protestant doctrines of salvation to modern capitalist patterns of investment and wealth accumulation). However, he also sought to show that the varying religious traditions or orientations that are found within or among the world religions were a matter of class differentiation.

The study of the local versions of the various world religions was also associated with efforts to theorize the relationship of the local community and its distinctive cultural traditions to the larger society and civilization of which it was a part. Some of the work of theorizing local and national religious and cultural complexity was done within the general notion of peasantry or peasant society. Unlike tribal societies that were essentially autonomous and complete in political, economic, and cultural terms, peasant societies were "part societies," in all of these and other respects. Another way of talking about the religion and culture of the peasant or village sectors was to use the term "folk," as in "the folk religion of Mexico" or "folk Catholicism in Italy." The meaning of such phrases was that the religious beliefs and practices at the local or village level were different from the orthodox ones of the official religious hierarchy.

The American anthropologist Robert Redfield (1957) developed such notions further by referring to the Great Tradition and Little Tradition. The Great Tradition referred to the overarching civilization found in cities, based on writing and books and created and perpetuated by literate elites, and essentially the same throughout a country or region. The Little Tradition was that of villages, based on oral transmission and partial or restricted literacy and characterized by diversity from one place—even one village—to another. Redfield developed the scheme with regard to Mexico and Central America, but his colleagues at the University of Chicago and elsewhere developed it further with regard to India, a land of thousands of villages and endless local variation in customs and beliefs.

However, it soon became evident that society, religion, and culture in complex settings involved more than the two levels that the notions of Great and Little Tradition specified. There were also towns, where the two levels of civilization interacted. Centers of administration and commerce, towns also came to be understood as locations of religious worship, organization, and learning, especially if they were pilgrimage sites as well.

Religion, Society, and Civilization in Rural Java

One of the most important and influential of the early studies of a world religion in a local setting was Clifford Geertz's account of Javanese beliefs and practices in the town of Modjokuto (a pseudonym), central Java, published as *Religion in Java* (1960). The densely populated equatorial island of Java in Southeast Asia is a Muslim country, as is much of the rest of Indonesia, which has the largest Muslim population in the world. However, to simply describe the Javanese as Muslims would be a great oversimplification of the situation Geertz described for the early 1950s. Islam had spread peacefully, mostly by trade and, as a result, the people who converted were somewhat free to pick and choose both what to accept and what to give up from their preexisting religious traditions. Some people in the town were relatively strict, orthodox Muslims, but others were not. He described Javanese religion as consisting of not only Islam but also of elements of Hindu and Buddhist traditions, as well as indigenous animist and magical ones, all of which had continued to exist and be important after the arrival of Islam four to five hundred years previously. Javanese religion was therefore syncretic, a blend of earlier and later elements.

But it did not consist of a homogeneous blend equally distributed throughout the population. Although the title of Geertz's book refers to the *religion* (rather than *religions*) of Java, he interpreted Javanese religion as consisting of three distinct variants, each in some sense recognized by the Javanese themselves and labeled by a term of identity, though later scholars have sharply disputed the religious nature of one of the variants. These three variants included the *abangan* tradition of magic and animism, the *santri* or more orthodox Muslim tradition, and the *prijaji* tradition of mysticism and high art. Furthermore, he linked each of these variants with a different class or status group within the population. This way of looking at Javanese religious complexity was based especially on Max Weber's sociology of religion, which held that different classes in complex or stratified societies had different sorts of religious needs or interests. In the case of the Javanese, society was stratified into three classes: peasant farmers, merchants and traders, and feudal rulers and administrators.

Geertz, however, also made use of Redfield's formulation of the Great and Little Tradition, between which there were mediators or "culture brokers." In the case of Java there were two Great Traditions, an older Indic or Hindu-Buddhist one and a more recent Islamic one. The peasant farmers followed the *abangan* variant. They had probably converted to Islam mainly because their kings had done so, but had otherwise gone on believing and doing much of what they had previously believed and done, or so Geertz suggests. Their religion involved beliefs in spirits and magical powers, but the main emphasis was on ritual, and the most important rituals were the neighborhood feasts held for birth, circumcision, weddings, funerals, curing, and other important occasions. Geertz suggests that what they chose to believe or not believe was less important than the performance of the correct rituals on the right occasions, with the right people invited (i.e., they were myth-ritualists as described by Robertson

Smith). *Abangan* religion expresses social values and promotes social solidarity, though it may also conflict with the ritual practices and identity of Javanese who follow the more orthodox version of Islam.

Geertz stressed ritual practices as well as institutions in his description of the *santri*, or more orthodox Islamic variant of Javanese religion. Islam had taken hold most strongly in those areas and among those groups associated with commerce rather than agriculture. This variant of Javanese religion was therefore associated with the trading classes of the town and, more generally, the coastal trading zones of the Island of Java. In this case, while the village feast was also important, the main thing was the performance of the five major requirements of Islam—the confession of the faith, the five daily prayers, attendance at the Friday prayer at the mosque, payment to charity, and the completion of the pilgrimage to Mecca for those who could afford it. Of the various Muslim institutions, the most important is the traditional boarding school or *pesantren*. Indeed, the term *santri* means student. While the *santri* version of Javanese religion stood against the other traditions, it was also internally differentiated into a more traditional or orthodox form and a more modern or reformist one (today there would be a "fundamentalist" version in addition to or instead of the latter). While Geertz discusses the differences in the beliefs or views of orthodox and modernist versions of the *santri* tradition (the former being closer to, and more tolerant of, *abangan* animistic beliefs and practices), he stresses organizations. Each version of Islam was associated with a main political party and other groups, including women's associations and boy scouts. Finally, he places great emphasis on the links between trade and markets and Islam.

The *prijaji* variant of Javanese religion was the elite or courtly counterpart to the peasant or *abangan* one. In the past the *prijaji* had been a feudal class of landowners, warriors, and court officials that under Dutch rule had become colonial administrators. Indeed, other scholars (Woodward 1989: 2) subsequently argued that the significant distinction in Javanese religion was simply between *abangan* and *santri*, and that *prijaji* referred to a class division in society, rather than a religious one. The *prijaji* variant consisted above all of the philosophy and practice of mysticism. This mysticism, while having an overlay of Islam, had Hindu-Buddhist roots and was focused on cultivating power and on developing and protecting the inner self. The other dimension of *prijaji* religion was aesthetics. The *prijaji* were patrons of the traditional arts of Java, including the shadow play and classical dance, which were also based on Hindu traditions rather than Islam. It is the *prijaji* variant that some subsequent scholars have argued is not really a religious category but only a social (or sociocultural) one.

Buddhism and Spirit Cults among the Burmese

Another early study involving a world religion in a local setting in Southeast Asia also stresses complexity but in a different way. This was Melford Spiro's (1967) account of Burmese religion, or what he terms supernaturalism. Burmese religion includes beliefs and practices relating to Buddhism. Buddhism in Burma as elsewhere is a sophisticated tradition based on the veneration or worship of the Buddha, who showed the way to enlightenment. It also involves he belief in the law of karma (the sum of good and evil done in this life and in previous ones, which determines one's fate in life and rebirth in the next). Religious practices include the support of monks, nuns, and monasteries and other good deeds as a means of earning merit, and the avoidance of various forbidden or sinful activities, including the taking of life, human or animal. Buddhism also stresses suffering and salvation.

But while the Burmese were Buddhists, there was more to their religion than just this, including an elaborate spirit cult and various other animistic and mystical and magical beliefs and practices. The general term for spirit is *nat*, and the most important are known as the thirty-seven *nats*, although this is a category label rather than a specific list of named spirits that everyone knew all of. Religious practices involving *nats* consist of making offerings to them, avoiding actions that offend them, and seeking their help through spirit mediums. The latter practices were highly developed. Spirit mediums, nearly always women, develop relations with *nats* that are thought of as a form of marriage. People approach the spirit mediums for healing or other types of assistance. The mediums in turn go into trances and invoke their spirits in order to overcome, cure, or provide other forms of help.

Like Javanese religion, Burmese supernaturalism consists of several traditions of belief and practice. However, unlike Geertz, who explained the complexity of Javanese religion by dividing it into three variants and relating each of these to a different class of Javanese society, Spiro is concerned with Burmese villagers, most of whom are farmers or peasants. He says nothing about other classes and their possibly different religious orientations. Buddhism and the spirit cults both exist among the same class of Burmese, but they are in conflict. He lists five ways that this is so, including morality (Buddhism is a religion of morality whereas the *nat* cults manifest values and practices that are amoral), sensuality (Buddhism teaches that desire is the cause of all suffering and advocates the subjugation of the passions, whereas the *nat* cults express the indulgence of passion), personality (Buddhism has serenity as the ideal mental state, while the *nat* cults reflect turbulence and violence), society (Buddhism is otherworldly and world-rejecting, while the *nat* cults are concerned with worldly or practical problems). While there appears to be considerable overlap among these various differences that Spiro discusses, the general point seems clear.

Spiro's (1967: 247–80) explanation of the relationship between Burmese Buddhism and *nat* worship is that they meet different sorts of psychological needs. He develops this point by drawing on a distinction made by Ruth Benedict regarding North American Indian cultures. This distinction was between Apollonian and Dionysian, which Benedict had gotten from the philosopher Nietzsche, who had developed it concerning Greek tragedy.

> [Nietzsche] discusses two diametrically opposed ways of arriving at the value of existence. The Dionysian pursues them through "the annihilation of the ordinary bounds and limits of existence"; he seeks to attain in his most valued moments escape from boundaries imposed upon him by his five senses, to break through into another order of experience. The desire of the Dionysian, in personal experience or in ritual, is to press through it toward a certain psychological state, to achieve excess. The closest analogy to the emotions he seeks is drunkenness, and he values the illuminations of frenzy. With Blake, he believes "the path of excess leads to the palace of wisdom." The Apollonian often had little idea of the nature of such experiences. He finds means to outlaw them from his conscious life. He "knows but one law, measured in the Hellenic sense." He keeps to the middle of the road, stays within the known map, and does not meddle with disruptive psychological states. (Benedict 1960: 79)

Benedict was discussing the religion and culture of the Zuni and other Pueblo groups of the American Southwest. Her general point was that these groups were psychologically Apollonian, even more than the Greeks so labeled by Nietzsche. In contrast, the other North American Indian peoples were thoroughly Dionysian. "They sought in every way to achieve an order of existence set apart from daily living" (Benedict 1960: 81). The many differences among the cultures of the various non-Pueblo North American Indian groups notwithstanding, they were all fundamentally Dionysian in their practices. "The most conspicuous of these is probably their practice of obtaining supernatural power in a dream or vision . . . On the western plains men sought these visions with hideous tortures" (Benedict 1960: 81).

But there was a fundamental difference between the North American Indians as described by Benedict and the Burmese as described by Spiro. While the former groups were *either* Apollonian or Dionysian, the latter were both; that is, Buddhism is Apollonian and the *nat* cults are Dionysian. In this regard, Burmese religion is similar to Greek religion, which, as Benedict pointed out, contained both traditions. Nor do the

Burmese *nat* cults and Buddhism form a seamless whole. Spiro asserts that ordinary Burmese were very aware of the differences between the *nat* cults and Buddhism and of various points of conflict between them. Moreover, all Burmese accept that Buddhism is the morally superior and more important part of Burmese religious life. Spiro does not estimate how much time and resources Burmese villages devote to Buddhist activities in contrast to those involving the *nats*, but presumably these are substantially greater.

Why have the Burmese retained the *nat* cults and other non-Buddhist traditions if they conflict with Buddhism and if the Burmese are as committed to Buddhism as Spiro emphasizes? Part of the answer is that Buddhism is relatively tolerant of non-Buddhist beliefs and practices, even ones that conflict with basic Buddhist doctrines and values. Another part of the answer is that the beliefs and practices of the *nat* cult address needs and serve interests that orthodox Buddhism does not. While the *nat* cults may be in conflict with Buddhism, they are also in some sense complimentary to it.

Gender and Religion in Korea

The two foregoing studies have attempted to explore and explain religious complexity in two different ways. Geertz explains Javanese religious complexity as a matter of the historical developments and of class or status-group differences in a stratified society. Spiro explains Burmese religious complexity as a matter of the same people (Burmese villagers) having differing religious needs of a Dionysian and Apollonian sort, and as satisfying these needs through the spirit cults, in the case of the first, and through Buddhism, in the case of the second. Neither Geertz nor Spiro attempts to explain religious complexity as having much to do with gender. For Geertz, the key to understanding Javanese religious complexity is the differences among the *abangan*, *santri*, and *prijaji* variants, and these are differences in class, not gender. For his part, Spiro makes some limited observations about gender. Most importantly perhaps, he notes that nearly all Burmese spirit mediums or "shamans" are women and that shamans tend to be looked down on. But he does not say if shamans have low status because they are usually women or for other reasons. More importantly, he does not say that Apollonian and Dionysian orientations are a matter of gender; presumably both women and men have both sorts of needs even if they do not have equal opportunities to satisfy them.

Over the past several decades, anthropologists have devoted much more attention to gender as a factor in religious complexity and in other things. To take another example involving Buddhism, Laurel Kendall's (1985) study is an effort to do this, especially from the perspective of women. This example concerns South Korea. To begin with, Korean religion as described and analyzed by Kendall has three main traditions or dimensions. Her study, like Spiro's, is focused on the rural or village sector of society rather than on the whole of it. If it were the latter it might be necessary to include other traditions. For example, there are also Christians in the area (as will be noted later, Korea has a large Christian minority, by national proportion the largest in Asia outside of the Philippines). Christians and Christianity, however, are peripheral to Kendall's concerns. As far as the non-Christian majority of rural Koreans are concerned, the three main traditions are Buddhism, Confucianism, and shamanism. Of these, Buddhism is also somewhat peripheral and mentioned mainly in passing, although it is undoubtedly an important part of Korean religion for it is strongly involved with matters of death and the ancestors, among other things. In contrast, Kendal's study is mostly about what she calls shamanism.

According to the distinction made in chapter 9 between shamanism broadly and narrowly conceived, the Korean version described by Kendall and others is more the former than the latter. Specifically, it seems to be somewhere between simple spirit mediumship and true shamanism. Kendall is critical of the concept of shamanism and of applying it to Korean practices but does so in part because it has become conventional. "The term shamanism and the adjective shamanistic have been broadly, indeed sloppily, applied to a vast spectrum of Korean religious activity" (1985: 29), as she puts it. At the same time, Korean practices have some affinity with classical north central Asian shamanism, which is not surprising given the geographical position of the Korean Peninsula. Most notably, Korean shamans (*mansin*) are recruited to the role through "traumatic possession sickness," which is another way of saying they are believed to be selected by the spirits rather than their own desires. This is one of the crucial features of shamanism. On the other hand, *mansin* do not appear to engage in soul flight, another of the main characteristics of classic shamanism. In any case, the central ritual activity of shamanism is the séance, in which the shaman dances, sings, and becomes the voice of spirits for the purpose of finding out what is wrong with a patient. They also put people in contact with those who have passed on.

This leaves Confucianism, which Kendall presents as the main contrast to shamanism in Korean village religion. Although the Koreans (including the villagers) are devoted adherents of Confucianism, it is a relatively late import into Korea from China. Strictly speaking, classical Confucianism is not really religion (in the sense of involving the supernatural). It is rather a philosophy or ideology of social organization and hierarchy, one that focuses on the respect, honor, and duty of children for parents and grandparents, and of social inferiors for superiors and everyone for government authority and scholarship. Confucianism becomes religion through the practice of ancestor worship, for the relationship between children and parents and grandparents does not end with death. Ancestor worship involves paying respect and making offerings to deceased parents, grandparents, and other ascending ancestors. This is done at temples and graves but most importantly at household altars. The Koreans fervently believe that dead ancestors want to be remembered and respected and they appreciate gifts of food and other things. They also continue to be concerned with the affairs of the living.

This brings us to Kendall's (1985: 26–28) main thesis, which is that Korean religious complexity is above all a matter of gender. Shamanism, as among the Burmese, is a female activity. Nearly all shamans are women and, while seances are often held for ailing men, they are organized by women. Men rarely become shamans (*paksu mudang*), and when male shamans perform they dress as women (down to their underwear!). On the other hand, ancestor worship is a male activity. Men perform the formal rituals of respect and offering at family altars, as is consistent with the patrilineal and patriarchal nature of Korean kinship. As shamans, women also have a lot to do with ancestors, who make frequent appearances at séances, but this does not count as Confucian ancestor worship.

Kendall's main thesis has two corollaries, one concerning the differing behavioral or emotional character of male and female rituals and the other involving the respective status of each. As ritual activities, shaman performances are serious but not exactly dignified. They are loud, theatrical, raucous, and often comical and therefore performed before an audience. Ancestor worship by contrast is quiet and dignified, unspectacular, and an audience is irrelevant. As for status, well, you can guess. Confucian ancestor worship has high status and is regarded as "real religion" and shamanism has low status and is not. Shamans themselves don't have any pretensions about their ritual activities. Kendall had trouble getting them to tell her about what they did because they couldn't believe anyone would be interested. She ended up telling them that she was studying shamanism because she was a woman and American university professors sent male students to study the more important male ritual activities; this they understood.

But while shamans and shamanism don't get much respect and this correlates with their female nature, it is again not clear that shamanism is looked down on because it is associated with women or for other reasons (or for a combination of both). And finally, while shamans and their activities are low in prestige, they are both popular. The villagers enjoy the séances and they like the shamans. Villagers like to visit with the *mansin* because they are usually entertaining and very knowledgeable about what is going on with the various families, and not only among the living, of course.

THE CONVERSION OF INDIGENOUS PEOPLES
TO AND WITHIN THE WORLD RELIGIONS

While considerable attention has been paid to the spread of old and new religions, the matter of who converts and why is less well understood. Here there are several possibilities. One is that people who are members of one world religion shift to a different one, either because they are coerced in some way or because they freely choose to do so; another is that people who are adherents of their own indigenous religious tradition freely or otherwise join or convert to one of the world religions. Yet another possibility is that adherents of an indigenous religion or members of a world religion become followers of a new religious movement—a development that we have already explored in the preceding chapter. A final possibility is that adherents of one version of a world religion abandon it to join another, but very different version of the same religion—as when Roman Catholic Christians convert to some variety of Protestantism, to use an example that will be considered below.

Of these possibilities, the involuntary conversion from one world religion to another is familiar from history (such as those involving Jews and Muslims during the Inquisition in Spain and Portugal or the purge of Christianity in Tokugawa Japan). Today, the involuntary shift from one established world religion to another does not appear to be very common and probably accounts for only a small part of the religious change that has taken place in the world in recent times.

There are various examples of people voluntarily converting from one religious tradition to a totally different one, although how substantial these have been sometimes depends on whether you consider absolute numbers or percentages. In China, for example, the number of Christians is variously gauged but even generous estimates amount to only a few percent of the population. There have also been substantial exceptions, ones involving both real numbers and significant percentages. In Vietnam, by contrast, there are an estimated 7.5 million Christians, fewer than the number for China but much larger as a proportion. It is even more so in South Korea, where Christians constitute about 25 percent of the population. The particularly large proportion of Christians in South Korea has been attributed to its colonial circumstances: Korea was colonized by Japan rather than by a Christian European nation and Christianity therefore came to be associated with anti-Japanese nationalism. The less impressive but still substantial size of the Christian community in Vietnam (which was an important factor in the civil war and the division of the country into North and South sectors before its reunification under the communists in 1975) cannot be attributed to the sort of anticolonial experience found in Korea. In this case the substantial numbers may be attributed to the success of early Catholic missionaries.

The Conversion of Indigenous Peoples in Southeast Asia

Developments in South Korea and Vietnam notwithstanding, much of the recent overall expansion of Christianity and other world religions has been based on the conversion of peoples who previously adhered to their own indigenous religious traditions. Southeast Asia is one area of the world where the transition from indigenous to world religions has been taking place. Here the changes have involved Christianity, Islam, and Buddhism, with the shift to Christianity probably accounting for most of what has occurred. And here also the pattern of religious change is fairly clear.

For a long time, religious patterns in mainland Southeast Asia (the present-day countries of Vietnam, Cambodia, Laos, Thailand, and Burma plus adjacent parts of southwest China—especially Yunnan—and far eastern India) have been closely linked to political, social, ecological, and ethnic ones. To oversimplify a bit, scholars generally divide the ethnic populations of the mainland into two main types. Different terms are used, but we can call them the lowlanders and the highlanders. The lowlanders occupy the plains and valleys and cultivate wet rice; they are organized into stratified societies and states traditionally headed by divine kings. The lowland populations are composed of a relatively few ethno-linguistic groups that include (1) the Thai of Thailand, the Lao of Laos, and the Shan of northeastern Burma (all speakers of Tai); (2) the Khmer of Cambodia; (3) the Vietnamese of Vietnam; and (4) the Burmese of Burma (or Myanmar). Mainly long influenced by India and (as noted above) formerly adherents of Hindu-Buddhist religious traditions, the lowlanders today are almost entirely Theravada Buddhists (Theravada being the southern tradition, or the "smaller vehicle" of Buddhism). The non-Theravada Buddhists are the Vietnamese, who were more strongly influenced by China than India and who have a religion and a traditional political system that is closer to the East Asian than the Southeast Asian pattern.

The highlanders are different in just about every important way. They live among and on the mountains, practice swidden or slash-and-burn cultivation of dry rice and other crops, were traditionally organized at the village level as tribal societies rather than states, are generally egalitarian, and migrate frequently. They traded with the lowland peoples but otherwise kept apart from them. They include many different ethno-linguistic groups, some of which are numerous and scattered over wide areas (in particular the Hmong, Mien [or Yao], Akha, and Karen groups in the northern region). Influenced more by China than India, the highlanders adhered to their own indigenous religious beliefs and practices that usually included shamanism.

The modern countries of mainland Southeast Asia were created in large part by European colonial rule—French in Vietnam, Laos, and Cambodia, and British in Burma and Malaysia. Thailand was not colonized but its modern borders were determined in part by the establishment of those of the surrounding countries that were. Each country now has a national ethnic population, which in most cases gives the country its name (Cambodia is an exception, as is Myanmar, although this is recent). Most of the countries also have what is (or amounts to) a national religion, and, in all of the instances in which this is so, the religion is that of its national ethnic population—Buddhism. As a communist state with more of an East Asian than a Southeast Asian religious tradition, Vietnam is the only mainland Southeast Asian country without a national religion, although if pressed to name one the Vietnamese would probably also say Buddhism. Though Laos is also communist and has a large (in proportion) population of non-Buddhist highland peoples, Buddhism also serves as a sort of national religion. Its national monument is the large golden Buddhist stupa of Pha That Luang outside of Vientianne, the capital.

This brings us to the pattern of religious conversion among of the highland peoples, who traditionally adhere to their own indigenous religious traditions. And here we have a seeming paradox. The traditional distance between these groups and the dominant lowland/coastal national populations has been breaking down through acculturation and integration. Roads are being pushed into the forests and mountains of the interior, national schools are being built all over, the highland and interior peoples are learning national languages and working or trading in lowland and coastal regions, while lowlanders and coastal peoples are moving into the interior and highlands in search of land or for various other (mainly economic) reasons. Though to varying extents and at different rates in different countries, these changes are occurring in most regions. Yet where religion is concerned, while the highland ethnic minorities have been converting for a long time (though also to differing extents and at different rates) it has generally not been to Buddhism but rather to one or another version of Christianity. There are exceptions. Many Karen (a large highland group who dwell on both sides of the Thai-Burma border (though mainly in Burma) have converted to Buddhism as well as to Christianity. But overall, the move to Christianity is clearly the dominant trend among the highland peoples.

Why have the highland peoples of mainland Southeast Asia generally chosen to convert to Christianity rather than to Buddhism, even though they are otherwise acculturating to the national lowland Buddhist societies? To answer this, we must ask the even more basic question of why the highlanders have converted at all. And here we need to begin by rethinking religious conversion, at least as it is usually thought about in Western terms. Westerners are likely to see conversion as a mainly or an entirely personal or familial decision based on religious or nonreligious considerations. We recognize that some people convert because they are seeking a more meaningful or satisfying set of religious beliefs and experiences or because, as is currently common in the United States, they have experienced a personal revelation (often referred to as being born again). But some people convert for more practical reasons or because of social pressures. Converting because of marriage, for example, is a well-known and generally accepted reason that may have little to do with religious motives. In any case, the implications and consequences are usually limited to individuals, families, and perhaps friends. Who cares what your neighbor does?

Conversion to Christianity in Northern Thailand

Such reasons for conversion exist elsewhere as well. But often Western experiences with, and notions about, conversion are not a good guide to what is occurring in the developing world where the frontiers of religious change now lie. For one thing, the conversion of people who have followed traditional indigenous beliefs and practices to Christianity, Islam, or Buddhism is usually more than an individual or a family process. Here you do care what your neighbor does. Sometimes villages split over conversion, with Christians not wanting to live together with traditionalists or vice versa. I was recently in an Akha highland village in northern Thailand, where Christian converts are required to leave. This is not so much because people care about what other people believe as it is about what they do. Many religious rituals are communal or village wide. If converts were willing to continue to participate in the traditional rituals no one would probably care much if they were also Christian or about whatever they believed and did, but this has not usually been the case.

To the missionaries and others who spread their religion, the answer to the question of why people convert may seem obvious: they choose to join a morally and spiritually superior faith that offers the hope or promise of eternal salvation and a better life in this world; they have moved away from backwardness toward progress, from darkness into light. To the anthropologist or to any scholar of comparative religion, the question is significant but the answer is not obvious.

Probably there is no single answer. The governments of some Southeast Asian countries would prefer the indigenous ethnic minorities to convert, especially to the national religion. This preference is part of a general desire for the indigenous minorities to acculturate to the national society, if not to be absorbed into it altogether. Beyond this, both the national governments and the dominant ethnic populations tend to regard membership in a universal religion based on writing as part of being modern or civilized, as opposed to primitive or backward. At least in some countries, such views (that indigenous religious beliefs and practices are backward) are conveyed to children in government schools and tend to be accepted by adults as well.

The members of the non-Christian dominant communities sometimes think of those who convert to Christianity as "rice Christians," which means they convert for financial or other materialistic reasons. Insofar as this means outright monetary or other material gifts to individuals, it has probably not occurred. Western and other Christian missionaries do in many instances attempt to provide assistance to the highlanders and to other ethnic minority groups. While in Chiang Rai (northern Thailand) in 2006 I met a group of American Baptist volunteers who were there to build churches in Akha Christian villages. I also happened to visit an Akha Christian village whose inhabitants also told me they had received or were expecting such assistance. In such cases, however, the conversion had already occurred and it would be difficult to know if the anticipation of material support was a factor or, if so, how important it was. In the past, Christian missionaries throughout Southeast Asia often established schools and hospitals to which people were attracted and for which they were grateful. In the case of mission schools there is the opportunity of influencing students.

But the role of missions in providing medical services and education was probably much greater in the past than it has been in the recent period. Previously, Christian mission schools and hospitals were all that existed in some regions, but this is no longer the case. In Laos and Vietnam, Christian missionary service activities have been greatly reduced or have ceased entirely as a consequence of the war and the policies of present governments. There is a strong mission presence in some areas (e.g., in northern Thailand) but here and throughout many regions government hospitals, clinics, and especially schools are now widespread.

According to Cornelia Kammerer (1990), who studied conversion in northern Thailand from 1979 to 1981 and again in 1986 and 1987, the shift to Christianity among the Akha has had an economic motive, although it is not one the usual one. Kammerer rejects the "rice Christian" hypothesis—that practical benefits provided by missions explain conversion—for the reasons noted above. Instead, she offers an explanation that focuses on the changing economic circumstances of the Akha.

The Akha in northern Thailand are a well-known hill tribe (as the highland ethnic minorities are known in Thailand). They are one of a number of indigenous groups that are spread over a wide area that extends from upper Burma through southern Yunnan (China), northern Laos and Thailand to northwestern Vietnam. In northern Thailand they are among the most visible of such groups. This is because their villages are now generally accessible by road and often visited by tourists and trekkers. Akha women, who wear distinctive costumes with striking metal and cloth head coverings, hawk beads, trinkets, and other handicrafts in the market places of Chiang Mai, Chiang Rai, and other towns throughout the region that are frequented by tourists. The energy and persistence that Akha women display in peddling goods to tourists, the long hours they devote to selling in urban night markets, and the time and effort they spend traveling from their villages to their business sites tend to support Kammerer's conclusion that the Akha in Thailand have been coping with changing and difficult economic circumstances. These include land shortages, government restrictions on shifting cultivation and the migration to new village and farming sites, and the elimination of opium poppy cultivation.

It is to these changing economic circumstances that Kammerer attributes the changing pattern of conversion to Christianity that she found. In brief, this changing pattern involved a shift from a pervasive unwillingness to convert she encountered in 1980s to a strong tendency to do so that was taking place when she returned some years later. Efforts to convert the Akha in northern Thailand by American Baptists had begun several decades previously. This was partly a result of the shutting down of their mission in Shan State in Upper Burma (Myanmar) in the mid 1960s (that followed the military takeover of Burma a few years before) and its redeployment to northern Thailand. For a long time the Akha turned a deaf ear to conversion efforts and remained devoted to their own religious traditions and customs. Since these were and are mainly a matter of practice rather than belief, the Akha were not moved by the Christian emphasis on belief or faith as the main basis for a religion. Indeed, the Akha had no word in their language for religion in any sense familiar to Western missionaries. Their word *zah* refers to ritual practices but not really to beliefs, and not only ritual practices but to customs in general. Akha notions of religion are thus consistent with what (as noted earlier) William Robertson Smith said a century before about ancient religion in general—that ritual practices were primary while beliefs were secondary.

The Akha eventually began to accept Christianity, according to Kammerer, mainly because they had become unable to afford their traditional religion or, more specifically, the many ritual activities that make it up. Most (she does not say all) converted to Christianity as a way of getting out of these customary ritual obligations. The traditional rituals are costly because animals are sacrificed and, in addition to the meat provided as a result, rice, other foods, and drink must be provided for guests. Smaller and cheaper animals (chickens) could be used in place of larger and more expensive ones (pigs), but there are limits to such substitution, and the preparation for the ceremonies also takes time. Although the various ritual expenditures are traditional, the Akha did not find them overly burdensome in the past. But more recently their economic adaptation, based on swidden cultivation, has come under stress.

As further evidence for her interpretation of the main reason for Akha conversion, Kammerer cites missionary attitudes to what has taken place. One the one hand, the missionaries are pleased that their long efforts have finally brought fruit. On the other, they are not entirely satisfied with the sort of Christians the Akha turned out to be. The missionaries had a great interest in discussing beliefs and faith and placed a lot of emphasis on Bible study as a means of improving faith and deepening understanding of Christianity. But while some converts have taken to discussions about belief and faith, most have not been very interested in these activities. Christianity in the late 1980s was a new form of *zah*, a new set of customs and practices and not (or not yet) a whole new way of thinking and believing.

This brings us back to the question of why the Akha and most other highland minority groups have opted for Christianity rather than Buddhism. The answer has several dimensions. One is that Christian missions (which for a long time have included both Westerners and local or other Asian Christians) have active programs that include instruction or information about Christianity, about what conversion involves and how to go about it. Two other related considerations are prestige and ethnic boundaries. The highlanders know that they and their way of life are considered inferior by the lowlanders and associate Buddhism with such attitudes. Christianity, as the religion of the rich and modern Western world, is just as prestigious as Buddhism and perhaps more so. In addition, converting to Christianity is a way of becoming modern while maintaining an identity that is separate from that of the dominant lowland ethnic populations.

The Conversion from Roman Catholicism to Evangelical Protestantism in Mexico and Central America

Religious conversion is now also occurring widely in Mexico and Central America and to a considerable extent throughout Latin America and the Caribbean in general. While in some ways reminiscent of what has been taking place among indigenous peoples of mainland Southeast Asia, the Mexican and Central American pattern is notably different. As seen above, in Southeast Asia the main pattern of religious change has been one of indigenous peoples converting to one or another version of Christianity for the first time. In contrast, in Mexico and Central America, where the indigenous peoples have been Christian for a long time, the contemporary practice involves conversion from one version of Christianity to another—from Catholicism to Protestantism. Moreover, the pattern in this instance has been conversion to evangelical and Pentecostal forms of Protestantism. Evangelical versions of Protestantism have several characteristics, including a commitment to a literal interpretation of the Bible, to personal salvation (or being born again), and to proselytizing or spreading the religion (or evangelism in a narrow sense). Pentecostalism includes these plus the ritual practice of glosso-lalia or "speaking in tongues" while, it is believed, being possessed by the Holy Spirit.

Why is such religious change taking place at this particular point in time? As with the pattern of present-day religious conversion in Southeast Asia, there is probably no single key to explaining what is happening in Mexico or Central America. The authors of a recently published volume (*Holy Saints and Fiery Preachers: The Anthropology of Protestantism in Mexico and Central America*) explore what has occurred in a series of case studies that attempt to explain what has been taking place overall and in various specific places. In his introduction to the volume, James Dow (2001: 2) writes that there are almost as many explanations for the growth of Protestantism as there are people writing about the topic. He goes on to say, however, that scholars and researchers tend to emphasize two factors in attempting to explain what has occurred.

One of these is the growth of a market economy throughout the rural area. This sounds at first like another example of Max Weber's thesis on the relationship of Protestantism to the rise of capitalism. However, in this instance the appeal of Protestantism is especially to the poorer classes, for whom it has two bases, one positive and one negative. The positive one is that Protestantism is associated with improving business skills and work habits through discipline. This association is based partly on the message that Protestants promote about themselves and partly on the association of Protestantism with North American wealth and economic power (and whether this association is real or more a matter of symbolism and im-agery does not matter). The negative side of the association of Protes-tantism with the growth of a market economy is that economic change has undermined the traditional rural practices of redistribution that are asso-ciated with folk Catholicism; specifically the practice of sponsoring the annual festivities held in honor of saints. Becoming a Protestant, as a way out of such wealth-draining obligations, has a particular appeal in regions where rural economic conditions have deteriorated.

The other way in which the success of Protestantism has been explained focuses on its particular appeal to the native or Indian communities. At first it seems odd that Protestantism should have such an appeal. Accord-ing to several researchers, however, while conversion to Protestantism is occurring among both Indian and non-Indian (usually referred to as *mes-tizo*) Catholics in Mexico, it appears to be considerably more frequent among the former than the latter. The largest numbers of Protestants live in the southeastern states of Mexico (Chiapas, Quintana Roo, Tabasco, and Campeche). Here nearly a third of the population considers itself to be non-Catholic, and here also there are very large Indian populations (Garma 2001: 59). The link between Protestantism and Indian populations also carries over into Guatemala where, as of 1995, more than a quarter of the inhabitants were Protestant (Dow 2001: 5).

The particular attraction of evangelical Protestantism to members of the Indian communities is attributed to several considerations. One concerns the nature of folk Catholicism, which refers to the traditional, syncretic beliefs, practices, and institutions that have developed over a period of centuries. It includes in particular economic burdens and responsibilities for the festivities of the veneration of saints, burdens that are generally referred to as cargo. While folk Catholicism is not limited to the Indians, it is one of the defining ethnic characteristics of the Indian communities where, moreover, the leveling or redistributive mechanisms of the cargo practices and the civil-religious hierarchy are most fully developed. The argument here is that the negatively based economic appeal of Protestantism has become particularly strong for these groups.

This interpretation of the motives of converts to Protestantism is essentially the same as Kammerer's explanation of the recent pattern of conversion of the Akha of northern Thailand. It is also reminiscent of the apparently practical appeal of the Bungan reform movement in Borneo discussed in chapter 10. There are, however, several problems with the economic explanation of conversion in Mexico and Guatemala, which not all researchers accept. One is that the spread of a market-based economy cannot be separated from other sorts of changes. Southern Mexico and especially Guatemala have been heavily affected by political conflict and Guatemala by devastating repression and bloodshed that, as noted in the previous chapter, seem likely to generate religious movements as people lose faith in traditional beliefs, practices, and identity and search for a new start. Another problem of placing great emphasis on economic factors alone is that these do not seem to explain the particular appeal of Pentecostalism or even evangelicalism as opposed to any other form of Protestantism or, for that matter, the abandonment of religious identity and participation altogether (which is also occurring, according to these studies).

Some researchers therefore argue that Pentecostalism has a particular appeal to the Indians because it is closer to their own indigenous religious experience mentality than are other forms of Christianity (Garma 2001: 59–60; Cook 2001: 161); that is, the Pentecostal emphasis on possession by the Holy Ghost and speaking in tongues is close to the indigenous emphasis on shamanism, altered states of consciousness, and the power of words. This is also an interesting possibility. It is not, however, offered as a complete explanation, for if Indian converts are simply seeking religious experiences like their familiar indigenous ones, which they already have, why should they bother to convert at all? The answer seems to be that in addition to the economic and political considerations noted above, Indian religion is under pressure from both the Catholic and Protestant churches. The Catholic Church was previously tolerant of Indian folk Catholicism but has become much less so; the Protestant churches often condemn traditional Indian beliefs and practices as heathenism and devil worship. For those who are influenced to convert because of such criticism or for other reasons, Pentecostalism may be the most popular choice because of its affinity with traditional religious forms.

Finally, it may be that for those who are prepared to accept religious change, including a new identity, fundamentalist Protestantism (and especially Pentecostalism) has been successful for another reason. This is because it is these churches that have been most active, energetic, and confident in their mission efforts. To the extent that this is the case, what is occurring in Mexico, Central America, and Latin America generally may have something in common with what has been taking place in the United States as well: the increasing size, confidence, and influence of fundamentalist versions of Protestantism at the expense of mainline churches.

NOTES

1. "Ashkenazi" refers to Jews of Eastern Europe whose traditional language is Yiddish, a German dialect. The Sephardic Jews derive from Spain, from which they were expelled (along with remaining Muslims).

2. A joke that was circulating about ten years ago goes as follows: Question: What do you get when you cross a Seventh-Day Adventist with an atheist? Answer: Someone who knocks on your door but then doesn't say anything.

REFERENCES AND FURTHER READING

Beidelman, T. O. 1982. *Colonial Evangelism: A Socio-Historical Study of an East African Mission at the Grassroots*. Bloomington: Indiana University Press.

Bellah, Robert. 1965. "Religious Evolution." In *Reader in Comparative Religion*, edited by William A. Lessa and Evon Z. Vogt, pp. 73–87. New York: Harper & Row.

Benedict, Ruth. [1934] 1960. *Patterns of Culture*. New York: Mentor Books.

Cook, Garrett W. 2001. "The Maya Pentecost." In *Holy Saints and Fiery Preachers: The Anthropology of Protestantism in Mexico and Central America*, edited by James W. Dow and Alan R. Sandstrom, pp. 147–68. Westport, Conn.: Praeger.

Dow, James W. 2001. "Protestantism in Mesoamerica: The Old within the New." In *Holy Saints and Fiery Preachers: The Anthropology of Protestantism in Mexico and Central America*, edited by James W. Dow and Alan R. Sandstrom, pp. 1–23. Westport, Conn.: Praeger.

Dow, James W., and Alan R. Sandstrom, eds. 2001. *Holy Saints and Fiery Preachers: The Anthropology of Protestantism in Mexico and Central America.* Westport, Conn.: Praeger.

Eickelman, Dale F. 1981. *Moroccan Islam: Tradition and Society in a Pilgrimage Center.* Austin: University of Texas Press.

Garma, Carlos. 2001. "Religious Affiliation in Indian Mexico." In *Holy Saints and Fiery Preachers: The Anthropology of Protestantism in Mexico and Central America,* edited by James W. Dow and Alan R. Sandstrom, pp. 57–72. Westport, Conn.: Praeger.

Geertz, Clifford. 1960. *The Religion of Java.* Glencoe, Ill.: Free Press.

Gellner, Ernest. 1969. *Saints of the Atlas.* Chicago: University of Chicago Press.

———. 1981. *Muslim Society.* Cambridge: Cambridge University Press.

Goody, Jack, ed. 1968. Introduction to *Literacy in Traditional Societies,* edited by Jack Goody, pp. 1–26. Cambridge: Cambridge University Press.

Harper, Edward, ed. 1964. *Religion in South Asia.* Seattle: University of Washington Press.

Hefner, Robert W. 1993. *Conversion to Christianity: Historical and Anthropological Perspectives on a Great Transformation.* Berkeley: University of California Press.

Kammerer, Cornelia Ann. 1990. "Customs and Christian Conversion among Akha Highlanders of Burma and Thailand." *American Ethnologist* 17(2): 277–91.

Kendall, Laurel. 1985. *Shamans, Housewives, and Other Restless Spirits.* Honolulu: University of Hawaii Press.

Keyes, Charles F. 1993. "Why the Thai Are Not Christian: Buddhist and Christian Conversion in Thailand." In *Conversion to Christianity: Historical and Anthropological Perspectives on a Great Transformation,* edited by Robert Hefner, pp. 259–83. Berkeley: University of California Press.

Kipp, Rita Smith, and Susan Rodgers, eds. 1987. *Indonesian Religions in Transition.* Tucson: University of Arizona Press.

Lienhart, R. G. 1982. "The Dinka and Catholicism." In *Religious Organization and Religious Experience,* edited by J. Davis, pp. 82–95. London: Academic.

O'Connor, Mary J. 2001. "Evangelicals in the Lower Mayo Valley." In *Holy Saints and Fiery Preachers: The Anthropology of Protestantism in Mexico and Central America,* edited by James W. Dow and Alan R. Sandstrom, pp. 25–56. Westport, Conn.: Praeger.

Redfield, Robert. 1957. *The Primitive World and Its Transformations.* Ithaca, N.Y.: Cornell University Press.

Schiller, Anne. 1997. *Small Sacrifices: Religious Change and Cultural Identity among the Ngaju of Indonesia.* New York: Oxford University Press.

Spiro, Melford E. 1967. *Burmese Supernaturalism: A Study in the Explanation and Reduction of Suffering.* Englewood Cliffs, N.J.: Prentice-Hall.

———. *Buddhism and Society: A Great Tradition and Its Burmese Vicissitudes.* New York: Harper & Row.

Weber, Max. [1922] 1964. *The Sociology of Religion.* Boston: Beacon.

Woodward, Mark R. 1989. *Islam in Java: Normative Piety and Mysticism in the Sultanate of Yogyakarta.* Tucson: University of Arizona Press.

Index

Note: Some terms that occur very frequently throughout the text (such as belief, magic, religion, ritual, sacred, soul, spirit, and spiritual) are indexed only regarding definitions or key uses. Page numbers in *italics* refer to illustrations.

About the Author

Robert L. Winzeler is professor of anthropology at the University of Nevada, Reno. He has been actively involved in research in Southeast Asia over the past four decades, especially in peninsular Malaysia and Borneo and most recently among the indigenous highland peoples of Thailand, Laos, and Vietnam. His research has been supported by grants from the National Science Foundation, the Fulbright Program, the National Institute of Mental Health, and the Henry Luce Foundation. He is the author or editor of six books, including *The Architecture of Life and Death in Borneo*.